CW00421606

'Succinctly but completely describing 50 of the most important management innovations in the past 150 years, Mol and Birkinshaw educate us on where and how managerial innovations arise. An amazing overview of the management practice landscape, Giant Steps in Management provides invaluable insights for organizations seeking better performance.'

Jeffrey Pfeffer, Professor, Graduate School of Business, Stanford University

'Never has it been more important for managers to innovate the way they manage. As this book so powerfully shows, management innovation – advances in how we manage – is a secret weapon in the search for competitive advantage. With a fantastic compendium of the 50 most crucial management innovations, this book will surprise, inform and inspire any manager who believes that they need to innovate the way they manage.'

Lynda Gratton, Professor of Management Practice, London Business School; author of *Hot Spots; why some teams, workplaces and organisations buzz with energy – and others don't*

'This book might be called "Everything you wanted to know about management, but were afraid to ask". It's an invaluable quick guide to the entire arsenal of techniques and models, and I recommend it to anyone who takes the job of management seriously. It is typical of the authors' work, in that it is clear, crisp and useful.'

Tim Brooks, Managing Director, Guardian News & Media Limited

'A stimulating book to encourage all of us to think about what really matters in management: distinguishing the radical new approaches that will work for your organization from the repackaged and the over-hyped. Yet, as the authors appreciate, "what works?" is even itself a challenging question: they frequently remind us that the influence of history and context is pervasive.'

Robin Wensley, Professor, Warwick Business School and Director of the Advanced Institute of Management Research

'This book is an excellent primer for those organizations beginning to explore ways to improve and evolve their own management practices. It will serve as an important casebook for UBS' ongoing management innovation work with the authors.'

Maria Bentley, Global Head of Human Resources, UBS Investment Bank

Giant Steps in Management

FT Prentice Hall
FINANCIAL TIMES

In an increasingly competitive world, we believe it's quality of thinking that gives you the edge – an idea that opens new doors, a technique that solves a problem, or an insight that simply makes sense of it all. The more you know, the smarter and faster you can go.

That's why we work with the best minds in business and finance to bring cutting-edge thinking and best learning practice to a global market.

Under a range of leading imprints, including *Financial Times Prentice Hall*, we create world-class print publications and electronic products bringing our readers knowledge, skills and understanding, which can be applied whether studying or at work.

To find out more about Pearson Education publications, or tell us about the books you'd like to find, you can visit us at **www.pearsoned.co.uk**

PEARSON
Education

Giant Steps in Management

Creating Innovations That Change the Way
We Work

Michael J. Mol and Julian Birkinshaw

Foreword by Gary Hamel

Prentice Hall
FINANCIAL TIMES

An imprint of **Pearson Education**

Harlow, England • London • New York • Boston • San Francisco • Toronto
Sydney • Tokyo • Singapore • Hong Kong • Seoul • Taipei • New Delhi
Cape Town • Madrid • Mexico City • Amsterdam • Munich • Paris • Milan

PEARSON EDUCATION LIMITED

Edinburgh Gate
Harlow CM20 2JE
Tel: +44 (0)1279 623623
Fax: +44 (0)1279 431059
Website: www.pearsoned.co.uk

First published in Great Britain in 2008

© Michael J. Mol and Julian Birkinshaw 2008

The rights of Michael J. Mol and Julian Birkinshaw to be identified as authors of this work
have been asserted by them in accordance with the Copyright, Designs and Patents Act 1988.

ISBN: 978-0-273-71292-3

British Library Cataloguing-in-Publication Data
A catalogue record for this book is available from the British Library

Library of Congress Cataloging-in-Publication Data

Mol, Michael J.
  Giant steps in management : creating innovations that change the way we work / Michael J.
Mol and Julian Birkinshaw ; foreword by Gary Hamel.
      p. cm.
  Includes index.
  ISBN-13: 978-0-273-71292-3 (hbk.)
  1. Management. 2. Organizational change. I. Birkinshaw, Julian M. II. Title.
HD31.M6156 2008
658--dc22
                                    2007033889

All rights reserved. No part of this publication may be reproduced, stored in a retrieval
system, or transmitted in any form or by any means, electronic, mechanical, photocopying,
recording or otherwise, without either the prior written permission of the Publishers or a
licence permitting restricted copying in the United Kingdom issued by the Copyright
Licensing Agency Ltd, Saffron House, 6–10 Kirby Street, London EC1N 8TS. This book may
not be lent, resold, hired out or otherwise disposed of by way of trade in any form of binding
or cover other than that in which it is published, without the prior consent of the Publishers.

10 9 8 7 6 5 4 3 2 1
11 10 09 08 07

Typeset in 9pt/13pt Stone Serif by 30
Printed and bound in Great Britain by Henry Ling Ltd, Dorchester, Dorset

The Publishers' policy is to use paper manufactured from sustainable forests.

Management innovation: *a company's ability to affect fundamental changes in its own internal way of working.*

Nothing about our current ways of working is inviolable. That's why managers are always trying new things, different approaches. There are management innovations underway all the time in large organizations. Many fail. Some work. A few make history. The most valuable ones are picked up and diffused across entire industries and countries. Even now, the power of management innovation – and its potential – continues to amaze us. It is the most overlooked source of competitive advantage.

Contents

About this book

How do you manage? What skills, ideas, tools and techniques do you use? And why? Think about it: how we manage organizations – and ourselves – is in a constant state of evolution. Managers are restless tinkerers and experimenters. They try new approaches. They fly kites. They pilot and trial. Along the way, the practices we use to manage our organizations change fundamentally. The way you manage today is significantly different from how people managed a generation ago.

Innovation is at the heart of management. It is the essence of great management.

Giant Steps in Management is a book about how management has innovated. It presents a thought-provoking selection of the most important management innovations of the last 150 years and examines their impact on management today. But we also consider how the innovation process itself took place, the role of key management innovators, and how these people overcame a bewildering array of obstacles.

Our progress to *Giant Steps* has involved a couple of forward steps followed by a number backwards and sideways. We have been consulting, teaching, writing, and talking about management innovations over the last decade. Along the way we have discovered that managers and companies that try to engage in management innovation face two key barriers. One barrier is that they are not always aware of what innovations have gone before and how these historical innovations shape today's environment. The second barrier is that managers lack a solid understanding of how management innovation occurs. *Giant Steps* addresses both issues.

We have identified the key historical innovations, describing in detail for each one why it was needed, what it attempted to do, how it came about, how it spread to other organizations, and what its implications are for current practice.

In *Giant Steps*, we examine the major management innovations of the last 150 years by area of activity: people management; financial management; customer relationships; and so on. Of course, these areas of activity are not watertight compartments, and many management innovations, by their nature, extend across multiple areas. But our research suggests that it is useful to categorize management innovations in this way because clear storylines emerge. In each chapter there is an overview that briefly describes the major trends in 150 years of history for that particular domain of management activity. Then we present a series of case studies – one for each of the most important management innovations in that area. The final chapter pulls the different strands of work together and lays out the agenda for management innovation.

We realize that any selection of management innovations has an element of randomness. Selections of this type always ignite debate. Some readers will have favoured management innovations we have overlooked or identified as not having enough impact on practising managers. Some may think we have included too many innovations, and would argue some of the cases we describe are not very innovative, or perhaps not even about management. And others may feel that our selection is too America centric: a challenge we would accept as valid, but hard to avoid. Pleasing everyone is not possible, but we remain open to discussion on management innovations in general, and on those included in this book in particular. Indeed, sparking such debate lies at the heart of our mission in writing this book.

How did we arrive at this selection of management innovations? First, we clearly identified what we meant by management innovation. Then we engaged in a broad-based search of the management literature to identify possible candidates. We looked at several lists of management innovations drawn up by other academics, in specific areas such as human resources, and one that appeared in *Harvard Business Review*. We also sought the help of various experts at the London Business School and elsewhere to help us determine the key management innovations in each of their areas. And then we checked back with practising managers to verify whether they had similar innovations in mind. This book describes what we consider to be the 'top 50' management innovations since the Industrial Revolution.

Once we had selected the key innovations, we documented each one in detail. So this book is based on literally hundreds of sources, managerial publications such as the *Harvard Business Review*, academic journals like the *Business History Review* and the *Journal of Operations Management*; websites of executives like www.schneiderman.com; and many books like Alfred Sloan's

My years with General Motors and Harry and Schroeder's *Six sigma: The break-through management strategy revolutionizing the world's top corporations*. From all these sources, we distilled our stories on the world's key management innovations. In the introductions to each of the chapters, we also mention an array of further management innovations that, important though they were, did not make our top 50. And as noted already, some readers might have included them in their top 50. The book concludes with a list of relevant reading. (For a complete list of references please contact us directly – michael@michaelmol.com.)

We believe there is a lot to be learned from these management innovations. They have shaped the way you work and the way we all think about management. You may be familiar with some of the innovations but not with others outside your own area of expertise. You may like to understand how management innovators went to work, what they did to overcome the obstacles they faced, and what became of them. You may want to know what caused these innovations to become so successful, which of them continue to be crucial to today's management practice and which have been superseded by subsequent management innovations. Or perhaps you are just looking for a good read. We hope that the management innovations we look at inspire you to think and act differently when you are practising management. There is, we believe, nothing so practical as a great management innovation.

We would like to acknowledge the assistance we received in documenting and describing these innovations from Steve Coomber, Stuart Crainer, Latchez Hristov and Ignacio Vaccaro. We are very grateful for their work. We received advice from a host of people, which has helped us improve the book greatly. We also want to acknowledge the Advanced Institute for Management Research (AIM), which has been the key source of financial support for this research.

Michael Mol and Julian Birkinshaw

June 2007

Foreword by Gary Hamel

What is it that allows a company to consistently trump its competitors? What does it take for an organization to achieve unprecedented levels of performance? What's the secret to building long-term advantage? These are questions that have long occupied the minds of business school researchers and corporate executives – and Michael J. Mol and Julian Birkinshaw think they have the answer. In *Giant Steps in Management*, the authors argue that it is *management innovation* – fundamental breakthroughs in how companies organize, coordinate, plan, motivate and allocate resources – that drives long-term success.

Consider a couple of examples. GE's rise to iconic status in the early years of the twentieth century was driven by its creation of the world's first modern R&D Lab. By bringing management discipline to the chaotic process of scientific discovery, the company was able to bring more new products to the market more effectively than any of its early competitors. And Toyota's long and uninterrupted reign as the best volume car manufacturer in the world owes much to its success in harnessing the problem-solving skills of all employees.

While thousands of articles and books have been written about the importance of technology and strategy innovation, the central role of management innovation in determining long-term success has, until now, been mostly ignored. This myopia is surprising, since, as Mol and Birkinshaw demonstrate, management innovation is more likely to create an enduring advantage than innovation in operating practices, products or business models.

In recent years, many researchers have studied the way in which new management practices get transferred from one company to another. Yet despite this interest in the *diffusion* of new management ideas, there has been little or no systematic research into the generative process through which new management practices get *created*. In lifting the veil on the generative process of management innovation, *Giant Steps in Management* provides today's would-be innovators with essential insights into the promises and pitfalls of challenging management orthodoxy.

What you will find here is more than an historical *tour d'horizon* of management thought. For that, one could turn to Alfred Chandler, Daniel Wren, or any of several other distinguished management historians. *Giant Steps* isn't a history of management *thought;* rather, it's the story of how modern management – the processes and practices that govern managerial work in your company and just about every other company around the world – actually got invented. While some of the famous cases – such as Alfred Sloan's introduction of the multidivisional structure at GM in the 1920s – are well known, most are not. In fact, most well-read executives and b-school professors would be hard pressed to tell you where any of our key management techniques – from strategic planning, to capital budgeting, to discounted cash flow analysis – actually came from.

Giant Steps in Management describes the origins of fifty key management practices which were invented in the last 150 years. You can read this book in two ways. You may want to dip into it, to understand the origins and underlying logic of, say, the Balanced Scorecard. Or, you can read it as a single volume. Each chapter tackles one major management challenge (such as people management and money management), and shows how the innovations in that area have evolved and coalesced over time. Why is it, for example, that innovations in quality and manufacturing processes appear to build so nicely on one other, whereas innovations in people management have seemed disjointed and have often failed to take root?

Today, with so many new challenges afoot, it is critical that we look back and understand the genesis of modern management. Some of the tools and techniques we've inherited from the earlier years of the industrial age may well prove to be timeless – but most will not. Indeed, I believe that, on average, what most limits the performance of any organization today is not its operating model, or its business model, but its *management* model. Understanding the origins of our legacy and beliefs is a critical first step in deciding which of those beliefs deserve to be honoured and revered in this new century, and which should be jettisoned along the road to the future.

For this reason, *Giant Steps in Management* is a vital resource for anyone who wants to take management innovation seriously.

About the authors

Michael J. Mol is a senior lecturer in Strategic Management at the University of Reading and a Visiting Researcher of the Management Innovation Lab (MLab) at the London Business School. He is an expert in the strategic management of large firms, particularly sourcing strategy and management innovation. He has written three books, including the recent *Outsourcing: Design, process, and performance.*

Julian Birkinshaw is Professor of Strategic and International Management at the London Business School, and co-founder of the Management Innovation Lab (MLab). He is a leading authority on how large companies can foster entrepreneurship and innovation, and he is the author of ten previous books, including *Inventuring, Entrepreneurship in the Global Firm* and *Leadership the Sven-Goran Eriksson Way.*

Introduction:
Giant steps in management

The field of management is never short of new ideas – or at least new riffs on old ideas. As we write this, the business bestseller lists include such tantalizing titles as *The world is flat*, *Blue ocean strategy* and *The long tail*; *Fortune* magazine is offering the inside story on Google's corporate culture; and the consulting firm, McKinsey, is highlighting its newest thinking on 'global trends and corporate strategy'.

As a well-read and thoughtful manager, you want to be on top of these latest ideas. You want to know how the business landscape is changing. And you are constantly looking out for that spark of insight that will give you, or your company, a competitive edge.

But at the same time, you have a healthy scepticism for all these new ideas and fads. How is this new insight going to help *my* organization? What do these concepts mean in practice? And how is this supposedly novel idea really different from what Peter Drucker was telling us 50 years ago?

The fact is, management ideas and management practices come and go. Some are driven by profound insights: Douglas McGregor's theory of motivation (Theory X vs. Theory Y) is one example, Michael Porter's theory of competitive strategy may be another; but the truth is that genuinely new and timeless insights in management are about as common as British victories at Wimbledon. Therefore possessing those insights is a big plus for every manager.

Some management ideas are spurred on by changes in technology or by major social or economic trends. Rather than offering timeless truths about management, these ideas are all about the 'new rules' that are needed to cope with the changing realities of the business world. So, for example, the last decade has seen an enormous body of thought – some good, much of it less so – examining the implications of the internet for business; there have also been studies of how management has to change to meet the needs of Generation Y, those young people who are now entering the workplace and becoming important customers.

Other management ideas are old wine in new bottles. Rather like the propensity of Hollywood directors for remaking classic movies in contemporary settings, management thinkers are very good at reconceptualizing old ideas, giving them a new twist, and packaging them for an audience that wasn't exposed to the original idea. Of course there are many classic ideas out there that today's manager needs to be aware of. But the sheer volume of books and articles in this category exacerbates the scepticism that managers feel about this whole genre. There is, simply, an oversupply of writing on management and too much of it is repackaging.

Diving for pearls

So how can you discover the pearls? How can you do a better job of making sense of management thinking – the current and emerging ideas that everyone is talking about, and the ones that are still lurking in your company or elsewhere, enshrined in a standard operating process many years after their original proponents have moved on? And how can you choose which – if any – of these ideas is right for your company today?

The purpose of this book is to give you a new understanding of the plethora of management ideas and practices out there, in the hope that you can evaluate and implement them more effectively. We do this by tracking the major *management innovations* through business history. These are the significant landmark changes in management practice that have shaped the modern company and the way we manage today. By documenting the rise of significant new management practices, we show how some areas of business have made great strides forward in their effectiveness, while others have got caught up in pendulum-like swings of fashion.

Inevitably, much of this analysis is historical – though not all, since we also examine the origins of many contemporary management innovations. Innovations such as six sigma, the balanced scorecard, customer relationship management, corporate venturing, outsourcing, supply chain management, mentoring, and open innovation are very much alive and well in companies today, even though the rhetoric around them constantly changes. So why should you read what is, in essence, a history book? There are two important reasons why a book that traces management history can help you today.

First, history gives us a better perspective on the present. In the well-known words of George Santayana: 'Those who cannot remember the past are condemned to repeat it.' So by understanding the lessons from previous generations of companies, we are better equipped to make well-informed decisions about the companies we work for.

Or to make this point more tangible, a better understanding of the history of management innovation can help you figure out where opportunities for future management innovations lie. For example, why does the field of human resource management go through cycles of concern for the well-being of employees every 30 years (called, at different times, the human relations movement, employee well-being, quality of working life, and empowerment), without ever entirely resolving those concerns? Why does the issue of customer focus never get fully resolved? To understand the key themes or tensions in any area of management your best starting point is an awareness of the prior struggles managers have worked through. In this book, there is no repackaging of old wine into new bottles, we simply investigate what the old bottles have to offer us. And to become a management innovator yourself, you want to know where the biggest opportunities are to be found – and where the biggest pitfalls lie.

Second, today's management practices are all built on prior practices. A useful analogy is the process of sedimentation in a lake or river estuary: new layers of sediment get laid down on top of old ones, but the old layers still influence the contours of the river bed, and they occasionally poke their way through to the surface. It's the same with management practices. Despite all the rhetoric about hierarchies disappearing in the workplace, we still litter our conversations with military-style terminology – *staff versus line*, *span of control*, *high-ranking officers*, and so forth. And regardless of how the pioneering Victorian thinker Frederick W. Taylor is regarded in the field of management today, his principles of scientific management live on in many organizations – through time and motion studies, Gantt chart planning, and so forth. In one mining company we are familiar with, the thinking inside the organization is still deeply influenced by Elliot Jacques' 'stratified systems theory' (SST), despite changes in ownership and the fact that it is more than 15 years since Jacques' involvement ended. If you want to put forward any new ideas in this company, you had better understand how they relate to SST first!

 # In search of management innovation

So what *is* management innovation? In the words of our colleague, Gary Hamel, it is about innovation in management principles and processes that ultimately change the actual practice of what managers do, and how they get it done. It is different to operational or process innovation, which is about how the actual work of transforming inputs into outputs, gets done.

Over the last few years, along with Gary, we have discussed management innovation with hundreds of managers. We know there are many different points of view on what it really means. It is easy to point to classic examples – total quality management, the multidivisional structure, capital budgeting – that everyone can agree about; but it is not so easy to draw the boundaries around the outer limits of what constitutes a management innovation. In particular, the boundary between operational, process and management innovations is blurry.

It is not our intention here to enter into an academic debate (we love doing that, just not here and now). Rather, our own research in this emergent area has led us to identify four important characteristics. This is important because it allows us to begin to make distinctions between innovations in these different areas. These are the four criteria we use to decide if something is a management innovation:

- *A management innovation changes the work of management: it leads directly to new management practices and processes.* Total quality management, for example, has a real impact on the everyday work of employees and their bosses, so it counts. But there are many management ideas out there – Porter's 'five forces' framework, the learning organization, and empowerment, for instance – that operate at a level of abstraction that does not immediately influence the work of management, so they don't make the cut. It is useful to think of two realms – the world of theory and the world of practice. So, for example, open innovation operates primarily in the world of theory, while Procter & Gamble's 'connect and develop' initiative operates in the world of practice. While we often end up using the 'theoretical label' for the sake of convenience, it is the practice that we care most about in this book.

- *A management innovation is something new 'to the state of the art'.* It is not just another implementation of six sigma or the balanced scorecard, it is a marked departure from existing practice, and it is launched without any known precedent. This is not to say that a management innovation has to be the first of its kind anywhere in the world; that would be an unreasonably high hurdle to cross. Instead, it should be seen as a bona fide attempt by a company to move away from the pack, and create something new.

- *A management innovation requires implementation.* An obvious point, perhaps, but there are plenty of great and not so great ideas out there that never get put into practice. In the world of technology, innovation is about *exploiting* ideas, not coming up with the ideas in the first place, and exactly the same point applies here.

- *A management innovation is undertaken to further the company's goals.* Again, this may appear to be self-evident, but it is useful to emphasize the point that innovation is focused around solving particular management problems, not just as an end in itself. Companies do not sell management innovations; they use them to sell something else. (Of course, once the innovation is in place it may have a large resale value as many consultants know.) And remember that 'goals' does not just mean financial goals – there are plenty of management innovations directed towards making employees happier, or developing a more socially responsible orientation.

Note, too, that we don't define management innovation in terms of success. Some work, some fail. For every successful management innovation – total quality management and so on – there are failures: Volvo's experiments in cellular manufacturing, for one. Of course, the innovations we discuss in this book were all successes, at least for some time, but that is because we are focusing on the ones that have made a big difference to the world of business, not because all management innovations have positive outcomes. Indeed, there is every reason to think that management innovation, just like other forms of innovation, has its share of failures.

 # Management innovation as a source of competitive advantage

The million-dollar (or more) question is simple: *How important is management innovation to company success?*

It is important. If a company implements a genuinely radical innovation, it can expect to reap significant rewards for many years. At the same time, it has to be acknowledged that long-term corporate success, whether measured in terms of profitability or competitive advantage, will always be a function of countless interacting factors, lots of which cannot even be managed.

There are three pillars to the argument that management innovation reaps rewards. First, take a look at the case histories that are recounted in this book. Procter & Gamble stole a march on all its competitors when it introduced brand management in the 1920s. To this day, P&G continues to be held up as the gold standard in brand management. VISA emerged in the late 1960s through an unprecedented collaboration between tens of thousands of banks, and is still today the dominant credit card organization. Toyota created many of the key elements of what we now call 'lean production' and, based on this platform, it still retains its competitive advantage in the mass market auto industry. If *sustainable* competitive advantage is the goal, then management innovation is one of the most promising routes to that goal.

Second, it is worth reflecting on the underlying reason why management innovation might lead to competitive advantage. Internal competences – all the things your organization excels at – can only become a source of advantage if they are hard for competitors to imitate, as well as being valuable. Our research suggests that management innovations are often different from technological innovations especially *because* they are hard to imitate. Executives from Ford and GM have paid countless visits to Toyota's factories over the years, and, in the case of GM, even established a jointly owned factory (NUMMI) with Toyota to better understand their Japanese competitor's secrets, but they have failed to replicate the Toyota model. Total quality management is so deep seated in its principles of human behaviour, and spans so many activities and functions across the organization, that it has proved to be almost impossible to imitate. A management innovation cannot be reverse engineered so easily. And to varying degrees this is the case with all the other management innovations discussed in this book.

Third, it is worth acknowledging one important academic study that attempted to track the productivity impact from information technology (IT) investments. This 2001 study 'Knowledge, work organization and economic growth' by economists Elena Arnal, Wooseok Ok and Raymond Torres, focused on two variables: the amount of money companies invested in IT, and the amount of effort they put into developing new work practices around their IT investments (in other words, management innovations). And the core finding of the study was clear: the companies that invested in management innovation *alongside* IT saw far greater productivity improvements than the companies that did one or the other. This study did not examine the specific innovations that had been put in place, but it offers concrete evidence that spans multiple sectors of the economy. So management innovation is what makes the invention and implementation of technologies more effective.

How does management innovation happen?

Management innovation is a crucial ingredient in improving personal and organizational performance. Yet, real management innovation still occurs infrequently. Of course, companies tweak compensation systems, rethink their structures, and improve their manufacturing processes all the time, but if there is a scale from 'incremental' management innovations, on the one side, to 'radical' innovations, on the other, then the vast majority of cases are clustered at the incremental end of the scale. The number of truly radical management innovations – of the type documented in this book – is very small, which is precisely why the innovations we discuss are so crucial to today's practice.

So why does radical management innovation occur so infrequently? Simply stated, the social and structural forces at work inside large organizations all favour the perpetuation of the status quo. We are all so conditioned by our working environment that we find it extraordinarily difficult to imagine, say, an organization without bosses. The management processes for such things as capital budgeting or talent management are so deeply ingrained in the fabric of our organizations that they are desperately difficult to challenge. And even if it is possible to conceive of a way of changing these existing mindsets and processes, it is still an uphill task to get people to buy into a risky new alternative.

Or think about it this way: if your company is faced with a problem that requires significant changes to how it works, is it more likely to ask a consulting firm like McKinsey to implement a variant of a 'proven' model that others have already bought, or is it more likely to try to seek out its own novel solution? Most feel safer and more comfortable with using the consultant-led solution, but almost by definition this leads to the perpetuation of existing 'best practice', rather than the creation of what we might call 'next practice'. Some companies – such as GE and Procter & Gamble – have enough self-confidence and competence to push their own novel practices, and their organizations are open to such novelty. But the majority prefers the risk-averse approach that restricts any sort of management innovation to the incremental end of the scale.

So what are the key elements that have to come together for management innovation to take place? There is no simple answer to this question; no recipe book or 'silver bullet'. But one of the key reasons for embarking on this study of historical management innovations was a desire to identify the common themes that come together whenever management innovation surfaces. In the chapters that follow, we describe the key drivers in each case, and in the concluding chapter we offer our thoughts on what the most important and consistent themes are. We also discuss *how* management innovation takes place.

1

Process

How can companies get the most output from their work processes, in terms of products that are desirable to customers, with the least effort? What are the processes that need to be undertaken to serve customers and how should they be designed? The objective of management innovations in the work process is to make companies more efficient and controlled.

 ## Introduction

The workplace is full of processes that transfer inputs into outputs. A company's ability to make its processes efficient and effective goes a long way to determining its competitiveness in the marketplace and more than one company has built its reputation around process excellence.

We start our story of process innovations with *scientific management*, and with the man some consider to be the forefather of all that is bad about management – Frederick Winslow Taylor. Taylor worked at the US steelmaker Midvale in the late 19th century, and later moved to Bethlehem Steel. Driven by a strong work ethic and a belief that it was iniquitous to waste effort, he timed activities to find out how they were best performed and introduced pay-for-performance schemes. The essence of scientific management was a simple proposition: let's measure the best way to undertake a given process, and redesign that process accordingly. While Taylor's relentless push for efficiency led many to believe he disregarded concerns for human motivation, he was enormously influential, and his ideas continue to influence the way firms manage the workplace.

The other celebrated innovation of the pre-war era was Henry Ford's introduction of the *moving assembly line* in 1910. Building on insights gleaned from other industries, most notably the 'disassembly' lines of local slaughter-houses, Ford used conveyor belt technology to 'bring the work to the men', rather than the men to the work. And he restructured the roles of individual employees around self-contained tasks, which greatly increased the output per worker. Scientific management and the moving assembly line took the world by storm and set the tone in manufacturing excellence for decades.

It was after the Second World War that the next major innovation in process management appeared. Facing a major rebuilding effort after the war, Toyota and other Japanese firms became fascinated by the potential for improvements that would enable them to take costs out of their production processes. This model subsequently became known as *lean manufacturing* (this name was first used in the book *The machine that changed the world*) and it focused on minimizing waste of materials and efforts. Lean manufacturing was really the umbrella concept. The real management innovations, many of which were first implemented by Toyota, were specific techniques such as just-in-time (JIT), *kanban*, and target costing. Just-in-time was the principle that inventory represents waste and deliveries of supplies should occur only when they are needed; the *kanban*, or card, was a signalling system for managing the flow of parts to the assembly line. Target costing was an accounting invention of the 1960s, which involved Toyota agreeing cost targets with its suppliers based on detailed insights into supplier designs and processes.

In the 1950s, Toyota and other Japanese firms also started experimenting with *total quality management* (TQM), a set of concepts that W. Edwards Deming and Joseph Juran had been promoting. TQM treated quality as the responsibility of every worker. The quality dimension was added as a natural extension to lean production, because by lowering the number of defects, waste was reduced further. TQM also incorporated an important dimension of statistical process control, which allowed for the identification of anomalies. TQM made manufacturing processes much more reliable.

While the principles of lean manufacturing and total quality management are still central to most manufacturing operations today, the last 30 years have seen a range of other process innovations – some highly successful, some less so.

One of the less successful innovations involved the 1970s' experiments in *cellular manufacturing* that Volvo, in particular, became well known for. Faced with high absentee rates and pressure from the Swedish government for quality-of-working-life initiatives, Volvo ditched the traditional assembly line, and instead created small cells of multiskilled workers to assemble the entire car. Cellular manufacturing produced some genuine improvements in worker satisfaction and quality, but ultimately these benefits were not sufficient to overcome the losses in absolute efficiency, and Volvo eventually abandoned these experiments.

Two important adaptations to the traditional mass production model, both originating in the 1980s, were mass customization and modularization. In both cases, the starting point was the need to deal with increasing diversity in customer demand while not sacrificing the efficiency benefits of mass production. *Mass customization* sought to take advantage of increasingly sophisticated computer automation processes to configure a product to its customer's exact specifications while still producing it on a production line. The concept of modularization was more relevant to the increasingly important world of software development. It sought to break down the development of a system into a series of discrete, but interconnected, modules, so that each module could be altered according to customer needs without triggering wholesale change across all the other modules.

Concurrent engineering, also from the 1980s, took some of the advances from lean production to the engineering arena. Concurrent engineering allowed for parallel development stages in the engineering of new products. Soft and hard automation were terms introduced around the same time to reflect the use of robots in automated production processes.

Business process re-engineering (BPR), first used by Ford in the 1980s, was a modern variant of Taylor's scientific management, although with an important dose of lean manufacturing added in. Other antecedents include a technique known as brown papering, which mapped the processes in organizations in an attempt to eliminate unnecessary steps. BPR essentially took a process perspective on the activities of the firm, and it offered a set of tools for streamlining the value-added processes undertaken by the firm and eliminating the waste.

In the 1980s and 1990s the supply chain revolution also got underway. *Supply chain management* (SCM), a term introduced by Booz Allen Hamilton in 1982, and then supply chain integration, pioneered by Dell in the early 1990s, extended the notion of efficient and controlled processes across company boundaries to include supply chain partners. These innovations sought to increase the efficiency of the entire supply chain, rather than focusing only on those activities owned by the firm.

The last major process management innovation is *six sigma*, introduced by John Smith at Motorola in 1987, and subsequently picked up by GE. Six sigma was a logical extension of total quality management, in that it applied statistical process control mechanisms to the elimination of waste in production processes. It nonetheless became one of the biggest management innovations of the 1990s, thanks in part to the effective way in which the tools and methods were packaged for other firms to use.

Taken as a whole, process management has evolved in a remarkably linear and straightforward way. Subsequent innovations typically build on prior innovations, and the improvements in efficiency and quality over the last century are undeniable.

Scientific management

Creating efficient work processes is an abiding obsession for managers. Witness the fascination in the 1990s with re-engineering and more recently with outsourcing. Maximizing outputs and controlling inputs lies at the heart of management.

In the late 19th century these issues had hardly been identified, let alone examined. Frederick Winslow Taylor changed this through observations of his fellow workers. His starting point was the identification of a number of problems. Taylor noticed that workers engaged in what was then called 'soldiering'. Instead of working as hard and as fast as they could, they deliberately slowed down. They had no incentive to go faster or to be more productive. It was in their interest, Taylor said, to keep 'their employers ignorant of how fast work can be done'. 'Nineteen out of twenty workmen throughout the civilized world firmly believe that it is for their best interests to go slow instead of to go fast. They firmly believe that it is for their interest to give as little work in return for the money that they get as is practical', Taylor wrote.

Taylor went on to identify another crucial problem: the workers had a notable advantage in that their superiors had no idea how long the job should take. No one had thought to examine the nature of people's work. Irritated by such brazen inefficiency, Taylor set to work. Armed with a stopwatch, he examined in intimate detail exactly what happened and how long it took. Taylor surmised that minute examination of a task would enable the observer to establish the best means of carrying out the job. A single, preferred, efficient means of completing the task could then be established and insisted on in the future. This was the basis of what Taylor labelled *scientific management*.

Stopwatch hero

Frederick Winslow Taylor was born in Germantown, Pennsylvania, on 20 March 1856 into an affluent Philadelphia family. Taylor's father was a lawyer from an old Pennsylvania Quaker family; his mother, Emily Winslow, from an old New England Puritan family. (Her father was a New Bedford whaler.) Emily was a prominent antislavery agitator and a campaigner for women's rights.

Educated in France and Germany, Taylor travelled throughout Europe before eventually returning to the Phillips Exeter Academy. (Taylor retained strong European connections throughout his life. He spent vacations in Brittany and shortly before his death saluted the French and Belgian attempts at repelling the German forces in the First World War.)

Despite his well-heeled background, Taylor began his working life at the bottom of the engineering ladder. He initially worked as an apprentice at the William Sellers Company in Philadelphia. In 1878 he went to work at the Midvale Steel Company, near Philadelphia. At Midvale, Taylor began as a clerk, though he soon moved back down the company's ranks to become a labourer. Taylor's role appeared to change almost monthly. In six years at Midvale he was keeper of tool cribs, assistant foreman, foreman, master mechanic, director of research, and, finally, chief engineer of the entire plant. While working he also reactivated his academic career. (He had been destined for Harvard before poor eyesight reputedly intervened.) Taylor spent three years (1880–83) studying engineering at evening classes at the Stevens Institute. He stayed at Midvale until 1889, and it was his observation there that formed the basis for his theories of what became known as scientific management.

He later worked at a variety of places, most notably the Bethlehem Steel Company. At Bethlehem he attempted wide-ranging changes. Not all of these were either successful or popular and Taylor was eventually fired in 1901.

Taylor was a man of devotedly practical intent, a problem solver. Indeed, Taylor was the *ultimate* problem solver. In an age that produced more than its fair share of dilettantes, Taylor was a veritable Renaissance man. The breadth of his insights and interests is, even now in an age of hyperbole, astonishing.

Taylor was an inventor. Most notably, working with the metallurgist Maunsel White, he developed the Taylor–White Process for treating tool steel. This revolutionized metal cutting and enabled the development of mass production techniques. Taylor's restless inventiveness spawned over 40 patents and made him a fortune. These covered everything from 1909's 'Apparatus for Moving Growing Trees and the Like' to a revolutionary

'Power Hammer', built for the Midvale Steel Company in the late 1880s; from an apparatus for grinding balls (1900) to a 'combined hothouse grapery and greenhouse' (1907).

Taylor was also a sportsman. Although he may not have been a wonderfully gifted natural athlete, Taylor brought dogged determination and inventiveness to all his endeavours. In 1881 he won the doubles at the US tennis championships. Not content, Taylor then designed his own tennis racket, which resembled a spoon. His patent pageant also included a lawn tennis net (Patent No. 401,082 issued 9 April 1889).

Taylor brought this level of commitment to all of his many and varied activities. He had a passion for order and efficiency – typically, at school he revelled in the neatness of Dewey's classification and subject index for libraries. 'He was not the steam roller that some people like to represent him as,' said one of his disciples, Henry Gantt, 'but he did believe that a strenuous life was the life worthwhile, and that it not only brought more financial compensation, but that it added to the usefulness and happiness of men.'

And Taylor was incredibly persistent. When, in 1906, Taylor presented his paper, 'On the art of cutting metals', to the American Society of Mechanical Engineers, it was the result of 26 years of experimentation. Taylor's experiments involved cutting over 800,000 pounds of steel and iron into chips with experimental tools. Records were kept of some 30,000 to 50,000 experiments costing the then enormous sum of between $150,000 and $200,000.

An inventor and sportsman he may have been, but, most of all, Taylor was an analytically driven solver of problems. For this reason, he is often acknowledged as the first management consultant – his business card at one point labelled him a 'Consultant to Management'. His faith in using the latest analytical tools to provide a solution to a business problem created the template for the modern consultant. Henry Gantt said that Taylor was: 'Endowed naturally with untiring energy and a wonderfully analytical mind, he concentrated all the power of that combination on the problem of determining the facts he needed ... He was interested in what had been done mainly for the indication it gave of what could be done.' (Another disciple of Taylor's, Harrington Emerson, later termed consulting 'efficiency engineering'.)

Management as science

Taylor's 'science' (which he described as 'seventy-five per cent science and twenty-five per cent common sense') came from the minute examination of individual workers' tasks. He made careful experiments to determine the best way of performing each operation and the amount of time it required, analyzing the materials, tools, and work sequence, and establishing a clear division of labour between management and workers.

Taylor anticipated the rise of reductionism, which had a great influence on 20th-century thinking. Reductionism is based on the belief that if a problem can be reduced to its smallest component, and that component understood, then it is possible to comprehend the whole. Scientists believed for a time that if they could understand how the smallest particle in the universe worked, then they would unlock all its other secrets.

Taylor's experiments laid the groundwork for the principles of scientific management, first published in 1911. Scientific management includes time studies, standardization of tools and implements, standardization of work methods, the use of 'slide-rules and similar time-saving devices' and much more. Taylor called these elements 'merely the elements or details of the mechanisms of management'. He saw them as extensions of the four principles of management:

- The development of a true science.
- The scientific selection of the workman.
- The scientific education and development of the workman.
- Intimate and friendly cooperation between the management and the men.

Taylor warned of the risks managers make in attempting to make changes in what would presently be called the culture of the organization. He stated the importance of management commitment and the need for gradual implementation and education. He described, 'the really great problem' involved in the change 'consists of the complete revolution in the mental attitude and the habits of all those engaged in the management, as well of the workmen.'

The introduction of Taylor's ideas at the Watertown Arsenal reduced the labour cost of making certain moulds for the pommel of a packsaddle from $1.17 to 54 cents. The labour cost of building a six-inch gun carriage fell from $10,229 to $6950. The logic was simple. Measurement increased production as everyone knew what they had to do. Increased production was achieved with lower costs and this led to bigger profits. The gap between the increases in production and pay was increased profit.

Mass market management

Taylor's ideas were picked up by Henry Ford, who used them as the basis for his model for mass production. Ford had created a manufacturing process in which cars mounted on cradles were pushed from one workstation to the next, while workers swarmed around them assembling components. To fill demand for the Model T, Ford had to scrap this system. In 1913, he redefined the work to stop the swarming. 'The man who puts in a bolt does not put on the nut; the man who puts on the nut does not tighten it,' said Ford. Partially assembled cars were also roped together so they could be pulled past the workers at a predictable speed. In a single year, production doubled to nearly 200,000 while the number of workers fell from 14,336 to 12,880. The forerunner of the modern assembly line was born and Taylor was its true innovator. Peter Drucker cited Taylor's thinking as 'the most lasting contribution America has made to Western thought since the Federalist Papers'. Taylor's influence, he suggested, was greater even than Henry Ford. The assembly line was simply a logical extension of scientific management.

Scientific management had an immediate impact. Taylor was celebrated and spoke to large audiences – especially in Europe. A host of disciples provided their interpretations of his theories. As Lyndall Urwick, the British champion of scientific management, noted in 1956:

At the time Taylor began his work, business management as a discrete and identifiable activity had attracted little attention. It was usually regarded as incidental to, and flowing from knowledge-or-acquaintance-with, a particular branch of manufacturing, the technical know-how of making sausages or steel or shirts.

Taylor's promotion of management as a science was also paralleled in the development of business schools in the early part of the 20th century. Taylor made management worthy of study. But with the fame of scientific management also came its detractors. Some critics have pointed at what they call the 'inhumane' character of scientific management, suggesting it treats employees as if they were robots. Others have taken aim at the use of scientific management principles in Nazi Germany and the Soviet Union. But in defence of Taylor, these are consequences he neither intended nor could have predicted.

Alive and counting

No manager would even consider using the term scientific management today when communicating with employees and we don't suggest that you should. But Taylor's ideas and principles are very much alive and kicking, and remain valuable. A 1997 *Fortune* article noted: 'Taylor's influence is omnipresent: It's his ideas that determine how many burgers McDonald's expects its flippers to flip or how many callers the phone company expects its operators to assist.' In your own company the redesign of work processes is likely to be a more or less continuous activity. Business process re-engineering, the brainchild of Hammer and Champy launched in the late 1980s, is another management innovation that partly builds on Taylor's work and revolves around work process redesign.

But there has been a change in the role that employees play in redesign activities. McDonald's fully expects its employees to contribute to the setting of decision-making rules. Managers must design work processes in conjunction with employees. Health and safety concerns have led govern-ments increasingly to impose limitations on how work processes can be designed. And as economies develop, the nature of work shifts towards activities that are harder to measure and where indeed strict 'scientific' rules may undermine productivity. Knowledge workers should be managed differently. So to an extent Taylor's ideas are perhaps more applicable now to low-wage countries, where more measurable activities remain. When you implement these principles, you can therefore only be as strict as the activ-ities and people allow you to be.

Moving assembly line

Henry Ford was raised on a farm, and initially tried his hands at being a machinist and a farmer. He then turned to engineering at Edison, eventually becoming its chief engineer. Outside of work hours Ford worked on automo-biles, and in 1903 he launched the Ford Motor Company. During the early years of the automobile industry, Ford Motor Company established itself as a leading contender, especially after creating its famed Model T.

The Model T was introduced in 1908 and Ford's associate Couzens set up an effective sales network, using dealers and branches. Ford and his key engineers, Galamb and Willis, constructed the Model T so that it was very suitable for mass production. But as the Model T grew in popularity, Ford began to encounter difficulties in trying to cope with demand using the established stationary production methods at its Highland Park plant.

The problem was twofold. The stationary production methods had worked well until demand became so large that diseconomies of scale started to emerge. They simply couldn't make the cars quick enough to meet the burgeoning demand. For instance there were 100 assembly stations for the chassis, which were spread over two 600-feet rows. Dynamic assembly teams moved from one station to the next and components were continuously moved around the plant on mobile trucks. This also implied that any late arrival would have severe consequences down the line. Wheels would be fitted onto cars prior to assembly, simply to be able to move the car around from station to station more easily. Hence Henry Ford had to look for another way of increasing capacity.

A second problem was that the size of the Ford Motor Company had become such that managing the workforce became problematic, as monitoring of employee efforts became more difficult. These monitoring and management difficulties were further enforced through the constant moving about of the workforce and the ensuing chaos. This problem forced Henry Ford to look for a completely different way of organizing his workforce.

Moving the metal

In order to overcome these problems, Henry Ford and his creative team of foremen, supervisors, and engineers came up with a principle that is best described as 'moving the work to the men' and that was put into practice through the moving assembly line. Instead of moving the workforce around to various assembly stations, Ford now moved goods around on conveyor belts to workers who were in fixed positions, repeatedly undertaking the same task. By doing this, Ford managed to increase the productivity of slow workers, as they were assigned simple and fast tasks. By following the principles laid out by Frederick Taylor when he introduced scientific management, he could also standardize and simplify all tasks, eliminating the need for costly fitters. Indeed, there was little need for prior qualifications to work on Ford's assembly lines.

Ford took some of his ideas from elsewhere. Chicago meatpackers had long used overhead trolleys for moving meat in what Ford called 'disassembly' lines. William Klann, head of the engine department at Ford, recalled that he had toured Swift's Chicago slaughterhouse and had then suggested to superintendent P.E. Martin: 'If they can kill pigs and cows that way, we can build cars that way and build motors that way.' Other sources of inspiration included the mechanical conveying system of the flour-milling and brewing industries. And other manufacturing companies like the Westinghouse Airbrake Company were tinkering with similar ideas. But nowhere was there the success that Ford experienced. In their design efforts Ford's engineers concentrated on the principles of power, accuracy, economy, system, continuity, and speed.

Forty Second Street

The assembly line led to drastic productivity increases at Ford. Prior to the introduction of the moving assembly line, in 1912, the Highland Park plant had produced 12 cars per man year. In 1913 this number went up to 14.1, followed by further rises to 18.7 in 1914 and to 19.5 in 1915. The number of hours of labour needed to produce the cars decreased even more rapidly. This allowed Ford not only to increase production substantially but actually to do so with fewer employees. Every 40 seconds a new T-Ford was produced and ready to leave the factory. Prior to the assembly line Ford Motor Company had already produced a healthy 78,000 vehicles a year but in the early 1920s this number had increased to an astounding 2 million cars, all of the same type and, famously, of the same colour, as Ford did not care about the colour as long as it was black. The costs per car had also fallen dramatically, making buying a car a reality for a large number of consumers in the United States.

But the implementation of the assembly line was not without troubles. As workers in the magneto department lined up facing the flywheels and working with one or two simple components, they were adjusting to severe changes. During 1913, Ford's engineers continued to make improvements, including the introduction of an elevated and motorized conveyor belt, which set the pace for the line. Because the moving line was so much more efficient though, an imbalance arose as the assembly operation could not keep up with component production. The line was then expanded to include assembly operations, initially in a crude manner. And an ever better understanding arose of how much time each activity would cost by using stopwatches, much like Taylor had done earlier.

Since every step along the way seemed to increase productivity further, the engineers kept pushing the boundary and turned Highland Park into a series of assembly lines. This has been likened to a 'mechanical ballet'. Ford himself said that 'every piece of work in the shops moves, it may move on hooks, on overhead chains … it may travel on a moving platform, or it may go by gravity, but the point is that there is no lifting or trucking … No workman has anything to do with moving or lifting anything.'

Spreading the Ford

There was initial resistance to Ford's innovation in some quarters. The wife of one worker wrote to Ford 'the chain system you have is a slave driver!', adding: 'My God! Mr Ford. My husband has come home and thrown himself down and won't eat his supper – so done out! Can't that be remedied?' In late 1913 Ford found himself forced to increase workers' salaries substantially, in order to let workers share in the productivity and profitability improvements at the company. The same woman wrote: 'That $5 a day is a blessing – a bigger one than you know but oh they earn it.'

Other car companies started taking up Ford's ideas with much vigour to the extent that even firms producing much smaller numbers, say 1000 or 2000 vehicles a year, introduced the moving assembly line. Until Toyota introduced its lean production practices, Ford's moving assembly line was the state of the art in the production of vehicles. The assembly line came to form the heart of production engineering. And within 10 years the system spread to other industries as well, like household appliances, and eventually to virtually all manufacturing firms. That Ford faced rougher times some 10 years after introducing the assembly line (see also the description of the divisional structure in Chapter 4 (pp. 100–103)) had mostly to do with Henry Ford's unwillingness to consider other car models.

The moving assembly line truly started the era of mass production. And mass production has an enormous impact on how firms are managed, what working life looks like, and what consumers can spend their money on.

Still moving

Ninety years onward from its invention at Ford, the moving assembly line is still very much a part of how production processes are managed. With the shift of manufacturing activities to developing countries and the introduction of more and more automation of tasks its role and presence have changed somewhat, but not very much. The moving assembly line is simply a superior way of organizing people and work, particularly in manufacturing.

But moving assembly lines help out in a variety of places too – think of the transport of luggage at airports. And the assembly line has found its way into previously unexpected areas of application, such as sushi bars. You can probably think of further applications that affect your own work. If you need to implement a moving assembly line today, there is a great deal of available guidance and advice. But it is good to remember the principle of Henry Ford: move the work to the men, not the men to the work.

 # Lean manufacturing

Japanese companies emerged from the Second World War in a poor state. They were short on resources, much less efficient than firms in the United States, and produced at a much smaller scale as well. In the 1930s Toyota

Motor Company, founded by Eiji Toyoda, wanted to produce passenger cars but the government instead forced it to produce trucks, mostly through craft methods. Partly due to resource constraints, Toyota only produced a few thousand vehicles even in the early 1950s. Furthermore, Toyota had great difficulties meeting the quality standards set by the US Army, its largest potential customer at the time.

In 1949 sales collapsed, and Toyota fired around a quarter of its employees. This induced a strike and subsequently the resignation of the Toyota President, Kiichiro Toyoda. In exchange for peace with the union, Toyota had to give out a lifetime employment guarantee. So Taiichi Ohno, an engineer who had moved through the ranks at Toyota in the 1930s and 1940s to become the assembly manager, saw himself faced with two problems in the late 1940s and early 1950s. One was to become more efficient and produce at a large scale. And a related problem was how to do that without reducing the number of employees.

The lean machine

Ohno chose to increase flexibility and efficiency through what is now known as lean manufacturing, alternatively lean production, or the Toyota Production System. He essentially saw the workforce as a fixed cost and started changing the system around them. The lean manufacturing system built around the premise of waste reduction and minimization of all inputs by using fewer labour hours, materials, space, tool investments and engineering hours. It eventually changed all of Toyota's activities, manufacturing, human resources, purchasing, engineering, and even finance and marketing.

Ohno placed machinery in the sequence of the manufacturing process, to guarantee optimal flow. These flexible machines were operated by multi-skilled workers so that a variety of products could be produced at large volumes. This helped Toyota combine craft and mass production principles, when its American competitors were still completely tied in to large-scale production. Ohno also introduced the *kanban* system and the principle of just-in-time production. Rather than pushing materials through the system from inventory, Toyota used a pull system: only when materials were needed somewhere would they be delivered. *Kanban*, a system involving cards as visual aids being placed around the plant, helped to produce the right number of parts and to lower inventories and defects.

The workers were organized in teams, as Ohno recalled in his memoirs:

In a soccer team with eleven members, the key to winning or losing is teamwork.
Even with one or two star players, a team does not necessarily win.
Manufacturing is also done through teamwork. It might take 10 to 15 workers,
for example, to take a job from raw materials to finished product. The idea is
teamwork – not how many parts were machined or drilled by one worker, but
how many products were completed by the line as a whole.

Ohno also redesigned supply chain relations. Ford and other US producers
had vertically integrated many functions but Toyota decided that working
together with suppliers and coordinating information with them would be
a viable and often preferable alternative to vertical integration. Toyota built
a pyramid model of suppliers, organizing them into tiers which managed
each other. It also established much longer term relationships with suppliers
than was customary.

Of his sources, Ohno said:

The tool used to operate the system is kanban, an idea I got from American
supermarkets. … Combining automobiles and supermarkets may seem odd. But
for a long time … we made a connection between supermarkets and the just-in-
time system. A supermarket is where a customer can get (1) what is needed, (2)
at the time needed, (3) in the amount needed. … From the supermarket we got
the idea of viewing the earlier process in a production line as a kind of store. The
later process (customer) goes to the earlier process (supermarket) to acquire the
required parts (commodities) at the time and in the quantity needed. The earlier
process immediately produces the quantity just taken (restocking the shelves).

Ohno naturally faced resistance from workers and others. He later wrote:

We naturally feel more secure with a considerable amount of inventory. Before,
during, and after World War II, buying and hoarding were natural behaviours.
… We could say this is the response of a farming society. Our ancestors grew rice
for subsistence and stored it in preparation for times of natural disaster. …
Modern industry also seems stuck in this way of thinking. A person in business
may feel uneasy about survival in this competitive society without keeping some
inventories of raw materials, work-in-progress, and products. This type of
hoarding, however, is no longer practical. Industrial society must develop the
courage, or rather the common sense, to produce only what is needed when it is
needed and in the amount needed.

The Toyota way

Ohno started experimenting with the arrangement of machines: 'This was a radical change from the conventional system in which a large quantity of the same part was machined in one process and then forwarded to the next process. In 1947, we arranged machines in parallel lines or in an L-shape and tried having one worker operate three or four machines along the processing route.' This new setup was accepted after some struggles. Then suppliers became involved in new product development:

We wanted to get away from having to produce everything around the end of the month, so we started by looking inside Toyota itself. Then, when outside suppliers were needed, we first listened to their needs and then asked them to cooperate in helping us achieve levelled production. Depending on the situation, we discussed the supplier's cooperation in terms of manpower, materials, and money.

This, together with the introduction of *kanban*, helped to reduce inventories and guaranteed a better flow of products. In 1953, the just-in-time system was applied across the machine shop but the *kanban* system was not used across the whole company until 1962.

One problem the system could not deal with initially was rapid and unexpected changes in the volume or nature of demand. Because much planning is required, even small changes can affect the overall performance substantially. Toyota partly solved this by rearranging the sequencing of orders by dealers. This involved the use of more aggressive selling techniques at times. Another issue was the quality of Toyota's products. In order to meet the demands from the US Army, and because Toyota wanted to start exporting its successful Crown model to the USA, Toyota set up a total quality control system in 1958. This system later became known as total quality management.

Following the car in front

It took a considerable period of time for Toyota to develop and implement its production system fully, but it took longer for the outside world to realize how successful it was and even longer for others to start copying it in even a remotely close fashion. Toyota and other Japanese producers managed to fly under the radar long enough to be able to grab large shares of all the world's car markets. Western observers generally did not bother to notice the Japanese firms until the late 1970s.

The academics Womack, Roos and Jones must be credited with the term 'lean manufacturing' through their 1991 book *The machine that changed the world*. In 1986 they were amazed by a visit to Toyota's assembly plant at Takaoka (Japan):

There were practically no buffers between the welding shop and paint booth and between paint and final assembly. And there were no parts warehouses at all. Instead parts were delivered directly to the line at hourly intervals from the supplier plants where they had just been made.

They also compared Toyota's plant with the mass production system at Framingham by General Motors:

Takaoka was almost twice as productive and three times as accurate as Framingham in performing the same set of standard activities on our standard car. In terms of manufacturing space, it was 40 per cent more efficient, and its inventories were a tiny fraction of those at Framingham.

From the early 1980s onwards western car manufacturers tried to replicate Toyota's success. One place where western firms tried to learn from Toyota was at NUMMI, a joint venture between Toyota and GM located in a 1960s GM plant in California. Womack, Roos and Jones:

found that NUMMI matched Takaoka's quality and nearly matched its productivity. Space utilization was not as efficient because of the old GM plant's poor layout. Inventory was also considerably higher than at Takaoka, because almost all parts were transported 5,000 miles across the Pacific rather than five or ten miles from neighbouring supplier plants in Toyota City. It was clear to us by the end of 1986 that Toyota had truly achieved a revolution in manufacturing, that old mass-production plants could not compete, and that the new best way – lean production – could be transplanted successfully to new environments, such as NUMMI.

But GM ended up learning not too much from NUMMI and other producers like Ford have struggled mightily to come to terms with lean manufacturing.

Everyone's lean

Lean manufacturing principles and practices are now used by manufacturing firms in a wide range of industries and countries, from the production of bicycles in China to the construction of olive oil extracting machinery in Italy and the upgrading of London's Tube network. Some governments have been actively trying to promote lean manufacturing among local firms, and the 'lean' concept has been applied to other business processes including innovation.

In smaller firms and the services sector lean production is gradually starting to be introduced as well. Interestingly, supermarkets are now among those trying to learn from Toyota, reversing Ohno's journey 50 years earlier. The notion of lean is so powerful because it captures the bare essence of what a transformation process should do: take as little as possible and turn it into as much as possible.

 # Total quality management

The quality of a product has, of course, always been an important characteristic and it takes little convincing that if a product is of insufficient quality, customers will simply walk away from it. But seldom was the need to improve product quality greater than in 1950s Japan. Since Japan had come out of the Second World War on the wrong end, it lost much of its productive capacity and resources and its standing in the world. Once Japanese manufacturers had made the conversion from military to civilian products they found there was little demand abroad for 'Made in Japan' products, which were seen as inferior in quality and shoddy, especially compared to products of the mighty US manufacturers.

And because domestic demand was small, exporting products was going to be key to the success of Japanese firms. These problems had sparked the introduction of lean production (see pp. 20–25) at Toyota and other companies. Although lean production eventually produced great efficiency and productivity benefits, it did not directly raise quality levels. Toyota, in fact, faced severe quality problems with its Crown model, losing domestic leadership to Nissan, and had to temporarily pull out of the US market completely. How could these Japanese firms raise their quality standards?

Zero defects

Their response was to introduce total quality control (TQC), now known as total quality management (TQM). TQM aims to improve the quality of goods and services and the effectiveness of an organization. It is an integrative approach, which builds a desire for continuous quality improvement into the organization and makes everyone responsible for achieving quality targets. Desired quality levels are defined from the customer's perspective. The objective is to then obtain these levels with zero defects. In order to achieve zero defects a continuous stream of improvements in processes is needed. Statistics provide a means of measuring defects and their causes.

Kaoru Ishikawa, one of the developers of TQC in Japan, distinguished five goals: seeking quality before profits; developing the potential of employees by training, providing positive feedback and delegating responsibilities; building a long-term orientation on customers; using measurements and data and communicating those throughout the organization; and developing a TQC system through which employees understand the quality consequences of everything they do. According to Ishikawa, producing at the highest quality 'is a responsibility that should be shared by all people in the firm'. So rather than putting a focus on inspecting work after it has taken place, the attention ought to move to prevention of defects by all workers and managers, regardless of whether they work in production or in some support function or in fact in a supplier organization.

Continuous improvements

TQM was developed over a long period of time and by a variety of people and organizations. In the 1920s the Hawthorne works of the Western Electric Company, part of the Bell System, started applying statistical quality control in the United States. During the 1930s sampling-based inspection was introduced to ensure some control over defects. But real progress was not made until 1950, when quality expert W. Edwards Deming was sent to Japan by the US government. Deming was happy to go because he did not find much demand for his services in the USA where companies believe they were performing well enough without worrying about quality. While Deming was in Japan, he met members of the Japanese Union of Scientists and Engineers (JUSE), who asked him to advise them on reconstruction and quality issues. Deming explained how many statistical variations in quality have common causes, which can be tackled. He also stressed the importance of worker pride and satisfaction and pointed at the system, rather than the worker, as the ultimate source of quality variations and defects.

JUSE members were eager to learn more and subsequently invited other American experts over. Joseph Juran, who came to Japan in 1954, discussed the importance of top management in planning and controlling quality so that it suits customer needs. Juran, who had personally worked on the experiments at Hawthorne, also stressed measurement and problem-solving techniques. Other quality experts included Armand Feigenbaum, who introduced the term

TQC in 1956 and promoted cross-functional teams, and Philip Crosby. JUSE then started spreading this wisdom through the large-scale training and education of its members, including top-level managers, in quality control issues. These people then became quality control instructors in their own organizations, which allowed them to spread the message to everyone.

TQC became a company policy at various companies in later years. When Toyota found it could not meet the quality standards of the US Army in 1958, it decided to implement TQC in 1959. Then executive VP Eiji Toyoda said that 'the ideal inspection is no inspection. If all the machines and equipment can assure the quality of products, inspection becomes unnecessary'. Toyota proceeded in three phases in implementing TQC between 1961 and 1965, first stressing the need to involve all workers, then moving towards cross-functional collaboration and finally developing a management system built around quality assurance and cost management. Matsushita Electric likewise introduced its zero defects principle in the early 1960s. In the 1960s these firms then added quality circles to their TQC systems as an additional tool. Quality circles involve regular meetings of groups of employees and managers, where quality problems are discussed and solutions suggested.

Exporting quality

On the back of TQC Toyota and Matsushita rose to great success in subsequent years and built large market shares in the US markets during the 1960s and 1970s, as did other Japanese manufacturing firms. Ironically, when American firms started analyzing the enormous success of Japanese firms in the early 1980s, they found it was built on quality techniques discovered in the USA and exported to Japan. US firms then started implementing TQM as it was now called and quality circles on a massive scale, focusing more on the management aspect than on the statistical techniques. At some point 93 per cent of the top 500 American firms had implemented some form of TQM.

TQM sparked the introduction of prestigious quality awards, like the Baldrige Award for companies with advanced quality practices. TQM also found its way to other countries. And it brought along the introduction and mass spread of International Standards Organization (ISO) certification in the 1990s. ISO certification, particularly ISO 9000, was used by organizations as a way of showing that they complied with important quality demands. But eventually disappointment over TQM set in at many companies, since the results delivered often did not measure up against the great promises. This was especially true for later adopters of TQM. In the Netherlands companies that won the King William I prize for quality, like Fokker and DAF, went bankrupt within a few years. It seemed that TQM was most effective when top-level managers really committed to it, the organization was open to it, and employees were really empowered to make a difference. So in the 1990s TQM gradually disappeared from the scene. In retrospect, many consider it to be little more than just another management fad.

And now ...

In recent years, TQM as a concept has given way to its successor, six sigma (see pp. 40–43). Quality remains a key priority for companies today. As a consequence of TQM every company now realizes that quality must be the product of everyone's efforts, not just of some quality expert like a statistician or engineer, who analyzes products after they are produced. Customers have come to expect high quality levels.

In many ways competition today increasingly revolves around innovation, the ability to offer products with a different touch, and customer experience, the ability of a company to offer a different touch while delivering a product. But delivering innovation and a good customer experience still require the commitment of every employee, which the TQM revolution has sought to achieve. While TQM itself is no longer en vogue, the principles from which it is built are still very much present in management today.

Cellular manufacturing

Manufacturing in the 1970s faced a number of challenges. In car manufacturing, for example, the methods were predominately the same as 50 years previously, when Henry Ford and Alfred Sloan were running Ford Motors and General Motors. By the 1970s, however, the assembly line approach was beginning to creak. Although updated and modified over the years many believed it was inadequate for the demands of the modern world.

To begin with, a new educated workforce was reluctant to work amid the repetitive tedium of the assembly line, many preferring instead to work in the growing number of white collar jobs. Those that did end up working in factories were often poorly motivated and uncommitted to the enterprise. Employee turnover was high, strikes were frequent, and absenteeism was rife. These concerns were particularly acute in the social democratic countries of Europe, such as Sweden and Germany, where even the least well-trained worker felt he or she was entitled to an interesting job.

The demands placed on manufacturers were changing too. Manufacturers needed to turn out more differentiated products, in lower quantities, and with shorter lifecycles. Companies like Sweden's Volvo felt that change was needed – a new approach to manufacturing that both created the flexibility to meet the new demands placed on manufacturers, while at the same time creating an engaging work environment.

Flexible cells

These new demands opened up the possibility of a new approach to manufacturing: cellular manufacturing. This revolutionary concept got rid of the traditional assembly line entirely, and put in its place a series of assembly systems with flexible cells at their heart.

The cells were made up of workstations and resources clustered around specific stages of the manufacturing process. This arrangement cut the amount of time materials were being moved around the factory floor, which, in turn, cuts costs.

As well as its operational impact, cellular manufacturing had a significant effect on the way people worked in factories. Rather than the soulless monotony of the assembly line, cellular manufacturing required highly skilled workers who were capable of multitasking, and able to use a variety of different tools and machines. This new style of manufacturing was more attractive to a modern well-educated workforce allowing, as it did, a degree of autonomy not possible with the traditional assembly line. As a result employee engagement was typically greater, commitment to the business purpose improved, and productivity usually increased.

Celling Volvo

The story of cellular management is inextricably linked with car manufacturer Volvo and Pehr Gyllenhammar, the man who was appointed chief executive of the company in 1971.

When Gyllenhammar took over at the wheel, Volvo was motoring in the wrong direction. Annual labour turnover at the Swedish auto manufacturer's main assembly plant in Gothenburg was 41 per cent, despite comparatively high wages for the industry.

As Gyllenhammar pointed out, in a 1974 *Time* magazine article: 'As people became more educated – and Sweden spends perhaps more money per capita for education than any other country – their jobs have become less complex. That does not make sense.'

The rapid job turnover meant increased training costs and a drop in product quality. Gyllenhammar needed to fix the problem or risk tarnishing the Volvo brand image of reliable, durable, high quality cars. So the CEO put together a team of young executives to come up with a solution and design a new manufacturing plant where 'machines would be the product of people and not vice versa'.

Two months later and the trouble-shooting team presented its results: cellular manufacturing and the Kalmar Volvo plant. The newly designed manufacturing plant cost $23 million to build, 10 per cent more than the traditional equivalent. It started production in 1973.

As the *Time* reporter who visited the plant in 1974 noted, the Kalmar plant was a radical departure from traditional car manufacturing. For a start it was quiet, quiet enough for the worker to listen to their personal stereos. Bicycles cycled around the factory carrying just-in-time parts. The most obvious difference, though, was the lack of an assembly line. Instead, workers were arranged in groups of 15 to 25 people, working on a single car frame for a Volvo 264 at a time, the frame transported from group to group via computer guided platforms – 250 in all.

Each team dealt with a particular part of the assembly process, the electrical system for example. Within this each team member worked on different aspects of the electrical system, rather than just doing the same thing all day, every day, over and over.

Swedish models

Unsurprisingly, the Kalmar plant attracted visitors from far and wide. In the first few years auto magnates from Umberto Agnelli, managing director of Italy's auto giant Fiat, to Henry Ford II, beat a path to the small Swedish city, famous until now for its castle and cathedral.

Some industrialists were quick to adopt the new techniques. Fiat set up a new engine assembly process at its Termoli plant, abandoning the fixed assembly line in favour of fixed position assembly islands or cells.

In the USA, certainly in the motor industry, there was some resistance to the idea. The feeling was that because of the much larger scale of operation, cellular manufacturing techniques would not suit the US market. While in Volvo's plant itself, the unions were pushing for more radical change, proposing that the teams abandoned the idea of a foreman, for example.

(The union got its wish in 1974, with the opening of Volvo's Uddevalla plant, where there were no supervisors, but group ombudsmen instead.)

The Japanese began to adopt cellular manufacturing – *seru seisan houshiki,* as the Japanese called it – in the mid-1990s. The Japanese experimented with a number of different cell forms, including spider, spiral, escargot, and heart, even a cell pattern that looks like a flower. Indeed, since that first foray into cellular manufacturing by Volvo, cell layouts have been constantly modified to provide the least, but most effective, distance between the workstations in a cell.

Cellular manufacturing today

Cellular manufacturing has proved a popular alternative to more conventional assembly line operations. Being part of the lean manufacturing wave it has a substantial following inside and outside the car industry. However, while there are many adherents of cellular manufacturing who argue it offers a combination of flexibility, efficiency of product flow, and employee empowerment and engagement that other systems cannot offer, there are still many critics.

In 2006 a paper on cellular manufacturing in Japan noted that Japanese plant directors and manufacturing managers raised a number of reservations regarding cellular manufacturing, including: problems controlling and monitoring work within cells; increased training requirements and associated costs; and an increase in tools and equipment required.

And what of Volvo's cellular manufacturing experiment? In November 1992 Volvo announced that it was closing both its Kalmar and Uddevalla plants, but keeping the traditional setup at Gothenburg open. The last car rolled out of Uddevalla in 1993, while Kalmar closed the following year. (Uddevalla has since been reopened.)

 # Mass Customization

Throughout the 20th century, mass production techniques like the moving assembly line (see pp. 17–20) lowered the costs of manufacturing goods. Great efficiency was achieved through a stable and controlled production system that focused on scale economies. As a consequence products like cars, televisions, and stereos became available to the masses. And as these products were sold on a larger scale, this allowed for further cost reductions. But by the mid-1980s some cracks in the armour of mass production were becoming visible to companies.

Because competition was based primarily on low costs rather than product differentiation, there was a continuous need to drive down prices and heavy competition ensued. Consumers no longer seemed content with the limited choice they were being offered. Another problem with mass production was the ease with which the system could be transferred to lower wage countries. In its pager business, Motorola was facing increasing competition from Japanese companies, which offered pagers at half the price their American counterparts were charging. In the bicycle industry Japan's National Bicycle Industrial Company (NBIC) in turn faced competition from even lower wage countries, like Taiwan. So these companies faced the task of how to change the basis of competition.

Manufacturing gets personal

Their response was mass customization – the production of personalized goods and services but on a large scale. Mass customization uses flexible processes and new technologies to produce large volumes of these person-alized items at relatively low cost levels. As a consequence, almost all customers should be able to get the exact product they were looking for. In its pure form, mass customization does not just involve producing a greater variety of goods; it is also a production process that is driven by customer needs and desires. In the process, inventory levels are reduced as products no longer need to be stored when they are produced only after customers express their demand. And because customers receive a product that is closer to their actual demand, they are willing to pay a premium price. Furthermore, mass customization to an extent replaces market research, as customers tell the company exactly what it is they want in the process of ordering the product.

Lighting the way

Mass customization did not emerge out of the blue in the 1980s. Companies had put in place many of its elements earlier. For instance, Lutron Electronics, facing competition and cost pressures from giant GE in the 1960s, offered a wide variety of electrical switches based on the demands of individual customers like interior designers and architects. This helped Lutron lead the American lighting controls market, and produce a range of patents in the process. GE eventually exited from this line of business. But in the 1980s flexible manufacturing systems had emerged that allowed companies in a range of industries to introduce mass customization.

In late 1986 the Japanese bicycle market was not growing at all. NBIC already offered more than 250 models to its customers and within these models customers could choose their preferred colours and a range of options. But now it was changing its ordering system. When NBIC's president visited a famous Osaka-based department store, he could see women ordering custom-made dresses, which were delivered within two weeks. Seeing an immediate parallel to NBIC's bicycle business, he started to focus more on the high end of the market, producing the Panasonic brand through the Panasonic Ordering System (POS). There was initial resistance from some senior managers, who thought the idea risky and costly and from external industry analysts, who simply said this approach could not be successful. But NBIC pushed on regardless.

Mr Hata, the project leader, worked with a small team of designers, engineers and workers. After only four months they produced a pilot plant and seven months after the president had taken up the idea, NBIC had a fully operational plant. Hata said:

We worked long hours. We proposed and debated many new ideas for days. We started with a few people, but as the project began to progress, more people were added. Within a few weeks we established a pilot plant in a large empty warehouse next to the factory. Still, numerous issues had to be addressed and solved, but as time went on we were convinced that the project was doable. We knew we had the capability, because many of us had spent most of our professional lives making bicycles.

Hata turned out to be right, as POS produced a complete turnaround at NBIC, which saw its market share rise significantly over the next few years.

Motorola's pager division similarly introduced mass customization. Its project, started in December 1987, was run by a cross-functional team of 24 people and involved setting up an automated, computer-integrated assembly line with lot sizes of one. The Motorola team looked for best-in-world experiences and avoided reinventing the wheel. Because of this use of outside inspiration the project was called Bandit. The new Bravo pager model could be produced in two hours and came in 29 million different ways. Manufacturing director Len deBarros said: 'We didn't want to look at just the manufacturing process. We wanted to revamp the entire business cycle, from the time a salesperson takes an order until the time the pager is packed and shipped.' The order time went down from two months to just 90 minutes. Motorola's pagers instantly became a fashionable product and Motorola itself improved its global market to over 40 per cent and in the process gained the Malcolm Baldrige National Quality Award in 1988.

Taking it to the masses

The news on mass customization spread quickly. By 1989 NBIC's story had been featured not only in the Japanese press but also in *Fortune*, the *New York Times* and the *Washington Post*, further increasing the fame and value of the Panasonic brand. By 1992 mass customization had become a theme for many businesses, as evidenced by the publication of consultant Joseph Pine's book *Mass customization: The new frontier in business competition*. Pine suggested the move from mass production to mass customization amounted to a true paradigm shift in how businesses make their money.

Many companies have started to take up mass customization, though it has not always been easy. As Lutron's founder Joel Spira describes:

While Lutron has been very successful at mass customization, it hasn't been easy. Managers have to deal with the consequences of choosing between standard modules and creativity in engineering: between customization and costs in production; and between order and chaos within each of the engineering, production, purchasing, and selling functions. As we have learned at Lutron: 'Chaos increases new business – order increases profits.' Although, on occasion, the tension gets out of balance, and management has to take some action.

Vive la différence

Mass customization is used by many businesses today, both in manufacturing and in services. Highly successful service companies like Starbucks and Subway run their operations on the basis of the mass customization model, catering for customers according to their wishes. BMW's highly successful Mini car is produced differently for every individual customer. Mass customization works particularly well in the high end of the market, as this is both where customer needs tend to vary more and where customers are willing to pay a premium price.

To implement mass customization, companies have to alter their marketing, production and logistics functions. In marketing a mechanism needs to be introduced through which customers can express their needs. Of course, the internet is an ideal place for such information to be collected. And customer relationship management (see pp. 130–133) is used to gather and process the information. The production system needs to be flexible and responsive, using a modular design as well as flexible manufacturing systems. And in logistics and supply chain management (see pp. 38–40), supply chain designs and relations have to be adjusted accordingly, for which further information technology is used.

Business process re-engineering

It is a truism to observe that in any industry there are leaders and laggards. But in the early 1980s there was a strong feeling of malaise in the USA, as observers noted the increasing number of industries, from automobiles to consumer electronics to semiconductors, where all the leaders seemed to be Japanese and all the laggards seemed to be American (and European). In trying to understand the reasons for these differences in competitiveness, one common theme that emerged was that Japanese firms seemed to have more efficient business processes. In the USA different subunits all had well-defined roles in processes, and each unit tried its best, but no one carried responsibility for the overall process. A long time ago the USA had been the birthplace of Taylor's scientific management (see pp. 12–17) but now a new drive for more efficient processes was needed.

Rethinking processes

The solution, which for a few years completely dominated business magazines, was business process re-engineering (BPR). According to Michael Hammer, its most well-known proponent, BPR was 'the radical redesign of core business processes to achieve dramatic improvements in productivity, cycle times and quality' and also 'the fundamental rethinking and radical redesign of business processes to bring about dramatic improvements in performance.' The essence of BPR is to take customer requirements, decide which processes are needed to fulfil those requirements, and design those processes from scratch. This often requires a change in mental maps as well, in order to turn customer requirements into the focal point.

Another aspect of BPR is that it seeks *radical*, not *piecemeal*, change. And BPR makes use of new information technology to automate processes where possible and necessary. As Hammer wrote: 'If I were re-creating this company today, given what I know and given current technology, what would it look like?' BPR is executed through a set of techniques like diagramming. It is generally a top-down process, driven by executives and experts. The improvements BPR seeks to attain include lower costs and cycle times, by removing unnecessary activities, the employees who execute them, and the hierarchical layers that manage them, and higher quality, through integrated processes that have clear ownership.

Pioneers of re-engineering

When Donald Petersen became Ford President and COO in 1980, the company was losing $1.5 billion so Petersen started a change programme. One of the areas in which Ford tried to reduce costs was its accounts payable department, which employed over 500 people in North America. Ford reckoned that by using new information technology and rationalizing some processes it could reduce that number by up to 20 per cent. But then it compared itself with Japan's Mazda, partly owned by Ford, and found that Mazda employed only five people in accounts payable, a huge difference even taking Mazda's smaller size into account. As a consequence the goalposts were adjusted significantly.

Analysis of what took place at accounts payable showed that much time was wasted on removing mismatches between different documents. Using BPR, Ford came up with 'invoiceless processing', which involved a database. This lowered the number of matches needed from 14 to three and automated the matching process. As a consequence Ford reduced its number of employees in accounts payable by 75 per cent and the reliability of the process became much higher. Indirectly the redesign also helped in lowering inventory levels and improving cash flow.

Mutual Benefit Life (MBL) used BPR for its insurance applications. The existing processes involved 30 steps, five departments, and 19 people. It also took five to 25 days and made things difficult for customers. MBL's president required a 60 per cent productivity improvement. MBL introduced shared databases, expert systems, and computer networks, and redefined its jobs and departments. It introduced case managers who took full control of the application process. In the few cases these individuals could not solve, they could consult with senior underwriters. The application time dropped to four hours and the turnaround of an application to two to five days. In the process the number of people required for applications also decreased significantly.

Hard times

Hammer and others started writing about BPR, sometimes simply referred to as re-engineering, in 1990. That turned out to be excellent timing, as the US and world economies went into recession in the early 1990s. BPR became hugely popular and faddish because it was seen as the solution for underperformance, low profitability, a bureaucratic culture, and other company ailments. Other successful examples of BPR use appeared, for instance at American Express. As it turned out, many companies had built up substantial slack in their processes and BPR was just the thing they needed to make these processes leaner.

But in the mid-1990s the tide started turning. The economy improved, as did the performance of most companies. Worse still, BPR became a synonym for downsizing. Many companies in need for an excuse to cut jobs announced they would engage in re-engineering. Hammer kept trying to turn the tide, suggesting even in 1999 that:

it has enabled companies to operate faster and more efficiently and to use information technology more productively. It has improved the jobs of employees, giving them more authority and a clearer view of how their work fits into the operations of the enterprise as a whole. It has rewarded customers with higher quality products and more responsive service. And it has paid big dividends to shareholders, reducing companies' costs, increasing their revenues, and boosting their stock values.

Still re-engineering

Like the term scientific management, re-engineering is hardly used by executives these days. But most large companies have gone through some form of process re-engineering over the past 15 years, and many of its principles are still in use today. Re-engineering has made companies leaner and more productive. Fewer non-essential processes are in place now than 15 years ago. Further use of information technology has increased the use of case managers and the like who own processes and are quite autonomous.

At the same time many feel that the real challenge facing companies today is to be more innovative, not necessarily leaner. And too much focus on the efficiency of processes can actually be detrimental to innovation. In rapidly changing environments a process focus can create resistance to change and undermine the ability to adapt to changing circumstances.

It is also worth noting that BPR gave very little attention to the tasks and skills of management that were needed to implement the new processes. James Champy wrote a follow-up book called *Re-engineering management*, which sought to tackle this issue, but by the time it came out the enthusiasm for re-engineering had passed.

Supply chain management

In the globalizing business world of the 1980s, it was increasingly important to deliver goods and services when and where they were needed. The just-in-time principle in lean manufacturing (see pp. 20–25) was an important part of this trend. But with consumer trends switching at a fast pace it was not a good strategy to hold inventory, even in small quantities, if this could be avoided. So companies faced an increasing need to deliver on demand.

At the same time a combination of growing competitive pressures and globalization led companies to outsource elements of their business to third parties (see pp. 136–138), where those outsourcing suppliers could add value and expertise at a lower cost than the company doing the outsourcing. And many of the best suppliers were based in other countries. This created an extended and fragmented supply chain dispersed across the globe.

As a result of these trends, companies started to realize they need to be as responsive as possible. But how could they meet the changes in demand, and be sure of delivering products to consumers at the right time and the right price, when they no longer owned or controlled all the elements of the production process? This was precisely the dilemma that consultants Booz Allen Hamilton were advising companies like Dutch electronics producer Philips on in the early 1980s.

Inventing the supply chain

Supply chain management (SCM), as it came to be known, combines logistics with strategy. It involves the management of two-way flows of materials, finance, people and information along the chain from the raw materials to the customer. In the modern world the chain usually stretches across countries and continents. At the centre of modern ideas about supply chain management are speed and flexibility. The concept is founded on the image of a chain with continual links between the different supply stages.

Effective SCM can lead to processes, people, and materials working more efficiently and so has a significant impact on costs. Simplifying the supply chain, usually through the use of technology, can often lead to improved services at highly competitive prices – something that computer manufacturer Dell achieved by electing to sell computers directly to the public. For major multinational companies, there is no doubt that global SCM is a highly complex challenge, but one critical to their competitiveness.

Linking the lexicon

The term supply chain management was coined by Keith Oliver, a consultant at US management consultants Booz Allen Hamilton. It was introduced in an article about Oliver in the *Financial Times* in 1982.

The origins of the term were bound up in a strategy meeting between a consulting team from BAH that contained Oliver, and a team from one of the firm's clients, Philips, the Dutch consumer electronics business. During the 1970s, Oliver had been developing his ideas about removing functional silos in a business to integrate the processes involved in producing a product or service.

Oliver's strategy team came up with the name 'integrated inventory management', or I2M, to describe the concept. The people at Philips were not that impressed with the new term, however. One member of the Philips team asked Oliver to explain what I2M actually meant. Oliver later recalled the exchange:

'We're talking about the management of a chain of supply as though it were a single entity,' Mr Oliver replied, 'not a group of disparate functions.'

'Then why don't you call it that?' Mr Van t'Hoff, the member of the Philips team said.

'Call it what?' Mr. Oliver asked.

'Total supply chain management.'

And so it was that the term SCM was born, when a set of practices was given a name.

Chain reaction

At Booz Allen Hamilton, Oliver disseminated SCM through his work with a range of clients both before and after the concept was given a name. These companies included manufacturers like Cadbury-Schweppes, Heineken, and Hoechst, as well as Philips.

A number of other early SCM initiatives have been documented demonstrating the way the concept began to gain ground. Wal-Mart, the global retail giant, was an early adopter of SCM. The company worked with its manufacturers, tasking them with managing its inventory, a practice known as vendor managed inventory. In turn it expected 100 per cent, or close to 100 per cent, order fulfilment rates on those items.

In the early 1990s, Hewlett-Packard, the computer business, linked distribution activities with its manufacturing activities, implementing a new distribution requirements planning system. And its competitor Dell took SCM one step further, to *supply chain integration*, when it increasingly started treating its suppliers as if they were part of Dell, thus tightly integrating relations and goods and information flows.

Appliance manufacturer Whirlpool introduced its supply chain management system in 1992 with the vision: 'Winning companies will be those who come the closest to achieving an inter-enterprise pull system. They will be linked in a short cycle response mode to the customer.'

With exposure in the management literature, the work of consultants like BAH, and the pressures of the global commercial markets, SCM proliferated rapidly.

Chain evolution

It was obvious fairly early on that supply chain management would be an important part of a company's competitive arsenal. Whirlpool, one of the early adopters, created a vice-president of logistics. Since then corporations have shifted SCM further up the corporate agenda.

As Oliver and Laseter pointed out, many companies, the ChevronTexaco Corporation, and H.J. Heinz Company, for example, elevated the role of chief procurement officer to the C suite alongside the COO, CFO, etc. At DuPont a vice-president (global sourcing and logistics) and chief procurement officer were appointed, while IBM created the new position, senior vice-president, who integrated the supply chain.

Understandably, the practice of SCM has evolved over time. Today, for example, logistics are being moved closer to the centre of many companies' operations. Take the example of TNT Logistics, part of the Dutch group TNT, which manages BMW's supply chain to its factory in Spartanburg in the USA. TNT handles supply from the point when a supplier sends a part, to the moment it is installed in a vehicle in the BMW plant. This means that the forklift truck drivers ferrying the parts around the assembly line are from TNT and not BMW. It is a sign of how roles in the traditional supply chain are growing increasingly blurred.

Six sigma

By the 1980s the importance of quality as a driver of success had become deeply ingrained in most executives' worldviews. Many companies had tried to tackle quality issues through the use of total quality management (see pp. 25–28). Although TQM had proven successful in some respects, it was found wanting in other areas. One common complaint was that TQM was internally driven, rather than focused on customers. Another issue was that TQM measured defects per 1000 products while in fact products should have far fewer defects than one per 1000.

Motorola was one company that still struggled with quality. In its communications division there were complaints about warranty claims from the field salesforce. Motorola also still lagged behind its Japanese competitors in the manufacturing quality of products. Managers in Motorola's operations did not see TQM as the solution to these problems. They felt there was scope for further improvement in the way the company managed its quality.

Sixth sense

Out of this opportunity emerged Motorola's quality initiative, which came to be known as six sigma – a method for continuously improving quality based on the use of hard data and statistical analysis. Six sigma focuses on identifying sources of variance and error in the process flow and subsequently eliminating those. The term six sigma stands for six standard deviations, which equates to 3.4 defects per 1 million opportunities (or DPMO), which is seen as an acceptable margin of error, although zero defects remains the ultimate goal. Six sigma involves aligning business processes with customer requirements through a structured model of which DMAIC (define opportunity, measure performance, analyze opportunity, improve performance, control performance) is the most well-known example. The data analyzed include both output and input data and together these produce a root cause of problems.

Six sigma differs from TQM in a number of respects. TQM included a less rigorous toolset, whereas six sigma has a clear sequence for using its tools. The objectives of TQM were organizational, rather than bottom line or business objectives. Six sigma is top-down driven with a strong need for executive commitment, unlike TQM's focus on self-directed teams. It is also said to be more closely associated with overall strategy and more cross-functional. Large-scale training systems have been set up around six sigma, including the awarding of belts similar to the system used in martial arts.

Galvin-izing success

Bill Smith was a top engineer and scientist in Motorola's communications division. When confronted with the problems with warranty claims, he devised a set of statistics and formulas because existing quality programmes were not sufficient to overcome this quality problem. Smith recognized that system complexity could well be a cause of the quality problems because it increased the number of failure opportunities. Motorola CEO Bob Galvin, who in 1981 had promised Motorola would deliver a tenfold improvement in quality, liked both the engagement of Smith as well as the detail of his proposals. Smith measured the reliability of processes by their mean time to failure and their quality by process variability and defect rates.

Six sigma was then implemented in the Schaumburg, Illinois, production facility. In Schaumburg, productivity increased 12 per cent a year for the next 10 years, poor quality costs dropped by 80 per cent, process defects by 90 per cent and the savings on manufacturing costs accumulated to a reported $11 billion. In 1988 Motorola collected the Malcolm Baldrige National Quality Award, to a large extent because of six sigma. Smith worked with Mikel Harry, now the most renowned six sigma expert in the world, to develop six sigma further. Harry went on to lead the Motorola Six Sigma Institute. Smith and Harry took some of their ideas from other quality experts who had visited Motorola during the 1980s, including Joseph Juran and Eliyahu Goldratt.

Selling six sigma

Motorola publicized the details of six sigma. But in the 1990s, after the untimely death of Smith, the six sigma initiative became less important to the firm. Motorola was a successful firm in the years after six sigma was implemented, although it had troubles competing in the mobile phone market. But instead of dying out, six sigma spread like wildfire. Mikel Harry left Motorola in 1994 to found the Six Sigma Academy. This allowed him to spread the concept without being constrained by his relationship with Motorola. The concept was taken up first by Allied Signal, in 1994, and then by GE Capital, in 1995. When he saw its potential, GE's Jack Welch made six sigma one of the company's key initiatives, and this helped to introduce the concept to a much broader audience. GE Capital's implementation also showed that six sigma might be as applicable to services as it was to manufacturing. Six sigma became a highly popular quality improvement tool that was implemented at organizations worldwide. Many books were published and both specialist and generalist consulting firms offered six sigma implementation advice.

Six peaks

Today the wave of six sigma implementations has probably reached its peak but interest in it continues. Companies have learned that implementing six sigma can be a challenging and lengthy task. Some of the challenges include the difficulty of finding high-quality data, prioritizing improvement tasks, getting close to zero defects in services, inconsistencies between companies in how six sigma and the belt system are used, and consultant overselling. The startup costs of six sigma make it less suitable for small companies. Because six sigma makes processes more efficient, like business process re-engineering (see pp. 35–37), employees may resist if for fear of job losses. Yet six sigma also seems to have brought many companies real improvements in quality levels and is a useful evolution in the management of quality.

2

Money

How can financial resources be allocated most effectively to new opportunities? How can the performance of existing activities be measured and evaluated? The objective of money innovations is to deliver on the financial objectives of the firm and its shareholders.

 ## Introduction

Innovation in the world of finance is a highly contentious topic: it is a great source of wealth creation for investment bankers, as they develop ever more complex and obscure derivative products, but it also creates opportunities for risk taking and illegal activity, as the cases of Barings bank, Enron, and others demonstrate.

While innovations in financial engineering tend to be the ones that make the headlines, our focus in this section is on the rather more mundane aspects of finance and accounting. Our objective is essentially to understand how firms make better decisions – by which we mean decisions that yield the greatest overall value to their owners. This includes decisions about allocating scarce capital to the most promising opportunities, keeping control of the profitability of different activities, and evaluating opportunities with different risk profiles. And, as with all the other aspects of business that we deal with in this book, many of the key innovations in this area go a long way back in time.

Managing the firm's finances

The customary starting point in the history of financial and accounting innovation is the invention of double-entry bookkeeping by Luca Paciolo in 1494 in Venice, which allowed the firms of the time to start keeping track of their assets and liabilities, rather than simply working on a cash-in/cash-out basis.

The next wave of innovations in accounting can be traced back to the 19th century, with the introduction of cost-benefit analysis as a means of evaluating the full range of costs and benefits before deciding to pursue a particular project, and then the emergence of *cost accounting* which allowed firms to keep track of detailed information on the cost drivers of various activities. In the early 20th century, the US chemical manufacturer DuPont introduced the concept of *return on investment* (ROI) which for the first time allowed different activities to be compared objectively. A few years later, *discounted cash flow* (DCF) was introduced as a way of factoring the time value of money into investment decisions. DCF had been developed as a concept in the 1870s, but it was first put into practice in the 1920s by AT&T, and most large firms only picked it up in the post-war years.

In the 1930s multinational firms, and especially the oil majors, started developing sophisticated internal transfer pricing systems to allow for trade between different units of the same firm, and to steer internal profits towards those countries with the most favourable tax policies.

By the 1960s the basic techniques of management accounting and capital budgeting had been put in place, but, of course, many challenges remained. The increasing complexity of companies made it much harder to allocate costs fairly across different activities; the need to keep control over diverse assets pushed companies towards highly standardized budgeting systems; and the increasing importance of 'knowledge' assets, rather than physical assets like plant and equipment, made it much harder to value firms. In response to these challenges, practising managers and academics began to experiment with a wide variety of innovative techniques.

One line of innovation sought to get a better handle on the true costs of a firm's activities, resulting in the introduction of *activity-based costing* (ABC) in the early 1980s. A second focused on overcoming the constraints of traditional budgeting systems. For example, Texas Instruments introduced the concept of zero-based budgeting in 1969 to encourage managers to start each budgeting cycle with a 'clean sheet of paper' rather than an incremental adjustment to the previous year's numbers. More recently the *Beyond Budgeting* Round Table was established by Jeremy Hope and Robin Fraser in the UK, building ideas first tried out by Swedish company Handelsbanken in the 1970s, to explore ways of eliminating the traditional budgeting process altogether. A somewhat related idea, which can be traced back to

Springfield Remanufacturing in 1983, is open book management, which involved communicating financial information to all employees as a means of increasing their understanding of, and therefore their commitment to improving, the financial results of the company.

The third line of innovation in management accounting was the introduction of systems for monitoring and valuing the firm's intangible assets. The most well-known approach here is the *balanced scorecard*, pioneered by US company Analog Devices in the late 1980s and subsequently rolled out on a worldwide basis by Robert Kaplan and David Norton. At around the same time the intellectual capital movement took off, thanks in large part to the pioneering efforts of Swedish company Skandia, and its Navigator model. Both approaches sought to develop reliable and valid measures of non-financial performance, especially with regard to customer relationships, employee capabilities, and internal processes.

Innovation in management accounting continues to take shape, driven by the truism that the increasingly important aspects of business (emerging opportunities, risk, intangible assets) are the most difficult to measure accurately. As Gary Hamel has observed: 'Companies should measure their success not by the fact that they are still around and making money, but by how many opportunities they have missed.'

Financial market innovations

While it is not our primary focus, let us offer a quick sketch of the financial innovations that have shaped the way firms relate to the financial markets. There is no obvious starting point for this discussion: firms have always relied, to a greater or lesser extent, on banks to support their investment activities, and over the centuries a sophisticated set of mechanisms has taken shape to cater to the various needs of savers and borrowers. The creation of the joint stock company as a legal entity, in 1856, for example, was a major institutional innovation that allowed individuals to invest in firms they did not work for, and it helped to spur enormous growth in the size of firms in both the USA and Europe in the latter part of the 19th century.

Perhaps the most important innovations in financial markets during the 20th century were those related to changes in the governance of firms. The dominance of the joint stock model in the post-war years led to the emergence of conglomerates (see Chapter 6) but, as these firms became unwieldy and their performance sagged, entrepreneurial financiers such as Kohlberg Kravis Roberts (KKR) introduced the leveraged buyout as a means of buying out shareholders largely through borrowing money, and typically selling off the parts of the acquired firm at a vast profit. KKR's acquisition of the Beatrice Corporation in 1976 is widely seen as the first case, and it spurred a wave of similar buyouts through the 1980s. The emergence of junk bonds as a high-risk/high-yield type of investment followed directly from this wave of leveraged buyouts, as did the poison pill, a defensive mechanism that many firms put in place to make their shares unattractive to hostile acquirers.

Other broad categories of financial innovation also stemmed from governance changes. Margaret Thatcher pushed the privatization of many formerly government-owned UK companies in the 1980s, and many other countries followed suit. Privatization often required vertical disaggregation as well – for example separating out the retail side of British Gas from the distribution and production sides of the company. More recently, the big trend has been the rise of private equity ownership as a valid alternative to the joint stock company – fuelled partly by the increasingly burdensome regulations on public companies, as well as by the enormous liquidity in the financial markets in the early 2000s.

The other side of financial market innovation is the approaches academics and bankers have used to value and repackage assets. Harry Markowitz introduced portfolio analysis in 1952 to show how diversification could help investors to optimize their portfolios. The capital asset pricing model (CAPM), developed by William Sharpe and others in the 1960s, defined the theoretically appropriate rate of return for an asset. Academics Robert Merton, Fischer Black and Myron Scholes introduced the Black–Scholes model for pricing options. These and other innovations led to dramatic increases in the understanding of risks and returns in the capital markets. When coupled in the late 1980s with increases in computing power and deregulation in financial markets, they spawned the creation of a baffling array of new financial products, from credit derivatives to collateralized debt obligations, that continue to evolve before our eyes.

The final innovation that we should acknowledge here is *economic value added* (EVA) which consultancy Stern Stewart introduced in the 1980s to help measure the true value of companies. EVA helped to improve the quality of analysis about profitability, which was useful to firm managers and financial market analysts alike. But it was not really that innovative: its core insight was essentially that the firm's cost of capital should be factored into an analysis of its profitability, and this idea had been in existence at least since the introduction of the CAPM. Nonetheless, Stern Stewart successfully pushed the concept, and developed a useful methodology for helping firms implement it, and as a result it became one of the most well-known financial innovations of the 1990s.

Cost accounting

During the industrial revolution, companies became much larger and more complex enterprises. The railway companies, for example, ushered in a corporate era of decentralized management and individually managed business units.

As a result, business owners and managers sought more information about their business in order to make sensible business decisions. This information gathering involved recording and tracking costs.

Until this point, the nature of business meant that managers were able to make rule-of-thumb decisions based on the variable costs of a business. As the name suggests, these costs varied, usually in direct proportion to production. The more trains a railroad company produced, for example, the more raw materials, energy and labour it used.

As organizations became more complex, however, other costs needed to be accounted for. With more complex organizations, fixed costs, such as storage and handling, heating and lighting, quality control, and the depreciation of plant and equipment, played a more important part in the decision making process. Louisville and Nashville Railroad was one company to face this challenge.

Predetermination

The invention of cost accounting made it possible to track, record and analyze costs associated with the products or activities of an organization. The practice of cost accounting evolved from simply recording historical costs, to apportioning a share of the fixed costs over a particular time period to the items produced in that time. This allowed businesses to evaluate the total costs of production.

The business could then set a predetermined cost, which factored a certain accepted level of costs for labour, overheads and other costs, as a standard cost. The standard cost is then used as a benchmark against which performance can be judged and efficiency measured. Thus if I think it should cost me X to achieve a certain task in a certain time, factoring in all the costs, I can then account for my performance on that task against this measure. Hence the use of cost accounting as a management tool, and the use of the term management accounting.

moting the use of cost accounting, noting: 'Many manufacturers
keeping cost accounts who hardly knew that there were such
years ago.'

exchanges between accountancy practitioners across the Atlantic
the use of cost accounting in the UK. Its establishment in the UK
by an official visit by a party from the UK to the USA in 1950, as
Anglo-American Council on Productivity.

constraints

companies proved in the 1980s that top-down cost control was not
the best route to manufacturing success. Instead they used an array
-up tools and techniques, from TQM to continuous improvement,
march on the USA. Standard cost-accounting methods were put
spotlight and, in some cases, found wanting. As a result, modern
began to emerge.

of constraints

-based costing (ABC) (see pp. 58–60) was developed during the
nd 1980s. And in the 1980s, Eli Goldratt proposed the theory of
nts, the idea that all businesses are constrained by bottlenecks.
esearch began to identify these constraints it became clear that
cost accounting was inadequate for making rational business
s, if throughput were to be factored in to the equation.

sult, a new type of cost accounting, throughput accounting, was
ed to manage throughput constraints and to squeeze as much as
from each unit of constrained resource. Throughput accounting
ts for three interrelated accounting variables: throughput – revenue
les; operating expenses – money used to keep the enterprise going;
ment – money expended to generate value.

hile throughput accounting is growing in popularity, standard cost
ting remains more widespread. And it has a profound impact on how
nies are managed.

turn on investment

1900 it was common for companies to operate a single activity, and to
te its performance by looking at their net earnings and the overall costs
ir operations. Other performance metrics that might be used included

Finky business

The story of the invention of cost accou
across both the USA and the UK. In the
taking account of costs hundreds of year
silver works, dating from 1598, for exam
mills where costing data were being used

In the USA, one of the earliest and most a
controls was the Springfield Armoury at S
mid-1800s. At the Lyman Mills, a textile
cost and financial accounting systems were

It is, however, Albert Fink, a German-born
who stands out as one of the seminal figures
cost accounting. In the early 1870s, Fink,
inches tall, was superintendent of the L
Railroad. His scrupulous record keeping al
analysis system, which he then used to a
efficiency of L&N's railroad operations us
unheard of at the time.

His innovations earned him the title of 'Fathe
in 1876, he published his work for the first tin
gation into the cost of passenger traffic on A
reference to the cost of mail service and its compen

Steel moles

In the 1870s cost-accounting systems spread th
in the USA, and then, via William Shinn, both so
mill and vice-president of the Allegheny V
Carnegie's steel business.

Carnegie wrote that, prior to cost accounting, 'w
the dark.' Cost accounting, he said, showed, 'v
who saved material, who wasted it, and who pro

Despite its success in the railroad industry, howe
reluctant to adopt the new accounting methods.
was never a fan of accounting, describing it as,
banking conspiracy'.

In the UK, the first issue of *The Cost Accountant* was
leading article the authors acknowledged the infl

War in pro
are today
things five

Increasing
promoted
was sealed
part of th

Costs and

Japanese
necessarii
of botton
to steal
under th
variation

The theory

Activity
1970s a
constrai
When
standar
decisio

As a re
develo
possib
accoun
from s
invest

But, w
accoun
comp

 Re

Befor
evalu
of th

operating ratio, cost per unit, and stock turn. The actual amount of money that needed to be invested to come up with these earnings was of relatively limited importance to the entrepreneurs who ran the firms of that era.

But as companies started to diversify their activities in the early 20th century, in response to antitrust legislation and driven by the new technologies produced in industrial research labs (see pp. 146–149), it became more necessary to compare the performance of various activities, in order to determine which ones should receive additional investment. It also became essential to control the budgets of various parts of the company. Around 1912 these problems emerged strongly in DuPont, an explosives company which was about to diversify into the emerging field of chemical products.

The ROI formula

The solution was as simple as it was effective. Return on investment (ROI), as pioneered by DuPont, measures the rate of interest returned on the outstanding investment during the course of a project or business. As a mathematical formula DuPont used $R = T \times P$, where R is return on investment, T is turnover (stock turn), and P is earnings as a percentage of sales. More recently, people have simply calculated ROI by deducting the costs of investment from the gains of investment and then dividing the number by the costs of investment. Managers using ROI ask the question which of the alternatives available for investing resources should be receiving those resources?

ROI makes it much more straightforward to compare the performance of multiple units or indeed multiple companies, perhaps operating in different industries. Its focus is not on measuring the productivity of the labour force, like Taylor's scientific management did (see pp. 12–17), or other specific resources of a company, but rather on the productivity of the financial capital that is needed to create and develop those resources. Once units are up and running, it is also possible to compare how they contribute to the company's overall performance. Because ROI is an objective measure, it reduces the amount of judgement needed to assess investment options.

Refining the method

Pierre du Pont and his associates found the standard solution for measuring returns at the time inadequate. It had been developed at GE and looked at earnings as a percentage of either costs or sales, missing out on how much capital was needed to perform an activity. DuPont had his people working on rates of return on capital from 1903 onwards but the method needed formalizing and refining.

Enter Donaldson Brown, an electrical engineer, trained at Virginia Tech, who had been working in the sales department between 1909 and 1914. His lack of formal accounting training probably served him well, as he came up with his own solution to the problem using his mathematical skills. Brown showed that even when prices stayed the same, and as a consequence return on sales was stable, return on capital moved in line with the volumes sold. He then developed his $R = T \times P$ formula of which he later said that R represents 'a final and fundamental measure of industrial efficiency'.

After Brown devised his formula, Coleman du Pont, the president, ensured that Brown became DuPont's assistant treasurer in 1914. To justify ROI DuPont's managers argued that 'a commodity requiring an inexpensive plant might, when sold only ten per cent above its cost, show a higher rate of return on the investment than another commodity sold at double its cost, but manufactured in an expensive plant.' As DuPont diversified, eventually moving to the multidivisional structure (see pp. 100–103), ROI gave top management a tool to compare the prospective and actual performance of its various business lines. This helped in planning, evaluating and managing the variety of activities the company now operated.

ROI conquers ROW

Following DuPont's success with ROI, and its move to the multidivisional structure, other firms started to take note of ROI and the DuPont system for measuring financial returns became the de facto standard for management accounting information. All kinds of firms implemented ROI, since it was not in any way company or industry specific. As they did so, the competitive advantage that ROI initially provided DuPont disappeared entirely, because ROI is a formula that is accessible and understandable to all and thus can easily be replicated. ROI helps to normalize different activities and it has been hailed by many as one of the key innovations ever to take place in accounting. Investors also took notice and started taking up ROI as a means of measuring the effectiveness of the various activities they invested in, which would later help in the development of the modern portfolio theory.

Sons of ROI

To this day ROI has remained hugely popular in the planning and control of investments. It provides an overall criterion for measuring the effectiveness of activities, which is comparable across all kinds of activities. ROI has also produced a variety of spin-offs like return on assets (ROA) and return on equity (ROE), which provide additional information. And the notion of a return has also been refined, with the introduction of earning before interest and taxes (EBIT) among others. The accounting and finance arms of companies have been built up around measures like these.

This does not mean that ROI and similar measures are without detractors. People have commented that working with ROI leads to too much focus on short-term financial success at the detriment of other important indicators of firm success like market share or customer and employee satisfaction. In addition if managers and employees are judged according to a single success criterion, they become highly effective at manipulating the outcomes of that criterion. The invention of the balanced scorecard (see pp. 60–64) can certainly be seen as a response to this singular focus on financial measures as success indicators. But none of that diminishes the innovativeness of the work performed by Brown and the DuPont Powder Company.

 # Discounted cash flow

The invention of return on investment at DuPont (see pp. 50–53) had presented a significant step forward in the ability to evaluate different investment options, because it allowed for an objective comparison of multiple investments that occurred simultaneously. Yet by the early 1920s it became clear to companies like AT&T that ROI had not resolved all problems in this area. Investments generated revenues and returns at different moments in time. In addition these revenues and returns might well differ from one year to the next. And it was obvious to many decision makers that holding some sum of money in hand today was better than carrying that same sum of money tomorrow or a year from now because the money could be reinvested in the meantime and there was no risk of the money losing its value through inflation, a problem that continued to bug the American economy and also countries like Germany. But how should one calculate today's value of receiving a sum of money in say a year from now?

Future proofing

The concept of discounted cash flow (DCF) was invented to overcome this problem. The essence of DCF is that money received in the future is discounted at some rate, generally referred to as the discount rate, to calculate its worth today. That interest rate should somehow reflect the speed with which money loses its value. That speed then depends on the availability of options for reinvesting the money to earn interest.

Underlying the notion of DCF is the principle that income as well as expenses in the future are worth less than at present. This way DCF helps to differentiate between investments that might have the same expected overall profits but where profits occur at different points in time. DCF will make projects where profits do not occur until the end of the project look relatively worse than projects where the profits occur early on in the project. In addition, DCF can also deal with projects of wildly differing lengths, as the outcome of using DCF on a project is simply one sum of money, the net present value (NPV) of the project. That NPV can be offset against the sum of money that is invested in the project initially.

A fishy business

In economics, academics had been talking about discounting since as far back as the early 1800s. But in business it was not until the early 1920s that companies really started paying attention to DCF, although there were some initial attempts in railroad investment in the 1870s by Arthur Wellington, a railroad manager who had written about the need for 'showing the justifiable present expenditure' of investments.

At its New York headquarters, AT&T had employed John Fish, a professor of railroad engineering at Stanford, and Eugene Grant, who was completing a degree at Columbia University, to work on its capital budgeting procedures. Fish and Grant were familiar with the work of Wellington and tried to apply it at AT&T. In 1923 Fish wrote a book that discussed investment analysis through the time value of money. But it was Grant, in particular, who introduced DCF to AT&T, before writing an improved version of Fish's book and then becoming a Stanford professor of engineering economics in 1930.

Justifications and disseminations

It proved hard for these academics to convince managers of the value of their work. Grant wrote that 'particularly where the situation is such that the results are not readily comparable with standard practice is there an inevitable tendency to a low grade of achievement in securing long-run economy.' 'He who has done well,' said Wellington, 'is shut off from adequate recognition of the fact.' The same is true of the one who has done poorly. The level of average practice is restricted not to the sum of the united abilities of all engaged in it, but to the average level of capacity and knowledge.

Only in the 1950s did DCF get more traction in the business world, both in the USA and elsewhere, and it did not become widespread until the 1960s. An important reason appears to have been the relative numerical complexity of DCF and the inability of economics professors to make DCF easily accessible and understandable for all. Among the early implementers were oil companies like Atlantic Oil, Standard Oil of Indiana and Continental Oil Company. At Continental Oil Company, an executive provided the following justification:

In the oil business, therefore, the making of capital investment decisions assumes considerably more significance as a part of top management's job than is usually the case. In our own situation it was apparent that the management judgement exercised in directing the flow of new funds into our business had a very significant bearing upon current and future earnings per share and a profound influence on the long-term growth and development of our company. We decided, therefore, that we should make a maximum effort to develop the best possible yardstick for comparing one investment opportunity against another and for evaluating the returns that particular projects would earn on the stockholder's dollar.

DCF assessed

DCF has proven its value as a support tool for investment decision making across a wide range of industries and firms. It helps companies to reduce the complexity associated with making decisions about long-term projects, and it is used in other key decisions such as on mergers and acquisitions, and by investors. Many mining companies, for example, swear by DCF as the only sound way of making decisions about whether to invest in new ore bodies.

The implementation challenges for DCF are twofold. First, a decision maker should be able to make some reasonable assessment of future cash flows and profits associated with a project. This becomes increasingly difficult as the project length and complexity increase. Second, a fair discount rate needs to be set that is based not only on environmental factors like inflation and interest rates, but also on a firm's other investment opportunities and willingness to take risks. At the end of the day, even technical management innovations like DCF require a great deal of managerial expertise to make them work.

Beyond budgeting

In the post-war decades, many companies found themselves growing rapidly, and they had to start building systems to keep control of their increasingly diverse operations. Strategic planning (see pp. 160–162) was one such mechanism, and along with strategic planning came a range of budgeting systems designed to provide senior executives with a detailed overview of the company's operations. This sort of detailed information was used in a variety of ways – it allowed the company to provide guidance to its shareholders regarding future performance, it helped senior executives to make investment decisions, and it allowed them to reward managers according to their performance.

But the budgeting process also created its share of problems: it led managers to focus internally, rather than on the needs of their customers, it encouraged managers to become risk averse, especially when their bonus was at stake, and it took a great deal of time. This was the problem facing Svenska Handelsbanken AB, one of the large Swedish banks, in the late 1960s. The company's incoming CEO, Jan Wallander, had sorted out a financial crisis in the bank, and was looking to put it on a secure financial footing. But he was faced with high levels of bureaucracy and a lack of responsiveness to customers.

Doing it our way

Wallander began his transformation of Handelsbanken by overhauling the company's basic business principles, which became enshrined in a publication entitled *Our Way*. Fundamentally, he believed that if you focused on customers and customer service then everything else would take care of itself. So he abandoned sales targets, and instead focused branch managers' attention on their customers. He decentralized authority to local branches. And he pushed for people to take responsibility for their actions.

In 1970 Wallander took his ideas one step further with the following directive: the company would no longer engage in any formal strategic planning process; neither would it prepare any more annual plans or budgets.

Budgets, Wallander argued, were narrow minded, internally focused, and defensive. As he subsequently commented: 'A budget will prove roughly right, and then it will be trite, or it will be disastrously wrong, in which case it will be dangerous. My conclusion is thus: scrap it!'

Instead of a budgeting system, branch managers were asked to prepare an operational plan with a small number of key performance indicators or 'fast actuals' – the cost–income ratio, return on equity, and profit per employee. And they provided rolling cash forecasts every quarter to give Wallander and the chief financial officer some early warning information about emerging issues.

Branches and regions were evaluated on the basis of actual performance (rather than performance against budget). The best region in each quarter was given a trophy, and individual branches were ranked, as a way of encouraging the poor performers to improve. But Wallander did not believe in high-powered incentives for his managers. Most employees received straight salaries, and a profit-sharing scheme allowed people to receive bonuses only when Handelsbanken had a higher after-tax return than the average of all the Nordic banks.

Spreading the word

Handelsbanken's innovative approach to internal budgeting and control became one of the cornerstones of its long-term success. By 2000, Handelsbanken had achieved world-class cost/income and cost/asset ratios, it was rated among the top 10 European banks by Moody's, and it had delivered a 20.3 per cent compound rate of return to its shareholders, compared to 16.8 per cent for a main rival, S-E Banken.

But while Wallander was very open about his new management approach, it was not actually picked up and copied by many competitors. Some found it too radical. And many struggled to understand how the company could perform so well without strong financial bonuses for individuals.

This situation changed significantly in the late 1990s when two UK consultants, Jeremy Hope and Robin Fraser, founded the *Beyond Budgeting Round Table* (BBRT). Building on their own experiences with inward-looking and expensive budgeting processes, Hope and Fraser began proselytizing about the possibilities of moving beyond budgeting, and they began to collect data about the emerging best practice in this area. Jan Wallander's work at Handelsbanken in the 1970s is still to this day seen as one of the most comprehensive and influential models.

The beyond budgeting movement picked up steam quickly under Hope and Fraser's leadership, and by 2002 the BBRT had more than 60 members. Many well-known companies implemented their own version of beyond budgeting. For example, the Swiss bank UBS eliminated its traditional budgeting system in its wealth management and business banking division in 2003, and this helped it achieve dramatic increases in its level of organic growth.

Beyond budgeting today

The beyond budgeting movement is strong today, but there are still very few companies that have fully embraced the concept. While alluring in principle, beyond budgeting is not as simple as it sounds. Sir Andrew

Likierman, an accounting professor at London Business School, comments that you cannot just eliminate budgeting because there are certain elements of it – including keeping track of performance, and monitoring future growth prospects – that no company can do without. Likierman argues, instead, that there is bad budgeting and there is good budgeting, and all you can do is encourage the latter.

Nonetheless, it is still something of a mystery as to why more companies do not embrace the beyond budgeting principles. At its heart, though, the problem here is one Machiavelli would have recognized: getting rid of budgeting is an unnatural act for senior executives, because it reduces their sense of control, and it dilutes their power. So it still takes an enlightened leader to embrace this sort of opportunity.

 # Activity-based costing

Traditional accounting systems first evaluated direct costs, such as raw materials or services purchased externally, then added in some percentage of indirect costs based on overheads occurring in various departments and other organizational units. This was called the two-stage costing system. Because it was assumed that resources were consumed in direct relation to the number of items produced, distortions often arose.

When these distorted cost estimates were used to determine the prices of products, these potential problems became real – some products would get sold at prices below the acceptable rate of return, while overpriced products would not sell enough, and the net effect on profitability would be highly negative.

In the early 1980s, when Japanese manufacturers started to flood certain western markets with low-priced products, companies like John Deere, a manufacturer of agricultural and other machinery, began reconsidering its costing system.

As easy as ...

Activity-based costing (ABC) was put forward as a solution to this problem. ABC attempts to determine the actual costs of any given product in a multi-product company. It achieves this by taking overhead costs from the general ledger and assigning them to specific activities. Once a product places demands on an activity, for instance when a product gets advertized, so-called cost drivers are applied and, based on the level of demand, costs are assigned to the product. Therefore ABC is better at assigning the resources put in to the outputs produced, in other words, at linking the provision and consumption of resources. This makes for more accurate pricing of products and often a rethinking of the product portfolio as companies discover which products drive their profits and which do not.

Deere hunting

Historically, cost accounting had moved through two stages, first only including direct costs but later also indirect costs. But for John Deere that was no longer enough. Farmland and commodity prices collapsed in the early 1980s and the second hand market was thriving. John Deere had a components division and started looking for ways to supply other companies and industries in a diversification effort. Frank Stevenson, division manager of Gear and Special products, said: 'We must dramatically increase our competitive position in the worldwide market. That requires a quantum leap in manufacturing quality and in reducing our costs.'

Keith Williams, who was manager of Cost Accounting Services, knew that the cost system was effective at the aggregate level but severely wanting when Deere was bidding for specific parts and components. So in November 1984 the situation at Gear and Special products seemed like an ideal testing ground to try out ideas Williams had about assigning overhead costs to products through a new experiment. A group of people set to work. Within six months, the activity-based costing study took shape. One of the key problems was the lack of an activity dictionary, so one had to be created. But by 1986 ABC was first formally introduced at Deere and in 1987 ABC was extended to other parts of the company.

Williams suggested:

Few things have generated more excitement. Even though it's still an allocation, it's such an improvement. Parts we suspected we were undercosting have turned out to be even more expensive than we had thought. It's proven what we suspected about the costs of material handling and transport expenses, and triggered our making layout changes. When it showed us the costs added by secondary operations, we brought them back onto the main floor.

As a consequence of ABC, Deere was able to make decision making more effective and changed its set of products.

Spreading the letter

Other companies that introduced ABC not long after John Deere included Weyerhaeuser and General Motors. At GM, corporate accountants' acknowledgement there was a product-costing problem and new transfer press technology combined to produce experiments in product costing. GM ran five separate experiments, using a non-accounting ABC sponsor and an ABC designer. Initially GM had to overcome well-known change problems like the not-invented-here syndrome, a lack of understanding, and a wait-and-see attitude. When GM rolled out ABC across the corporation, after successes in the experiments, the sponsor proved to be the key to success.

As these companies were experimenting with ABC, they relayed their stories to academics, most notably Harvard Business School's Bob Kaplan, who would later also be a key figure in the rise of the balanced scorecard (see pp. 60–64), and Robin Cooper. Kaplan and Cooper labelled the invention activity-based costing and started spreading the word through their writings and presentations. In the early 1990s the Institute of Management Accountants commissioned a study into ABC. GM executives spoke about their experiences with ABC at conferences. Then ABC really took off. As ABC data started to be used in a more strategic fashion, the term activity-based management (ABM) also emerged. ABC and, to an extent, ABM became widely used in business around the globe.

Alternative acronyms

ABC was a major advance in management accounting because it allowed cost analysis to become a more important aspect of setting a company's strategy. ABC worked particularly well in organizations that were concerned about their costs and that might also be going through business process re-engineering or total quality management efforts. But implementing it could be challenging because designing an appropriate cost model was laborious and required a deep understanding of the organization. And in some organizations, ABC encountered substantial resistance, leading to definitions of ABC like 'another big cut' and 'avoid being counted'. When implementing ABC, companies should therefore bring on board not only accountants and the people responsible for specific activities but also organizational change specialists.

Balanced scorecard

Every manager knows the mantra 'what gets measured gets done' and, throughout the last century, this truism has been reflected in the development of a complex array of ratios, measures, analytical tools, and software packages. Most focused on measuring financial performance. Measurements of other more abstract elements of corporate performance – such as customer loyalty or employee satisfaction – were generally neglected.

The balanced scorecard was introduced as a strategic management and measurement system that linked strategic objectives to comprehensive indicators. It recognized that companies have a tendency to fixate on a few measurements, which blinker their assessment of how the business is performing overall. The balanced scorecard helped to focus management attention on a range of key performance indicators, to provide a balanced view.

The art of balance

Art Schneiderman was a manager at the American company Analog Devices. Originally an aerospace research scientist, Schneiderman was strongly influenced by Jay Forrester's system dynamics concepts during his MBA training at MIT's Sloan School. He then spent six years as a strategy consultant with Bain working on quality management projects in Japan.

Armed with insights into Japanese continuous improvement techniques and a system-wide perspective on the functioning of the organization, Schneiderman then approached Ray Stata, CEO of Analog Devices, about working for the company. His timing was exemplary as Stata had just spoken to a major customer who was irate because a key shipment was late. Stata was unusually open to ideas, Schneiderman recalls: 'You can't innovate in an environment that is not open to innovation, and that means from the very top, from the CEO all the way down through the organization. And it was clear that Ray was interested, he recognized that TQM was important. It was the right environment for me and it was the right time for him.' Schneiderman was asked by Stata to develop a quality improvement process to be incorporated into the company's five-year strategic plan.

Schneiderman developed something he labelled the Corporate Performance Audit, an annual plan that identified a number of non-financial elements that needed to be managed to reach quality targets in five years. It was then decided that this needed to be reviewed annually and then quarterly.

Taming monsters

Alongside Ray Stata at Analog was COO, Jerry Fishman (later to become the company's CEO and president). While Stata was interested in innovation and how the organization and its people worked, Fishman was more focused on financial performance and the bottom line. Insiders referred to the Stata–Fishman partnership as 'the two-headed monster'. 'Opposites work very well together,' reflects Schneiderman. 'Except when you're in the middle. And it became very apparent to me early on that I was in the middle and I had to not only manage Ray but I had to manage Jerry.'

The differing approaches of the company's two leaders were abundantly clear at the monthly business meetings, which were chaired by Schneiderman. 'I would always put the non-financial performance measures first on the agenda, followed by the financial measures, and Jerry Fishman would switch them around.'

Schneiderman had visited Motorola and seen how Motorola integrated its non-financial performance measurement review into financial business meetings. This proved helpful when Jerry Fishman challenged him to find a way to make them both happy. A few days later, while at home in the evening, Schneiderman saw a television commercial that emphasized how a certain type of candy was a combination of two different products: peanut butter and chocolate. As he recalled:

Suddenly the light bulb lit: combine the financial and non-financial metrics as a single agenda item. So I added a small number of key financials at the top of the scorecard, and the problem was solved to everyone's satisfaction.

It was agreed that there would be no more than three financial measures and then non-financial measures on a slide. It was then suggested that the name Corporate Performance Audit needed to be changed to the Corporate Scorecard. Soon each division at the company had its own scorecard in support of the Corporate Scorecard. 'That is how the Analog Devices scorecard was born,' says Art Schneiderman. 'It evolved, but not a great deal. What changed over time are the things that went on the scorecard, not the financials but the non-financials.'

Cracking the code

Art Schneiderman's Corporate Scorecard was developed in 1987 and then implemented at Analog. Given more responsibilities, Schneiderman approached Robert Kaplan, the Marvin Bower Professor of Leadership Development at Harvard Business School, to seek out his insights into activity-based costing. Kaplan visited Analog and Schneiderman gave him a background presentation on the company. Later, Kaplan invited Schneiderman to sessions he taught at Harvard that used Analog as an example.

The scorecard was a relatively minor part of this but it was the one that attracted the audience's interest.

Kaplan, and his co-author David Norton, used Analog Devices as an example in an article in the *Harvard Business Review* (though the company was not actually named). This process, Kaplan argued, allowed Schneiderman's innovation to become more effective: the concept 'had become codified, generalized, and shown to be applicable to a much larger audience than the originating company'. Schneiderman acknowledges that, without meeting Kaplan, his innovation might have withered and died inside Analog Devices.

The Kaplan and Norton article – 'The balanced scorecard' – appeared in the January/February 1993 edition of the *Harvard Business Review*. It was the first step in the mass popularization of the concept. Thousands of companies implemented the scorecard in one form or another. And the scorecard has also spread to governments and other not-for-profit organizations, where it is particularly suitable because financial considerations are often of lesser importance.

Cockpit management

Kaplan and Norton compared running a company to flying a plane. The pilot who relies on a single dial is unlikely to be safe. Pilots must utilize all the information contained in their cockpit. 'The complexity of managing an organization today requires that managers be able to view performance in several areas simultaneously,' said Kaplan and Norton. 'Moreover, by forcing senior managers to consider all the important operational measures together, the balanced scorecard can let them see whether improvement in one area may be achieved at the expense of another.'

Kaplan and Norton suggested that four elements need to be balanced: the customer perspective (how customers perceive the company); the internal perspective (what the company excels at); the innovation and learning perspective (how the company can continue to improve); and the financial perspective (how the company looks to shareholders).

According to Kaplan and Norton, by focusing energies, attention and measures on all four of these dimensions, companies become driven by their mission rather than by short-term financial performance. Crucial to achieving this is applying measures to company strategy. Instead of being beyond measurement, the balanced scorecard argues that strategy must be central to any process of measurement – 'a good balanced scorecard should tell the story of your strategy.'

Tools and practice

Because the balanced scorecard is of relatively recent origin, there really is not much difference between how it was first applied at Analog Devices and developed by Kaplan and Norton and how companies use it today. The big wave of scorecard implementations is behind us now but Kaplan and Norton's ideas do not really feel outdated, just replaced by different priorities. Yet some important lessons have been learned on how to implement the scorecard.

The originator of the idea, Art Schneiderman, left Analog in 1993 and has some mixed feelings about the popularization of the concept:

In my subsequent consulting, I discovered that the big problem that organizations have in implementing the balanced scorecard, is that they don't have tools in place for achieving the goals. The scorecard is not the key thing, it's how you're going to implement the changes – that's the key thing. You have to have a well-documented, well-understood process that you refine each cycle, you work on the scorecard, on how you're going to do it and then, how are you going to achieve the goals that you come up with.

And Kaplan argued more recently that the balanced scorecard can only be a true success if it lies at the heart of a firm's strategy and drives its decision making. If, on the contrary, the scorecard is adopted simply because shareholders or others pressurize management into it, the scorecard is not likely to be a great success. So if you are thinking about implementing a scorecard system, make sure you have the implementation tools and that it fits your strategy.

Economic value-added

With the rising importance of public companies, advanced finance techniques, and shift of power to shareholders that all emerged in the 1980s, it became ever more important to measure whether companies create value for their shareholders. Corporate executives and shareholders were constantly searching for metrics that would allow them to measure and manage corporate performance effectively. But these metrics did not always reflect the true position of the company in terms of value creation. Without a true measure of value creation, however, it was difficult for shareholders to make investment decisions. Equally, it was difficult for the company executives to explain how the decisions that they made affected the value for the investing shareholders.

On top of this there was the related issue of pay. If the goal of the company is to create value for its shareholders, how could the company provide incentives for its employees to do this? If it were unable to make a link between the decisions of employees and the creation or destruction of shareholder value, then the company might have been rewarding its employees for destroying shareholder value. For companies like Coca-Cola facing these problems, the obvious solution was to find a measure that ties individual performance to the creation of shareholder value.

Adam and EVA

Roberto Goizueta, former CEO of Coca-Cola, once described the purpose of his company thus: 'We raise capital to make concentrate, and sell it at an operating profit. Then we pay the cost of that capital. Shareholders pocket the difference.'

If this statement is the essence of what companies do, then determining whether they are creating value for their shareholders involves accounting for the cost of capital. This is the idea at the heart of economic value added (EVA), defined as the difference between the after-tax return on capital of a company and its cost of capital. Surprisingly, many companies are unaware how their capital is employed – let alone what the cost of employing it is.

Finding out the cost of borrowed capital is simple enough. Over the short term, it is the interest paid, with an adjustment to reflect tax deductibility. Calculating the cost of equity capital is a little more problematic, however.

At first glance many people would say that money provided by the share-holders is free, as the company does not have to pay for it. There is a cost associated with equity capital, though. If the shareholders had not invested their money in company A, they could have invested it elsewhere. There is, therefore, an opportunity cost associated with equity capital, equivalent to that which the investor could get through capital appreciation and dividends by investing in a portfolio of companies of equal risk to company A. Fail to reward the investor with an amount at least equivalent to the opportunity cost and the shareholder is likely to invest elsewhere.

To work out the cost of capital, you also need to know how much capital there is in the organization. As well as property, plant and equipment, etc., plus working capital, supporters of shareholder value calculation, such as the EVA, suggest ignoring generally accepted accounting practice, and including capital tied up in R&D, marketing, training, and similar investments. This increases the capital base and also adjusts the operating profit calculation. EVA then, is calculated by taking the operating profit and deducting the cost of capital.

The Stern business of value

The term EVA was trademarked by consulting firm Stern Stewart and Co. in the mid-1980s, though the underlying concept was well established in the academic literature many years before. G. Bennett Stewart, who co-founded Stern Stewart in 1982, is credited with Stern's association with the value-based management system.

'Back in the 1980s restructuring and LBOs were such a dominant force that you never heard much about EVA, but when LBOs faded from the market place we retooled our practice,' says Stewart in a 1994 *Industry Week* article. 'What gets measured gets managed. If you change the way a company measures performance, you will change (executive) behaviour. Most companies lose track of capital accountability. There is too little concern about managing the assets on the balance sheet.'

Stewart describes EVA thus:

Take sales, deduct operating expenses, and you have earnings. All EVA is, is subtract one more expense, the cost of financing the assets on the balance sheet. What is left over is a measure of how efficiently the business is being managed and how to assess new capital projects.

Robert Goizueta was an early fan of EVA, introducing it at Coca-Cola in 1987. 'When I played golf regularly, my average score was 90, so every hole was par five,' Goizueta says in a 1993 *Fortune* magazine article. 'I look at EVA like I look at breaking par. At Coca-Cola, we are way under par and adding a lot of value.'

Using EVA to guide corporate strategy, Goizueta ditched a roster of businesses returning less than the cost of capital, covering products such as wine, pasta, and plastic cutlery. Instead, he invested in the soft drinks business earning 29.4 per cent on capital, almost 2.5 times its cost. At the same time he increased borrowings which, at the time, were cheaper than the cost of equity, and also squeezed more productivity out of existing assets.

EVAdoption

Adoption of EVA was quick: at least 300 companies in the USA were using the measure by 1997. In a 1996 survey by Manufacturers Alliance, 30 per cent of all senior executives who responded said that they already had EVA in place, while another 10 per cent were evaluating the measure.

In the early 1990s, EVA was championed by a number of companies besides Coca-Cola, including AT&T, and Quaker Oats. It is not just EVA, however, that has been adopted by organizations. EVA itself has its origins in concepts like the residual income method of performance measurement, developed in the 1960s by David Solomons, a former Wharton Professor of Accounting, and can be traced back to the writings of English economist Alfred Marshall in 1890.

Many other management consultants offered value-based management metrics, including the Boston Consulting Group's cash flow return on investment (CFROI) and the discounted cash flows championed by McKinsey. With the support of big management consultancies and increasing pressures from shareholders value-based management principles quickly spread across the globe.

The results

Economic value added is alive and well, part of a range of value-based management tools that have been adopted by organizational supporters of the approach. Although it has its critics, there is research to suggest that companies that use EVA outperform those that do not. For example, one study that compared adopters to non-adopters, revealed that, in a three-year period prior to adopting EVA, stock market performance was similar, while in the four-year period afterwards, EVA companies outperformed their average non-EVA competitors by 28.8 per cent.

EVA has also been widely adopted as a means of linking performance to pay, by creating EVA targets for individuals. For example, Tata Consultancy Services, one of the leading information technology companies in the world, adopted an EVA-based compensation system in 1999.

Many large multinational organizations continue to adhere to a value-based management approach, developing corporate strategies, based in part on the ability to create shareholder value through the effective use of capital. A good example is 3M, the US conglomerate, where George Buckley, who became its CEO in 2005, is a firm believer in the benefits of EVA.

3

People

How does a company recruit the best people? How can it make its employees effective in their work? And what can it do to ensure that employees share the company's purpose? The objective of people innovations is to get the most out of a firm's workforce.

 ## Introduction

Management innovation is an elusive phenomenon in the complex world of people management. Unlike some of the areas of business covered in this book, where change occurs in an ordered and progressive way, the changes we see in the way firms actually manage their employees are complex, often rather subtle, and always cloaked in a language that obscures more than it illuminates.

There are two aspects of the people management field that make it unusual. First, it appears to be highly cyclical, so we see plenty of supposedly new ideas about managing people that come along from time to time, but these can almost always be traced back to earlier waves of thinking. So, for example, the empowerment movement of the 1990s is not discernibly different from the participative management school of thought that straddled the years of the Second World War, and the concepts of the quality of working life movement in the 1960s draw unmistakably from the corporate welfare movement of the 1890s.

The second distinctive aspect of people management is the extent to which talk seems to substitute for action. While it is relatively easy to follow the way *thinking* about motivation or empowerment has evolved over the years, it is much harder to map how these changes are linked to meaningful changes in *practice*. Indeed, there are plenty of examples of new theories emerging in the field of people management where there have been no demonstrable changes in the way work actually gets done. As a case in point, the famous 'Hawthorne Studies' conducted in the Western Electric plant in Illinois in 1924–7 led to a revolution in the way people thought about human motivation, but the record on what changes they stimulated in management practice is remarkably limited.

All of which serves as a caution to the reader that the management innovations discussed in this chapter are less precise in their origins, and often older, than the ones we discuss in many other parts of the book. In some cases we have focused on a particular case that exemplifies the changes underway at the time – the quality of working life initiatives at General Foods' Topeka plant are an example of this. In other cases, we are able to be much more explicit about the origins of a particular practice – for example AT&T's pioneering work on *assessment centres*.

The evolution of people management: a three-act play

To make sense of the innovations we have chosen to feature, it is useful to provide a quick sketch of the history of people management in organizations. Progress here has not followed a predictable path, and for every two steps forward in one era there have typically been one and a half steps back in the next. In fact, one can usefully identify three major waves of waxing and then waning interest in people management issues.

Act 1. The earliest detailed records of how employers started to take the welfare and motivation of their employees seriously are found in the 1800s, with a number of well-known companies in different countries all taking great strides in what became known as *corporate welfarism*. We discuss the 1830s' innovations of Krupp in Germany in detail, but similar innovations were put in place by William Lever in Liverpool in the 1880s, Richard and George Cadbury in Birmingham in the 1890s, and Milton Hershey in the early 1900s in Pennsylvania. This era gave rise to such innovations as pensions, healthcare programmes, company housing, and other benefits. These innovations were all intended to take better care of employees, with a view to making them more productive and happier in their work, as well as to raise the moral standards of the company. One can certainly debate what motivated the likes of Alfred Krupp to invest in corporate welfarism – some would suggest it was a deep 'social conscience', others would argue, more cynically, that it was driven by a desire to get more productive use out of employees. Either way, the corporate welfare movement led to the introduction of a host of benefits that previous generations of employees had not had access to, and gradually these changes worked their way through from a small number of pioneering companies to other parts of the industrial sector.

The late 19th century was also an era in which many of the other foundation stones of the modern organization were put in place. One innovation, pioneered by the American railroad companies, was the emergence of *professional managers*, as distinct from the owner–managers who predominated until this time. Another important innovation, which also helped the rise of the professional manager, was the introduction of *business education* programmes, as pioneered by Joseph Wharton in the 1880s.

The emphasis on employee welfare dipped in the early years of the 20th century as the era of *scientific management* took hold. As we discuss elsewhere, scientific management became the dominant way of improving productivity and performance in the USA and in many parts of Europe, and during this period there were no meaningful innovations in the area of people management. Processes suddenly mattered more.

Act 2 is generally referred to as the human relations movement. It took shape in the late 1920s and continued to be the dominant way of thinking about people management issues through the 1960s, though with many twists and turns along the way. The human relations era started with the now famous Hawthorne Studies of employee motivation at Western Electric's Illinois plant – where the productivity of a small group of employees was carefully scrutinized while adjustments were made to the working environment. The interpretation of these experiments has been hotly debated by academics ever since, but the research was the key stimulus for a new set of ideas about how employees could become more involved in their work. The initial studies by Elton Mayo, Fritz Roethlisberger, and William Dickson were followed later by an explosion of interest in human motivation from such seminal thinkers as Abraham Maslow, Frederick Herzberg, and Douglas McGregor, among others.

But while there were plenty of new theories put forward through the 1930s about motivation, employee involvement and so forth, there is little evidence that genuinely new ways of working were put in place. One exception is the *performance-related pay* or gain-sharing experiments in the USA, the most famous of which is the *Scanlon Plan*, which sought to bridge the divide between workers and managers in unionized settings.

In the period immediately after the Second World War, the human relations field took off in earnest. As Stanford Professor Stephen Barley observed, 'corporate experimentation with strategies for enhancing loyalty, motivation, and satisfaction blossomed almost overnight'. This period saw the founding of the US National Training Laboratories (NTL) that gave rise to *T-groups* as a methodology for bringing social psychological principles to bear on group dynamics. The T-group methodology was quickly picked up by such companies as Exxon. Assessment centres also emerged in this period. The idea of formally assessing prospective managers was first tried out during the war by the British and American armies; the idea was then picked up by AT&T, a company that pioneered this concept in the private sector.

The human relations movement was also highly influential in the UK, largely through the efforts of the Tavistock Institute, founded in 1947 to conduct applied research on the social dynamics in the workplace. Under the leadership of Eric Trist, the institute became most well known for its concept of socio-technical systems, which essentially meant that one needed to understand the interaction between the social and technical elements of an organization to make it function more effectively. Socio-technical systems thinking had a profound influence on management practices on both sides of the Atlantic. The Tavistock Institute also became famous for the research conducted by Elliot Jacques in the Glacier Metal Company that led to his development of stratified systems theory, a model of management that equates an individual's position in the hierarchy with his/her ability to handle complex jobs with long time horizons.

The tail end of the human relations movement saw major innovations in the nature of factory work. One set of initiatives took place in Scandinavia, through the Norwegian industrial democracy project and the Swedish quality of working life movement, the most famous example of which was Volvo's *cellular manufacturing* experiments (as we describe in detail on pp. 28–31). Another set of initiatives took place in US factories in the 1960s around the '*quality of work life*' concept, with the most well-known example being General Foods' dog food plant in Topeka, Kansas. While Topeka was not the first factory to experiment with socio-technical principles in the organization of its work, it represents an important focal point for our understanding of how these principles were put in place, and the challenges companies faced in making them stick.

These and other innovations continued to take shape throughout the 1960s and 1970s, but they lost ground to other schools of thought that favoured the rational or system-based approach to management. A combination of factors, including the emergence of computers and the technocratic mindset that dominated government policy during the Cold War led to the rise of *operations research*, *strategic planning*, and management science as disciplines. Of course, there were still ongoing debates about people management issues during this period, but once more they occurred in the shadow of these technology- and system-driven movements.

Act 3 began in the early 1980s. Americans had begun to worry about the rise of Japan as an economic powerhouse, and by the apparent decline in their overall competitiveness, and this malaise was captured beautifully in a number of influential books, notably *In search of excellence*, by Tom Peters and Robert Waterman, which went on to sell 5 million copies. This and other books reminded managers, once again, of the importance of the human side of the organization, and especially the value of developing a supportive organization culture. Two major innovations that mirrored this increased emphasis on the softer side of the organization were *mentoring and executive coaching* and *360-degree feedback*. Both these practices took off in the 1980s, though in each case it is possible to trace the original idea further back.

The 1990s saw a continued emphasis on people management issues, often under the banner of empowerment (even though the concept of empowerment is no different to the earlier concept of participative management). While there was no shortage of innovative activity during this period, most of the novel practices, such as Brazilian company Semco's experiments with workplace democracy and open-book management, can be traced back to the pioneering efforts of companies in previous eras.

Corporate welfarism

By the early 19th century, the industrial revolution had produced true manufacturing companies and along with them a working class of employees. Traditionally, the company was seen as providing employees with wages only. But these people had demands for more than just wages. The government, church, and other institutions were unable and perhaps also unwilling to meet these demands. Therefore social problems arose during the 19th century in such towns as Essen, in the middle of Germany's heavily industrialized Ruhr area. These included issues like a lack of fire protection, hygiene, education, and proper housing.

When Alfred Krupp's father, who had run a small steel company called Krupp, became ill and passed away, Alfred left school and was suddenly charged with running the company against this background of deprivation. But there was substantial demand for Krupp's products, which included cast steel, tanner's tools, coin dies and rolls. Although Essen-based Krupp only had seven workers in 1827, it wanted to grow rapidly. But to do so, it needed to find a sustainable way of attracting personnel. So Alfred was faced with the question of what he could offer potential employees.

More than wages

By 1836 Krupp had come to the realization that it needed to offer employees more than just wages. Instead it would have to start caring about the welfare of its employees. Hence it started a sickness and burial benefit fund, which received contributions from the company, from fines workers had to pay when breaking rules as well as a small contribution paid by workers themselves. This fund was first voluntary but was made compulsory in 1853. This was the introduction of corporate welfarism, alternatively known as welfare work, welfare capitalism, industrial paternalism, and industrial betterment. Corporate welfarism allowed Krupp to co-evolve relatively peacefully with the local Essen community and in 1860 it had 1800 employees locally, a number that rose to 41,500 in 1913.

Corporate welfarism was later extended to many other areas. The American Bureau of Labor Statistics defined corporate welfarism in 1919 as 'anything for the comfort and improvement, intellectual or social, of the employees, over and above wages paid, which is not a necessity of the industry nor required by law'. The idea behind corporate welfarism is that it can help to increase employee motivation and work commitment, as well as improving loyalty and lowering turnover. These can all lower labour costs and increase a company's output. Furthermore they may limit strikes, the growth and influence of the unions, and efforts by the government to regulate the labour market and help improve a company's public relations. In later years the fear of socialism was another reason why corporate welfarism became popular, especially in the USA.

More and more

Krupp never really engaged in a conscious experiment with corporate welfarism. Instead it used a piecemeal approach, adding to its existing arrangements over time. After its illness and burial fund, it introduced better healthcare for its employees in 1860 by paying doctor's fees and providing a 30 per cent discount on medicines, followed by the construction of a Krupp hospital in 1872. In 1885 the pension fund was extended and the company's contribution to it increased substantially. In 1892 retired employees could live rent free in houses provided for by Krupp. Retirement at 65 came in 1895 and a disability programme was introduced in 1896. Krupp started providing food in 1899 and schooling and housing in 1900.

In 1903 Krupp even opened its own dental clinic. Krupp essentially started looking after employees' welfare from the moment people entered the company until the day they died.

Corporate welfarism spread rapidly across Germany and the rest of Europe but also in the United States, where Vanderbilt and other railroad tycoons introduced the Young Men's Christian Associations (YMCAs) in the 1870s. The Bancroft company provided cheap housing and food for workers. S.D. Warren introduced the eight-hour working day and provided workers with athletic facilities. George Pullman, of Pullman Palace Car Company, even constructed a whole community for employees to live in. Endicott Johnson was another company which later introduced welfarism, including elements like profit sharing and employee stock ownership. Johnson likened corporate welfarism to a happy family, because 'a business concern ought to be like a family as much as possible', and advertized with that image. Owner George F. Johnson was portrayed as the head of the family. Its labour turnover was only around 40 to 60 per cent of the industry average.

But some opposed these changes on moral grounds or out of self-interest. The Boot and Shoe Workers' Union for instance wrote:

We have a few real Mussolinis in our shoe industry. One of the most prominent of these is the head of the Endicott Johnson Company. This executive exercises absolute control over the earnings and lives of several thousand employees and their families. All power is exercised at the top and yet the executive seems to wish to sell the idea of a super management to his employees so as to enthuse them with greater confidence in his dictatorship.

Other people questioned whether the economic performance of these companies had really improved as they did not seem to outperform their competitors much because their cost levels were higher. And it was not always clear whether the commitment of workers increased as a consequence.

Beyond welfarism

The term corporate welfarism is no longer part of the business vernacular, and some of the programmes introduced by companies as part of corporate welfarism have now been taken over by governments or insurance companies. Yet the principle that companies ought to provide non-wage benefits to their employees is alive as ever, particularly in highly developed countries where there is a shortage of skilled employees. What is often referred to as the war for talent forces organizations to come up with contract offers that extend far beyond just wages. Business magazines frequently publish lists of the 'top companies to work for' and these lists focus, essentially, on the perks and benefits that employees today value.

Today's companies may be offering anything from company cars, insurance deals, holiday entitlements, company restaurants, or use of the internet for private purposes. But that is only the beginning: a company also needs to be a fun place to work for, and offer opportunities for personal development. And although a paternalistic attitude is eschewed these days, a company has become a home away from home for many of us.

Professional managers

Until around 1845 managing a company was the responsibility of its owners. These owners might employ foremen, but they would retain all management responsibility. By 1845, however, some companies had started to grow in size considerably. This was especially true of the relatively new railway industry. It was growing rapidly on the back of substantial demand and advanced new technologies, constructing miles and miles of railroad every year. It transported large amounts of cargo and, increasingly, people over long distances. This was a complex task requiring much administration and many decisions. In other words, a more complex managerial structure was called for, as well as people with some degree of competence in executing these tasks.

Furthermore, the fact that railroads were so geographically dispersed implied that activities on the ground would have to be managed locally because quick decisions were often called for. The railway companies therefore operated as multiunit companies, adopting regional divisions which can be seen as a forerunner of the M-form (see p. 101). But an owner can only be present in one location at a time. So companies like the London & North Western Railway in the United Kingdom and the Pennsylvania Railroad in the United States were faced with the dilemma of how to manage their operations. And in the UK the government had also just enacted the Railway Clauses Consolidation Act, which stipulated lower maximum rates and fares in an industry already facing overcapacity and much competition.

A sense of calling

The solution to these problems would prove to be the hiring of professional managers, in the words of *Economist* journalists John Micklethwait and

Adrian Woolbridge: 'People who didn't own the organizations they worked for but nevertheless devoted their entire careers to them. They had a high sense of their calling (some even looked down on the mere amateurs who had founded the companies).' Of course, there had been managers before but they would be owners or in some instances aristocrats. Now being a manager was turned into a profession, much like being a doctor or a lawyer.

A prime example of one of the earlier professional managers was Captain Mark Huish, who was made general manager of the London & North Western Railroad in 1846, being a former army officer and secretary of various railway companies. Huish was given responsibilities hitherto unheard of for a non-owner of the company. His assignment was to 'secure the harmonious working of the whole of the traffic'. The Pennsylvania Railroad and other US railways followed the example of their British counterparts some years later.

Power games

Huish's appointment had a substantial impact on the London & North Western. He helped develop new technology but also the notion of railway management, writing papers on railway accidents, in which he was the first to take up safety systems and the electric telegraph. However, as Huish and other professional managers gradually became more powerful, the same directors who had appointed them wanted to get their power back. These directors were generally aristocrats and to an extent this was a social class conflict. Then other railways started opposing Huish and his position of power and in 1858 he had to resign from his post.

At Pennsylvania Railroad professional managers began to be appointed in large numbers in 1850, when there were already dozens in place, because the board found it was unable to handle all the company's business effectively. They would soon come to powerful positions as well. In theory these professional managers had as their sole goal the long-term performance of the company. But a similar problem started to manifest itself, as it became less and less clear how the owners could direct managers to a course of action they were seeking and how they could ensure that these managers would not be working for their own, rather than the company's, benefit.

All professionals now

The number of railway companies employing professional managers grew rapidly, as did the number of managers they employed. Professional managers contributed to not only many technological innovations, but also organizational innovations like accounting and information systems and were generally thought to be improving the performance of the firms they worked for. Professional managers also turned out to be more effective in the coordination between railroads, which helped increase safety and interoperability. As the great business historian Alfred Chandler commented:

The close cooperation between the managers of the first modern multiunit enterprises in the United States contributed impressively to increasing the speed and regularity of transportation and decreasing its costs.

Professional management spread quickly to other industries and along with the profession came a need for business education (see pp. 78–80).

Omnipresent managers

Who isn't a manager today? Apart from managing directors of companies there are football managers, nursery managers, restaurant managers, and train managers. One can be a crisis manager, a turnaround manager or an interim manager. We recognize there are many management styles, some more and others less desirable. Professional managers, along with business education, are the only management innovations without which this book would never have been written as they have created the demand for knowledge about management innovation. We no longer wonder whether professional managers are needed.

Yet management has never quite managed to remove itself from the firing line. The conflict between owners and managers, often referred to as the agency conflict, has continued to persist. Managers get fired if their performance is seen as not adequate. Employees display varying degrees of happiness about the managers they work for. And the word management itself has become value laden.

To be an effective manager today requires the ability to do many things simultaneously. To manage relations with those lower or higher in a company's hierarchy, with outside partners, with shareholders and stakeholders like governments, non-governmental organizations and the media. To motivate other people to achieve desired tasks. To take risky decisions that will, hopefully, benefit the company. Meeting these challenges is a tough challenge and one that only the skilful or lucky few manage to do.

Business education

Some 30 years after the introduction of professional managers (see pp. 75–77), the number of manufacturers in the USA was growing, as were the size of the workforce and the size of companies. Rapid technological change was a prime underlying reason for these changes. So the need to delegate responsibility to a corps of managers was as great as ever. As a consequence companies started to feel a greater need for managers who could perform their tasks well. How could individuals be made to become better managers?

This question was pressingly on the mind of Joseph Wharton. Wharton had started his career as an apprentice bookkeeper but moved on eventually to make a fortune in the metals industry. Wharton had become a director of the Saucon Iron Company, which was renamed as the Bethlehem Iron Company and then Bethlehem Steel, the same company where Frederick Taylor would do most of his work on scientific management (see pp. 12–17). Wharton found it very difficult to recruit business leaders for Bethlehem. There were so-called 'commercial colleges' around at the time, which offered a three-month training course in business arithmetic, simply bookkeeping and penmanship. In Wharton's mind these colleges produced clerks and not educated business leaders. He thought that 'an intellectual hiatus exists in the business life of the nation'.

In the beginning

Wharton was convinced that a new type of business education, with a liberal arts foundation and a social science focus, was needed to obtain intellectually trained and broad-minded business leaders for the future. So in 1881 Wharton decided to donate $100,000 to the University of Pennsylvania, for it to establish a school for educating businessmen and public leaders, so that large firms and governments would have a pool of potential employees to choose from. That made the Wharton School at the University of Pennsylvania the first real business school, and implied a significant departure from the existing model of business education. Instead of focusing on technical skills, Wharton thought that financial management and social and people skills were important to the success of businesses and the school set out to train students in this area. Formal business education was a natural extension to the rise of professional managers, as it helped to train people to become better managers, which should help to improve the performance of the firms they worked for, so Wharton reasoned.

As soon as Wharton made his donation, the school started operating but not without a fair share of troubles. Existing faculty members who came to work for the school out of the liberal arts department had employed different methods in the past from the practical approach Wharton wanted. After two years many of them were released by the university administration and then substituted by instructors who were more familiar with business subjects. These people started building a curriculum that varied substantially from the classical curriculum seen in other subject areas. Staffing remained a problem for a long time, especially in areas like business economics where there was no clear established field of study.

And there were additional issues. The arts and sciences faculty tried to put in restrictions on the subjects that could be taught at Wharton. Wharton initially also had problems with funding as the donation was large but not enough for the school to be sustainable in the long run without other income sources. Finally, other members of the university were concerned that the academic and scholarship standards at Wharton would be lower than elsewhere in the university.

Expanding classes

After overcoming its initial problems, the Wharton School became a successful enterprise. Yet the funding needed to establish a business school was so substantial, and the resistance from traditional academics in other fields so large, that it took some time for other universities to follow suit. In 1900 the Amos Tuck School of Business Administration was established at Dartmouth College following another donation and the observation by Dartmouth College president William Jewett Tucker that where previously 90 per cent or more of the graduates had gone into law, medicine, ministry, and teaching, this had fallen to only 64 per cent in 1899, with many more graduates choosing a career in business. Since he saw this as a lasting trend, it was decided Dartmouth College should also be opening a business school.

As the demand for formally trained business leaders kept growing, other US universities followed the University of Pennsylvania, including Chicago (in 1898), the University of California at Berkeley (in 1898) and Harvard University (in 1908). In other countries, it would take many more decades. In the United Kingdom, business schools for instance did not emerge until the 1960s, with the country's two leading universities only entering the fray in the 1990s.

And now the world

The business education industry has continued to grow rapidly. Almost all universities now have a business or management school. But growth has not just been limited to the university sector, with many private companies now offering business education as well, either internally or to other companies. Curricula have evolved over time, as has the notion of what it takes to be an effective manager. The dominant vehicle for business education today is the Master of Business Administration (MBA) degree. Although MBA degrees have often been criticized on all kinds of grounds, for being too shallow or leading to the wrong skill sets, students seem as willing as ever to invest large sums of money into taking these degrees. The same is true for other degree and non-degree business education. Joseph Wharton would have been pleased to see his vision come to life.

 # Performance-related pay

Determining pay rates is a challenge for any organization. Historically, during times of labour surplus, companies could afford to pay as little as the market would bear. During times of labour shortage, however, the balance of power shifts and organizations need to attract the best employees from a smaller pool of talent.

At the same time, regardless of external market conditions, firms need to be able to motivate individuals within the business to perform to their potential. If employees are paid the same, regardless of performance, the best individuals are likely to become disenchanted and leave. So to maximize individual and, therefore, organizational performance, organizations throughout history have experimented with various formulas for rewarding employees in ways that related to their output. For example, during the 1500s some guilds tried paying their employees on 'piecework' rates, which rewarded individuals for the units of output they produced rather than the number of hours they worked. Variations of the piecework model were adopted during the Industrial Revolution on both sides of the Atlantic.

During the 1920s and 1930s, the challenge of creating appropriate incentives for employees became acute. Scientific management techniques had enabled companies to enhance their productivity, but often at the expense of their employees. Management thinking, and in particular the so-called human relations movement, had started to re-emphasize the human side of the equation in the design of work. Yet trade unions had become more powerful, and frequently resisted productivity-related initiatives from company managers. How, given these tensions, could companies create appropriate systems for linking employee pay to the performance of the organization?

The Scanlon Plan

The most well-known solution, though by no means the only one, was the brainchild of Joe Scanlon. Scanlon had a colourful career; he was a boxer, cost accountant and union president before becoming a lecturer in industrial relations at MIT. On the way, he invented the Scanlon Plan, designed to allow workers to share in the fruits of their productivity, while providing them with an incentive to work harder.

Scanlon was president of the local steelworkers' union when a local plant in Ohio was threatened with closure. Scanlon brought workers and management together to thrash out a union–management productivity plan. A productivity level was agreed by both union and management. If the workers managed to work more productively, at a lower cost per unit, then they received a bonus from the savings. A key aspect of the plan was that it was not competitive and, rather than promoting the individual over the team, rewarded the efforts of the collective enterprise.

The plan worked and, better still, made the plant profitable. One suggestion made by the union production committee saved the plant $150,000 in a single year. Scanlon was transferred to the union head office so that he could advise other steel plants about his new productivity plan.

Working for the union as trouble shooter, Scanlon took his ideas to a number of companies. In 1945 he implemented his system at the Adamson Company, Ohio, a manufacturer of steel tanks. A year later, and the Adamson Company was 500 per cent more productive. After dividing up the bonus, the managers doubled their previous income.

Machine tool motivation

Next, Scanlon moved on to the Lapointe Machine Tool company, in Massachusetts, producing a 61 per cent productivity gain inside of 20 months. Not long after, Scanlon tried out his plan on a company that was already successful, and not suffering from union problems. There were motivation problems, however, tied to the use of what was at the time the standard type of incentive plan, which rewarded individual performance over the team's. Over the first 12 months, the workers earned a bonus every month but one, with the best result a 27 per cent improvement over their usual wages.

By the 1950s, 60 plants across many different industries had implemented the Scanlon Plan. Enthused by his success, Scanlon took up a position at MIT, where he was able to interact directly with the leading thinkers of the day, including Douglas McGregor, who subsequently wrote the highly influential book, *The human side of enterprise*. Scanlon died in 1956, and his ideas were published posthumously in a 1958 book by Frederick Lesieur called *The Scanlon Plan: A frontier in labour–management cooperation*.

Broader influence

The Scanlon Plan exemplified two important principles of performance-related pay: a direct link between the performance of the collective (e.g. the factory) and the individual's bonus; and a joint worker/manager scheme that encourages both sides to work together towards a common objective. However, it did not provide a panacea to the problem of paying individuals for performance: it was quite unwieldy to put in place, and it did not discriminate between hard working employees and those who were taking it easy. Partly because of these problems, the Scanlon Plan did not get adopted in a comprehensive fashion. Today there are still some 25 companies that are paid-up members of the Scanlon Plan Institute, but for most companies, the Scanlon Plan is an interesting historical story, rather than current practice.

But the broader effect of Scanlon's innovation on the field of management is much greater than the Scanlon Plan Institute would suggest. During the post-war years, as the human relations movement really took off, many companies experimented with their own approaches to performance-related pay, often building explicitly on Joe Scanlon's ideas.

For example, at the other end of the corporate ladder from where Scanlon started, senior executives embarked on their own highly leveraged compensation schemes in the latter half of the 20th century. A spate of takeovers in the 1980s pushed senior executives across the world to tie pay to stock performance, rather than take bonuses for hitting financial targets. It was a move that trickled down to other employees, to a lesser extent, and led to the increased use of stock options as part of the total cash compensation.

Taking stock

The rationale behind stock options is that they align the interests of the individual executives to that of the company by giving them a stake in the future value of the company. Critics, however, point out that, in a rising market, as during the 1990s, directors still gained, even if their company badly under-performed, when judged against the industry average for their sector.

In 1990, an article in the *Harvard Business Review*, 'CEO incentives – it's not how much you pay, but how,' argued that that there was very little connection between how much CEOs were paid and their company's performance. More recent research by Ruth Bender at Cranfield School of Management, published in 2004, showed that many firms use performance-related pay because their peers do, rather than for motivational reasons.

Finally, in the 2000s, a stock option backdating scandal surfaced, where directors were caught backdating the granting of their options to a date where the stock price was lower than that on the actual issue date. This has undermined confidence in this type of executive performance pay system.

These problems illustrate a fundamental truth with performance-related pay: it is impossible to create a scheme in a large company that motivates all workers, while still being perceived as fair and in the interests of the share-holders. Companies continue to experiment with various models to alleviate the weaknesses of their current model, and increasingly we see companies such as the Body Shop, Patagonia, and Whole Foods Market, which attempt to appeal to non-financial employee motivators such as a higher sense of purpose.

Assessment centres

As management grew more professional during the 1950s and 1960s, a new challenge emerged – finding appropriately talented candidates for managerial positions. The problem was that many candidates came from specialist areas with little general management experience. How could you assess whether a person was suitable for a particular position if the position required different skills from those skills they used in their existing work? Moreover, what if there was no opportunity to demonstrate the skills required in their existing job: for example, a salesman moving to sales manager; or a scientist to a managerial position.

Even when the applicant had some training for or previous experience in a managerial post, to what extent would that person's CV predict their actual performance? Neither was the challenge just about organizations filling existing positions; they also needed to create a pipeline of talent for the future. Companies needed to create a process for identifying candidates with high potential, so that these people could then be fast tracked, and groomed for senior management. But what would be the best way to evaluate people's skills and potential?

Talent spotting

One solution that organizations developed to meet this selection need was the assessment centre. An assessment centre is a location where a process takes place that uses a number of tests (objective, projective, and situational), interviews and other methods to make judgements about the abilities of the people being assessed. Assessment centres used to identify high potential internal staff are also called development centres.

Applicants for a position or high potentials identified by HR attend an assessment centre and undergo a battery of tests, possibly over a period of several days. The information gathered about the candidates is collated into an assessment report, and the report is provided to management so that they can make a decision regarding the people who were assessed.

At some point in the future, the progress of the people hired or fast tracked as a result of decisions made using the assessment centre process can be compared with a control group of people hired or fast tracked without the help of the assessment centre process. Ideally, the assessment centre decisions will be linked to better outcomes.

Officer selection

Some suggest the concept of the 'assessment centre' dates back to the research into personality by Professor Henry Murray at Harvard University during the 1930s.

The first use of multiple assessment procedures on a significant scale, however, was by military organizations for the recruitment of officers during the Second World War. This included the German Officers' Programme, and the British War Officer Selection Boards (WOSB's). Perhaps the most famous was the programme devised by the American Office of Strategic Services (OSS) in 1943 to select intelligence agents for service during the Second World War. A summary of the work was later published in *The assessment of men*, written by members of OSS.

Contributions by the military to assessment centre techniques included the leaderless group, the combining of a variety of tests together, the use of several assessors and the collating of opinions, and various situational exercises.

The Management Progress Study

Like other military innovations, such as strategic planning (see pp. 160–162) and operations research (see pp. 172–174), the assessment centre soon made its way into the business world. The first instance was a research study at the telecoms company AT&T in 1956 called the Management Progress Study. The aim was to discover the factors that determined career success by studying 422 people from six Bell System operating companies.

The research used psychological assessments including clinical interviews, samples, paper-and-pencil tests, group problems and leaderless group discussions, during three and a half day assessment centre sessions. Each group contained 12 people. The research programme extended over four years from 1956 to 1960. It was on publication of the research that the term 'assessment centre' finally became part of the management lexicon.

Following this AT&T, impressed by the research results, extended the programme to the Michigan Bell Telephone Company in 1958 as the Personnel Assessment Program (PAP). The programme then spread rapidly to other Bell companies. Soon other organizations, such as Standard Oil, General Electric, and Sears Roebuck, also became aware of the benefits and implemented centres.

Assessment centres today

The use of assessment centres is widespread today. As noted in an article by William C. Byham for the International Congress on Assessment Centre Methods, for example, hundreds of manufacturing plants use, or have used, assessment centres to select staff. Byham cites the example of car manufacturer Toyota assessing 22,000 applicants to staff its 3000-person plant in Kentucky.

Assessment centres also make use of technological advances to improve their reliability and validity, such as videoing the behaviour of individuals being assessed, for example. Also, organizations have tried to make the process less cumbersome and expensive by incorporating the elements of the assessment centre process into the everyday working lives of employees when assessing high potential, as opposed to sending all managers off to a separate location, which may adversely impact on the operational performance of the organization.

Although in widespread use as an HR tool for personnel evaluation and selection, assessment centres have been placed under some degree of scrutiny recently, in terms of their fairness and validity.

Given that the decisions taken as a result of performance in an assessment have a significant impact on individuals' careers it is no surprise that they have been the subject of challenges in the courts. Partly as a result, a taskforce in the USA was assembled to consider practices within assessment centres and subsequently issued a document entitled 'Guidelines and ethical considerations for assessment centre operations'. This, in turn, was endorsed by the International Congress on Assessment Centre Methods.

T-groups

In the late 1940s the world was recovering from the devastation caused by the Second World War. After an intense period of global conflict, many countries, such as the USA were trying to come to terms with internal conflict between different communities.

At the same time, the traditional mechanistic view of organizations as machines with employees as the moving parts, was waning with support for a more humanistic view of organizations as communities growing. As this view took hold, people-related issues rose to the fore in the field of management.

What was required, it seemed, were new ways of understanding people's behaviour; and new types of training to deal with more human-related issues, such as conflict between people and inappropriate or unproductive behaviour.

Time for T

For a few years in the 1950s, the answer to these problems appeared to be training groups, or T-groups. Introduced by German-born psychologist Kurt Lewin, T-groups encouraged learning by getting individuals to assess their own views and behaviours and their impact on others in a group setting. In particular it focused on feelings and the communication of feelings.

T-groups defied easy description, as they were designed to be highly informal and unstructured in nature. They were facilitated by trainers, although the trainers saw themselves as having very limited involvement in what went on. The idea was that as the individuals interacted and struggled towards some sense of group identity, they would challenge their perceptions of how they and others felt. The T-group also allowed them the space and trust to try out different behaviours.

The trainers helped the group's learning process, prompting, occasionally interpreting, offering theories, opening up to the group in order to encourage the group members to open up, providing feedback and, sometimes, challenging individuals.

Boyish enthusiasm

In the 1940s Kurt Lewin, a professor of child psychology at the Child Welfare Research Station in Iowa, carried out research at boys' clubs in Iowa City. Groups of boys were given leaders with different leadership styles and the ways in which the groups responded and worked were recorded by Lewin and his colleagues. This research found that the more democratic groups worked most effectively. This hardly seems a staggering conclusion but in an era still dominated by scientific management, corporate dictatorship was the order of the day.

In 1946 Lewin was working as a director of the Massachusetts Institute of Technology at its new Research Center for Group Dynamics. Lewin was asked by the American Jewish Congress Committee on Community Interrelations and the Connecticut Interracial Commission to help train community leaders to help create better relations in their home communities.

The training, in New Britain, Connecticut, involved three continual learning groups. Each group had a leader, an observer, and various participants. The observers recorded results, and then discussed them together later on.

At one point, a number of participants asked to sit in on an observer session and Lewin agreed. During the ensuing discussion a female participant disagreed with an observer's interpretation of her behaviour earlier that same day. A discussion followed on behaviours and their interpretation, and after the success of this discussion, similar sessions became the focus of the conference. Lewin had discovered a new method of learning – by experience in the group discussion, rather than by lecture.

Freezing progress

Lewin believed that bringing together groups of people was a very powerful means of exposing areas of conflict. The theory underlying T-groups, and the Lewin model of change, was that behaviour patterns needed to be *unfrozen* before they could be *changed* and then *refrozen*. T-groups were a means of making this happen.

Keen to take the idea forward, Lewin began making plans with his associates to establish a 'cultural island' where T-groups could be examined more closely. A suitable location – an old school in Bethel, Maine – was identified shortly before Lewin's premature death of a heart attack in 1947. The

National Training Laboratories for Group Dynamics were established in Bethel and proved highly influential. An entire generation of human relations specialists became involved. These included Warren Bennis, Douglas McGregor, Robert Blake, Chris Argyris, and Ed Schein. 'NTL crackled with intellectual energy and the heady sense that some major discovery about the real nature of groups was taking place,' recalled Warren Bennis, going on to pay tribute to Lewin's colleagues Ronald Lippitt, Kenneth Benne, and Leland Bradford who turned NTL into a reality.

After the success of the first conference, over 100 participants turned up to the conference in 1948 and many more were turned away. There followed a rapid expansion, with labs opening across the USA, and many large corporations such as Exxon becoming active supporters. In the UK, a similar movement was gathering momentum, based around the Tavistock Institute and the work of management thinkers such as Eric Trist and clinical psychologist Melanie Klein. With the network almost doubling during the 1960s and the NTL publishing *The Journal of Applied Behavioral Science*, the growth continued until the 1970s.

At the margins

In 1975, the NTL's then director retired. The NTL was going through a period of difficulty, the membership were unhappy with the board and the organization came close to dissolution. A major reorganization left the NTL with a new-look board, but intact.

Today the NTL still exists but the T-group concept has been somewhat marginalized. Some have criticized aspects of the T-group's process, such as sensitivity training. A number of research papers have questioned whether the T-group process was psychologically damaging. But, more broadly, the T-group was gradually superseded by a range of more outcome-oriented development activities. Increasingly, companies felt they could not allow their senior executives to disappear for several weeks at a time engaging in self-reflection, and opted instead for the more focused offerings of business schools and other training organizations.

But the influence of NTL's T-group methodology on a generation of business school professors should not be underestimated. Many of today's standard approaches to self-reflection and group work can be traced back to Kurt Lewin's original ideas back in the 1940s.

Quality of work life

The 1960s were a decade of significant social upheaval in the business world. The post-war years had seen dramatic increases in productivity and economic well-being in North America and Europe, and yet these improvements had not always been matched with a sense that the quality of working life – for the majority of people – had actually improved.

In terms of management thinking, the so-called human relations movement, which had begun in the 1930s, was still in full swing, and indeed (though its advocates did not know it at the time) nearing its end. In the United States, the ideas of leading organizational thinkers such as Douglas McGregor, Ed Schein, Chris Argyris, and Warren Bennis encouraged a continued focus on the 'human side of the enterprise'. In Europe, the situation was more fragmented, but there were several hotbeds of activity. In the UK, the pioneering work of Eric Trist and others at the Tavistock Institute led to important ideas about 'socio-technical systems' that combined concerns for social dynamics with the technical imperatives of the workplace. And in both Sweden and Norway the importance attached to a high-quality working environment led to important innovations in management practices – such as Volvo's experiments in cellular manufacturing discussed earlier (see pp. 28–31).

But for many companies there was a gap between the rhetoric of a high quality of working life and the reality of their actual management practices. While many experiments were put in place during this period, the level of satisfaction with their outcomes was decidedly mixed.

General Foods and Topeka

Perhaps the best known quality of working life experiment was at General Foods' Topeka, Kansas, factory. This was not the first innovation of its type, and it was only a qualified success, but because of the vast amount of publicity it received at the time it came to typify the management innovation efforts of this era.

In 1968 the US consumer products company General Foods had its share of labour problems and inefficient work practices. Two senior plant managers, Lyman Ketchum and Ed Dulworth, were running a dog food plant in Kankakee, Illinois that was grossly overcrowded and had abysmal labour relations. But unlike most of their counterparts in other plants, Ketchum and Dulworth were deeply dissatisfied with the status quo. They had taken part in T-group training at the National Training Laboratories (see pp. 86–88), and they had been introduced to the concept of socio-technical systems and the quality of working life movement in Europe.

A new vision

Ketchum and Dulworth started introducing socio-technical thinking at Kankakee, but their big opportunity came in 1969, when they persuaded senior executives at General Foods to invest in a brand-new dog food plant. Topeka in Kansas was chosen as the location and Ketchum and Dulworth were given responsibility for designing it from scratch around socio-technical principles. There would be no supervisors, just self-directing teams with a rotating leadership role. Authority would be based on capability and the willingness to pitch in, rather than on pay grade. Traditional status differentiators – separate dining rooms, bathrooms, and parking spaces for management – would be eliminated. Teams would have the power to make changes to their work practices without seeking permission from higher ups, and they would be given time away from the production line each week to dream up better ways of churning out Fido's dinner.

While the concept for Topeka was visionary and groundbreaking, it was built on strong foundations. Ketchum and Dulworth picked up practical tips from Procter & Gamble's Lima, Ohio, plant, and they drew on the expertise of Richard Walton, a professor at Harvard Business School who had been an NTL trainer.

The gleaming new Topeka plant was opened in 1970, and it quickly started setting records. Production costs fell by 40 per cent compared with Kankakee and absenteeism shrank from 15 to 2 per cent. Richard Walton proclaimed it an 'unqualified success'.

Curing the blue-collar blues

Soon management scholars and plant managers from across the country were sniffing around the Topeka plant, trying to ferret out the secrets of its unrivalled performance. Before long, Ketchum and Dulworth's cure for 'blue-collar blues' was being touted in the pages of the *Harvard Business Review*, in the *New York Times*, in America's weekly magazines and on television.

Not bad press for a couple of guys running a dog food plant. But the external adulation was never matched by similarly effusive praise from within General Foods. Within five years, both Ketchum and Dulworth had been pushed out. Senior executives seemed more interested in preventing the Topeka virus from spreading to other factories than in using it as a model for the rest of the company. While employees loved the notion of a less stultifying and more engaging workplace, Ketchum and Dulworth's peers weren't about to try something so radical in their own plants. Nevertheless, despite a succession of often unsympathetic owners – General Foods, Anderson Clayton, Quaker and Nestlé – the Topeka plant has stuck with its team-based management system.

Back to the future

While the terms quality of work life and socio-technical systems are only used occasionally today, the underlying concept that a factory should balance the social needs of its employees with its technical imperatives is firmly established, and indeed gets periodically reinvented with new vernacular. Most large companies now embrace these ideas, often under the label of 'self-directed work teams' or 'high-performance work teams'. For example, Rolls-Royce, the UK engine manufacturer, has achieved at least 30 per cent gains in productivity over the late 1990s and early 2000s through its introduction of self-directed work teams.

But there is still very often a large gap between the rhetoric and the reality of socio-technical systems, and there are plenty of cases of factories that have implemented these ideas for a few years and then lapsed back into a command-and-control mentality. The reason is that these sorts of system require managers to devolve power, rather than retain it, and they require workers to take responsibility for their own destiny; and to do this consistently means changing – in many cases – the habits of a lifetime. There are real benefits to the socio-technical way of working, but it is fragile and requires constant attention.

Mentoring and executive coaching

Traditionally, capital was seen as the key source of competitive advantage of a company and people were mostly pairs of hands. But over time this started to change and by the 1970s more attention started to be paid to human capital. In a world where people and the knowledge they bring were becoming a critical organizational asset, great emphasis started to be placed on personal development. College training, a variety of commercial courses and in-house training were the key learning options available to all employees.

But what about those higher up the organization? What about senior executives wanting to hone their leadership skills? And what about those executives earmarked for better things, or those who simply wanted to get up the corporate ladder a little faster? The higher up you were, the harder it was to do personal development. For a start, who would deliver it? The issues tended to be more around leadership style, personal effectiveness, and interpersonal skills, such as empathy, communication and listening; it was hard to get this from someone in the organization in a junior position. How then, could the learning needs of senior executives be met?

A propensity for intensity

Mentoring and executive coaching are two closely related management innovations designed to meet the learning needs of senior executives, and rising talent within organizations, in particular; although people at other levels of an organization also benefited from them. Mentoring has been defined as 'an intense relationship, lasting eight-to-ten years, in which a senior person oversees the career and psychosocial development of a junior person'.

There has, however, been some debate over whether mentoring within formal mentoring programmes can be described in the same way as informal mentoring. A formal mentor has been described as 'a person who oversees the career and development of another person, usually a junior, through teaching, counselling, and providing psychological support, protecting, and at times promoting or sponsoring'. The point about formal mentoring programmes is that, unlike informal arrangements, formal mentoring is structured, often to the extent of prescribing the mentor and monitoring the programme.

Executive coaching, which later followed mentoring, is closely related to formal mentoring. As with mentoring, definitions vary but the common denominator is that this coaching involves one-on-one relationships with executives, focusing on behavioural changes to hone leadership skills; enhance personal effectiveness; or correct unhelpful behaviours – and, ultimately, improve job performance.

In his book *Coaching: Winning strategies for individuals and teams*, Dennis Kinlaw defined coaching as:

A disciplined personal interaction with one or more persons which produces winning results for individuals, teams, and organizations by focusing and refocusing them on performance goals and facilitating their achievement of these goals.

Old mentors

Informal mentoring has been in existence for thousands of years, many military leaders and future kings have benefited from the process, after all. Aristotle, the Greek philosopher, was mentor to Alexander the Great; Julius Caesar mentor to Mark Antony. But in a corporate setting the first mentions in management literature of formal mentoring are connected with the implementation of a formal mentoring programme at the Jewel Tea Company in Chicago.

As far back as 1931, the company began a mentoring programme in which MBAs joining the company were assigned to a senior manager who acted as a mentor. At the time, management development consisted of training programmes and job rotation, so this was a progressive development. The mentoring programme at the Jewel Company enabled three consecutive presidents to be appointed under the age of 45. Over time the programme was gradually expanded as needs kept changing and by the 1970s, when human capital came to be seen as a core asset, it started to get noticed.

The programme was described in a *Harvard Business Review* article in 1978. 'Executive responsibility involves assisting the people down the line to be successful. The boss in any department is the first assistant to those who report to him,' said Franklin J. Lunding, former president and first beneficiary of the mentoring programme at Jewel.

From grassroots to boardroom

Mentoring spread rapidly in the 1980s to areas of work as diverse as consulting, politics, and sports. Executive coaching started later, in the late 1980s and early 1990s, but the most dramatic growth has been in the last five years or so. Its spread has been hastened by endorsement from the highest corporate echelons. Coaching has also drawn on the work of academics like psychologist Harry Levinson, Kurt Lewin with his Field Theory, and MIT's Ed Schein.

One of the main reasons for the growth of executive coaching, apart from its efficacy, were the efforts of one of the world's leading proponents of the practice – Marshall Goldsmith. Goldsmith is one of the world's best known executive coaches, having written over 23 books on the subject, including *Coaching for leadership* and the most recent *What got you here won't get you there*, and having coached over 70 major CEOs.

Coaching is certainly no longer the same 'grassroots movement' that *Fortune* magazine called it in 2000. The number of high-profile leaders using a coach has elevated the reputation of coaching from that of a run-of-the-mill management fad. Senior executives who have enlisted the help of a coach include among many others: David S. Pottruck, ex-CEO of the Charles Schwab Corporation; eBay Inc. CEO Meg Whitman; Henry McKinnell, ex-CEO of Pfizer; John Chambers, CEO of Cisco; and Jim Padilla, COO of Ford Motor Company.

Coaching the world

Formal mentoring now has corporate support on all continents. Executive coaching, however, is most prevalent in the United States, but is spreading globally. A 2002 survey of human resources professionals by the HR consultancy the Hay Group found that over half of the 150 organizations polled from Asia, Australia, Europe, and North America increased their use of coaching in the previous 12 months; 16 per cent had used coaches for the first time.

Reservations about the practice remain in some quarters, executive coaching remains largely unregulated, for example. The International Coach Federation (ICF), established in 1995, is the closest thing to a professional body for coaches. The ICF estimates that there are over 15,000 coaches in North America, and the ICF has over 11,000 members in 82 countries, against 1500 in 1995. Yet demand for mentoring and coaching is as high as ever.

360-degree feedback

The annual appraisal was once a bureaucratic chore to be completed as speedily as possible. Every year, at an appointed hour, a manager sat in an office with their direct superior. The manager's performance over the previous year was discussed and dissected. The manager emerged from the room and headed back to their desk, until the next year. But by the 1970s it was no longer clear this approach was good enough.

The appraisal's *raison d'être* is straightforward: to improve an individual's – and, therefore, an organization's – performance. But to do so, the appraisal has to be responsive to individual needs. The traditional method of getting a periodic report from an individual's direct superior proved to be a very limited approach, susceptible to subjective bias. In order to be able to develop, an individual must have an objective assessment of their strengths and weaknesses. Otherwise how can employees know which areas to focus on, in order to improve performance?

Only perform

The appraisal is now seen in the broader ranging context of 'performance management'. This means that it must embrace issues such as personal development and career planning, in addition to simple analysis of how well the individual has performed over the last year.

Extending the range of this approach is the increasingly fashionable concept of 360-degree feedback. This involves a manager's peers, subordinates, bosses, and even customers, giving their views on the manager's performance, usually by way of a questionnaire.

The attraction of 360-degree feedback is that it gives a more complete picture of an individual's performance. Different groups see the person in a variety of circumstances and can, as a result, give a broader perspective than that of a single boss. This, of course, relies on a high degree of openness and trust – as well as perception. One way to achieve that is for the feedback to be anonymous.

Weis and means

The idea of getting feedback from different sources in order to appraise performance is not new. An imperial rater was used during the Wei Dynasty, in 3rd-century China, to evaluate performance of people at the imperial court.

Much later – in 1950s North America – management theorists, as part of what was known as the human relations school began to focus on what motivated employees in the workplace. Clinical psychologist Frederick Herzberg, for example, coined the phrase *job enrichment*, suggesting that true motivation in the workplace came from factors such as achievement, job satisfaction, personal development, and recognition. The 360-degree feedback tool was part of a range of tools developed with personal development and employee motivation in mind.

In terms of the individual most closely associated with the invention of the 360-degree feedback process as a corporate tool, it is probably industrial and organizational psychologist Clark Wilson. He developed 360-degree feedback tools following the development of multilevel surveys in the 1970s, through his work with the World Bank. The first 360-degree instrument was called the Survey of Management Practices (SMP), and it was developed by Wilson for use as a teaching tool in his management class at the University of Bridgeport Graduate School of Business in Connecticut. The first company to adopt Clark's SMP was the DuPont Company in 1973.

Pickup

By the mid-1970s the list of companies had expanded to include Dow Chemicals, a number of utility companies, and Pitney Bowes. Human resources consultants began to pick up on the concept as well, which further contributed to its wider use.

By the time Walter Tornow was writing about 360-degree feedback in 1993, the subject was widespread enough to command a special issue of *Human Resource Management* devoted to the subject. It was clear that the concept was used throughout industry as a tool for a number of purposes. There were at least 16 well-known 360-degree feedback instruments available, plus many more that were less familiar.

By 2002 the list of companies that responded to a survey of corporations using 360-degree feedback included many of the world's leading companies, including Deutsche Bank, Citigroup, BP Amoco, Bestfoods, Anheuser-Busch, Dell Computers, Ford, Kellogg's, Nestlé USA, and PepsiCo.

Corporations also began to adopt 360-degree feedback for uses other than gauging the strengths and weaknesses of an individual for personal development planning purposes. The 360-degree tool was used as part of performance appraisal, to determine suitable assignments for individuals, as part of a succession planning process, and even to engineer organizational change.

All around

Modern organizational structures with flattened hierarchies make it even more difficult for supervisors, if there are any left, to assess the strengths and weaknesses of individuals beneath them in an organization. As a result, the 360-degree feedback tool is more popular than ever. Its popularity is borne out in popular management literature and self-help books and from its support by leading HR practitioners such as executive coach, Marshall Goldsmith.

Research at Ashridge Management College, into the growth of 360-degree feedback suggests that successful use of the concept requires a number of factors – a clear strategic rationale; top management support and involvement; a culture geared towards behaviours and attitudes rather than simply performance; sensitivity; a genuine and wide-based willingness to achieve change; and willingness to discuss any issue.

4

Internal structures

What is the most effective way of organizing a large company? And how should the various parts of the company be related to one another? The purpose of innovations in internal structures is to improve communication and information flows to ensure that the whole is more than the parts.

 ## Introduction

There are entire libraries of books concerned with various aspects of organization structure. In one famous book by Gareth Morgan, *Images of organization*, metaphors as diverse as a machine, a brain, a living organism, and an iron cage are used to shed light on the way work is conducted inside the firm. Thankfully, however, this variety and eccentricity is for the world of theorists rather than how firms are structured in practice. Nonetheless, there have been some dramatic changes in internal firm structure over the past century, and smaller changes are continuing to occur all the time.

Internal structure is one of the least sexy aspects of business. Employees can all see the problems of deep functional silos, multiple lines of reporting, and bureaucratic procedures, but their benefits are rarely acknowledged. However, the reality is that structure can deliver very real benefits – it enables information to flow effectively to the relevant parts of the organization, it reduces duplication of effort, and it can create very sophisticated levels of coordination. The challenge companies face is one of delivering on these potential advantages while keeping the costs of bureaucracy as low as possible. And a variety of innovative approaches to doing this have been experimented with over the years.

Taking a broad sweep through industrial history, the major trend has simply been the need for firms to develop innovative new structures to cope with the increasing scale, complexity and scope of their operations. Before the Industrial Revolution the vast majority of firms were small, owner-operated entities where coordination was achieved through a simple informal structure with the owner at the apex. As the economist Adam Smith observed more complex operations would be handled by multiple companies, which interacted in markets. As firms grew in size into hundreds and thousands of employees, a form of functional specialization was adopted in which work was grouped into specific tasks and coordinated through a hierarchical system that had its origins in the organization of the armies of Ancient Greece.

The first definitive innovation in firm structure in the last century and a half was the creation of the *divisional structure* in the 1920s by such firms as GM and DuPont. Essentially, the limits to coordination through a functional structure had been reached, so Alfred Sloan, the CEO of GM in the 1920s, took the critical decision to break up the company into five self-managed divisions, while leaving certain administrative responsibilities at the corporate centre. This new structure allowed GM and others to grow much larger without losing control of the diversity of their operations. This divisional structure was subsequently refined in the 1960s through the invention of *strategic business units* at General Electric and elsewhere, which were smaller units operating in specific product–market combinations. Divisions then came to consist of a set of such business units. Business units proved to be much more responsive to change in the marketplace and easier to manage, although an additional layer in the organization also increased the costs of organizing.

While the multidivisional structure offered enormous benefits, it also led to a lack of communication between divisions and a duplication of effort. To try to get the best of both worlds (i.e. functional *and* divisional structures), firms began experimenting with various versions of the *matrix structure* in the post-war years. The first known matrix structure was put in place by aircraft manufacturer McDonnell in the early 1950s, as a way of reconciling the demands for efficient delivery of specific projects (e.g. an aircraft order from the US government) while also achieving high levels of functional specialization for each different activity. In this structure, teams of employees essentially worked for two bosses – one project boss and one functional boss.

Other forms of matrix structure soon followed. International firms, such as IBM, Dow Chemical, and Digital Equipment, created global matrix structures during the 1970s with reporting lines to strategic business unit heads, on one side, and country heads, on the other. Professional services firms, like Citibank and McKinsey, developed matrix structures with their service lines, on one side, and their city or country-based resource pools, on the other. More recently, firms such as Citibank and Hewlett-Packard have experimented with global account structures, which overlaid the demands of a global customer against the country-focused sales organization. And during the 1990s many firms experimented with some sort of horizontal organization in which the activities that collectively represented a specific business process, such as order fulfilment, were overlaid on a traditional functional structure.

In addition to these high-level structures, there have also been innovations in how to structure individual projects and activities. One model that became commonplace in research and development organizations was what academics Kim Clark and Steven Wheelwright labelled the tiger team – a highly autonomous unit somewhat akin to a *skunk works* (described on pp. 149–151). As the capacity to communicate and work interactively on a global basis took off, so did the virtual team. And a number of innovations have been tried over the years to facilitate rapid problem solving. The most well known of these is the quality circle, which we discuss as part of total quality management. Another celebrated example is the workout team that GE first created in the late 1980s as a non-hierarchical model for resolving internal operational inefficiencies.

All these innovations are what we might call *formal* structures, because they rely on clear lines of accountability and responsibility as a means of getting things done. But there is a whole other dimension to structural innovation, namely the *informal* systems and mechanisms through which work gets coordinated in large organizations. Unfortunately, it is much more difficult to identify the landmark innovations on the informal side of the organization because, to varying degrees, informal mechanisms are always –and have always been – a key part of any effective organization. For example, the term *network organization* became popular during the 1990s as a way of characterizing the multiple lines of contact and influence that managers need to have to get things done, but this was nothing more than a label for what had already become, and perhaps always had been, standard practice in most large organizations.

Despite all this, it is useful to note three informal structural innovations. First, the *transnational model* was very much in vogue during the early 1990s, particularly in global firms, with ABB as its standard bearer. ABB's innovation involved a dramatic decentralization of the individual business units, coupled with a very tight set of facilitating systems, and a strong culture to build coordination between the units. As such, it attempted to create a 'matrix in the mind of the manager' rather than through formal reporting structures. Second, Danish hearing-aid company, Oticon, created the spaghetti organization also in the early 1990s. This was a project-based structure not unlike the original matrix, but it was unique because the projects were defined on a bottom-up basis with individuals selecting themselves onto projects, rather than on a top-down basis. Third, the concept of a *community of practice* was established in Xerox in the late 1980s and became popular during the 1990s. A community of practice is essentially a group of like-minded people working in different parts of the organization who choose to share ideas and insights to facilitate their individual learning. Such communities have existed (in some form) for as long as organizations have been around, but by recognizing their existence and by understanding their value, Xerox and other firms were able to nurture their development.

The divisional structure

In the early 20th century, many firms began to look to product diversification as a means of enabling their further growth. Constrained by antitrust legislation (that limited their ability to buy up direct competitors) and invigorated by their new-found industrial research capacity (see Chapter 6), the dominant mode of expansion was into related business areas. DuPont and General Motors were leading examples of this trend. In 1920 DuPont gradually expanded its product range away from its original explosives business towards plastics and paints. GM had, through a series of mergers, assembled an impressive range of brands, although it was not competing effectively with market leader Ford, which had established its lead through the moving assembly line (see Chapter 1) and a focus on providing a low cost car, its renowned Model T. In 1920 GM was operating more or less as a holding company.

Product and brand diversification caused a host of new challenges, primarily because of the increased complexity and scope of operations that it created. The dominant existing 'U-form' or functional structure relied on a division of labour among functional departments. Adjusting these departments to deal with multiple products proved to be hard. In addition, it was almost impossible for top management to retain the desired oversight of such a complex business. As suggested by economist Oliver Williamson: 'The ability of the management to handle the volume and complexity of the demands placed upon it became strained and even collapsed.' Both at DuPont and at GM there was therefore a need to gain synergies from having multiple businesses in-house without affecting their decision-making autonomy.

Divide and rule

In response to these problems DuPont and GM more or less simultaneously developed the divisional structure, alternatively known as the M-form organization or simply the divisional form of organizing. The divisional structure involved setting up separate product departments or divisions, each of which would tackle a different and clearly defined market. These would be led by a general manager, with full authority over the product or products in that division, including development, production and sales, but no authority beyond the division's boundaries. The general manager was made responsible for divisional performance and divisions operated as profit centres.

Meanwhile the central office, or headquarters, of the company grew substantially and became responsible for standard setting, monitoring the performance of the divisions, and major personnel and strategic investment decisions. It was also involved in forecasting future demand, including how to segment the overall market. The central office would set goals for the divisions. Because it was much better informed than external capital markets through the auditing process and could use the internal hierarchy to enforce decisions, the central office could add value to the operations of the various divisions.

The divisional structure produced several benefits. A company's CEO no longer needed to process all available information and could be concerned much less with daily operations. This implied the CEO could be much more concerned with strategic direction and with allocating resources between divisions. Because of this detachment and increased transparency, the chances of one product being favoured over another on political or personal grounds were reduced. Resources would simply be allocated to the investment opportunities that made most sense. This was further enabled by the emergence of more objective success measures like ROI (see Chapter 2). The division's general manager would be operating much closer to the product market and could therefore take more effective decisions on how to proceed in that market.

Sloan ranging

GM was first to officially put the divisional structure in place, on 3 January 1921. It was first proposed by Alfred Sloan at the end of 1919 in a memo intended to tackle the problems associated with the rapid expansion of GM. Sloan, who had taken a mechanical engineering degree from MIT in 1895, had started his career at Hyatt Roller Bearing Company. He managed to purchase the firm and later sold it to United Motors, where he became a president, before United Motors merged into General Motors.

Sloan later said: 'I drafted the "Organizational Study" and circulated it unoffi-
cially. It became a kind of "best seller" in the corporation all during 1920; I
received numerous letters from executives requesting copies of it.' As a consequence, Sloan had few problems pushing through his ideas, although GM
President Pierre du Pont introduced some amendments, related primarily to
the composition of the executive committee, which needed to contain
enough individuals with automotive experience to convince the divisions of
its legitimacy. GM operated separate divisions based on market segments for
each of its five automobile brands, Cadillac, Buick, Oldsmobile, Pontiac, and
Chevrolet, as well as for its truck, parts, and components divisions. The implementation of Sloan's ideas took some four years, until he was finally
convinced that both efficiency and integration had been achieved.

DuPont introduced its divisional structure in September 1921. It had been
tinkering with the idea since 1919 following the recommendations of a
committee that had been established to tackle the difficulties associated with
operating in such a variety of industries. DuPont president, Iréné du Pont,
initially opposed the proposal, instead propagating the 'principle of specialization'. But an experimental structure used for the paints business proved to
be so successful that the whole company eventually moved towards it.

DuPont like GM before it set up a central executive committee and central
departments in sales, engineering, product development, accounting and
research. These departments advised the core operating departments in
cellulose products, paint, pyralin, explosives, and dyestuffs. A major cultural
change accompanied the structural change at DuPont because the company
used to be highly centralized and had now decentralized responsibilities and
decision-making powers.

New standards

The divisional structure proved successful both at DuPont and at GM,
where, along with other innovations like market segmentation and Henry
Ford's refusal to change his low-cost strategy, it helped the company unseat
Ford Motor Company from its industry leading position.

The subsequent spread of the divisional structure to other firms was not rapid
but it was, nonetheless, decisive. Early adopters included Jersey Standard in
the petroleum industry and retailer Sears Roebuck. The companies adopting
the divisional structure early on mostly operated in new industries like cars,
chemicals and electronics or in existing industries that were affected by rapid
technological and demographic change like petroleum and chain stores. Over
the next four decades the divisional structure spread to more or less every
large firm, and to many smaller firms, in the United States and elsewhere.

The divisional legacy

Organizing a single firm into divisions produced such large and obvious benefits that it became the dominant model across most industries. At the same time, though, the divisional structure did not solve all the communication and coordination problems thrown up by size and complexity. One problem with the divisional structure was that divisions themselves often became large, and contained a variety of products and customers, so many firms moved to a strategic business unit (SBU) structure to create focused units that operated in specific marketplaces (see below). Another disadvantage of the divisional structure was the focus on vertical information flows, and thus the relative lack of communication *between* related activities in the different divisions. As a result, firms increasingly began to complement their vertical structures with horizontal structures and informal networks – as subsequent sections describe.

In some ways, the divisional structure has become seen as similar to the U-form it replaced – cumbersome and rigid. It allowed firms to achieve unprecedented levels of scale and scope, but it did not overcome the problems of bureaucracy that afflict all formal structures. As they say, you can't live with it but can't live without it.

Strategic business units

The divisional structure (as described on pp. 100–103) became the dominant organizational form in the 1960s, as companies throughout North America and Europe adopted it. Building on the basic principles devised by Alfred Sloan at GM, corporate planning involved centralized objectives being set and disseminated to divisions, which in turn drew up plans and objectives of their own to meet their higher level objectives.

It became clear during the 1960s, however, that this process was flawed in a number of ways. In particular, plans at a divisional level tended to differ from one division to the next. Some divisions would take an over-optimistic view of what was achievable, while others would be over-cautious, ensuring that targets were met by setting them too low.

When the plans were considered as a strategic whole by the senior team, it was very difficult to get any real sense, an accurate overall picture, of what was actually happening in the divisions. This planning mish-mash, driven by targets rather than strategic objectives, resulted in impressive revenue growth, but very little increase in profits.

What was needed was a way of providing a more coherent organizational strategy, while, at the same time, still allowing managers further down the corporate hierarchy, who knew the business on the ground, to have an input into the strategic planning process.

Good intentions

The strategic business unit (SBU), as it became known, offered a solution to these problems. Based on the same principles as the divisional structure, the SBU was highly focused, designed to serve a specific marketplace. The underlying idea is that a diversified firm can be managed as a portfolio of business units, with each business unit developing a strategy that best serves its interests, while at the same time ensuring that the strategy they adopt also serves the interests of the corporate wide strategy.

The firm then has the job of distributing capabilities and resource to the SBUs in a way that maximizes performance for the company as a whole. The development of portfolio analysis, through such tools as the Boston Consulting Group matrix, helped to make this process of resource allocation more efficient.

New plans

In the corporate world, the SBU model can be traced back to General Electric (GE). In the 1960s, GE notched up substantial growth in revenues. Despite its success in racking up sales, it posted a disappointing and comparatively small increase in profits during the same period. In fact, between 1962 and 1970 return on assets at GE actually fell. Action was required to address the situation. So, in 1971, GE's senior executives gathered to decide on a new corporate planning system.

The result was a decision to re-engineer the company using strategic business units rather than persisting with an organization structured along the traditional group and divisional lines. At GE this meant reorganizing nine groups and 48 divisions into 43 strategic business units. These strategic business units cut right across the group, division, and profit centre lines. So, for example, food preparation appliances in three different divisions were combined to form a single SBU.

Expanding SBUs

Within a few years of General Electric putting SBUs at the heart of its business structure, many other companies also adopted an SBU approach to structuring their business. However, although the basic premise was the same, the term used to describe the components of the new structure varied from company to company.

Union Carbide, the giant chemicals corporation, was an early adopter of GE's new organizational concept, for example. The company took 15 of its groups and divisions and first rearranged them into 150 of what it termed 'strategic planning units'. Subsequently, these planning units were combined into nine new units, designated 'aggregate planning units'.

Adopters didn't just use different terms to describe the concept, they also altered the concept to fit their circumstances. The idea was that SBUs should have strategic autonomy. In reality, however, that didn't always happen. At General Foods, another firm that latched onto the SBU approach early on, SBUs were initially delineated along product lines, regardless of the fact that many served overlapping markets. General Foods later organized the units according to menu segment, however.

While the basic elements of GE's SBUs were retained, SBUs took on other names and modifications to suit corporate circumstances.

Hardly remarked

Today strategic business units are an unremarkable element of the business world, indeed they are such so much a part of the modern corporate landscape that they have become a required element of the average MBA core class.

Firms have also become more sophisticated in their approach towards SBU implementation. Firms have learnt that if they are to get the full benefits from adopting the SBU approach then they need to change management systems to align development and reward SBU managers in ways related to the performance of their SBUs.

Companies are also more adept at apportioning resources to SBUs. A number of management consultants have developed planning tools to aid resource allocation to the SBUs. The two best known are the Boston Consulting Group Matrix, with its cash cows and dogs, and the General Electric/McKinsey matrix.

The tyranny of the SBU

However, like any other formal organization structure, SBUs have their weaknesses. By focusing effort towards the existing and well-defined product/market spaces that the firm is serving, the SBU structure makes it very difficult to see opportunities that emerge in the 'white spaces' between

those units, or opportunities that cut across them. When Gary Hamel and
C.K. Prahalad wrote their famous article 'The core competence of the corporation', they remarked that most companies struggled to identify or derive
value from their core competencies because of the 'tyranny of the SBU' that
blinkered executives to opportunities beyond their target market. Partly as a
result of this challenge, many companies have developed lateral structures
that attempt to forge more explicit links between their business units.

Matrix organization

In the early 1950s aerospace research procurement by the US government was
becoming considerably more professional. The government was starting to
impose additional demands on aerospace contractors, though not nearly as
many as today. One of its demands was that companies ought to set up what
was called a 'project management system'. Contractors were forced to provide
the government with an organization chart for every individual project,
including an idea of how the project was directly monitored by top executives.

The system was intended to govern how projects were run at contractor
companies and especially to ensure that government agencies could speak with
a single contact inside the company to lower coordination costs. That contact
person was the project manager, who was responsible for managing costs and
deliveries. While this was clearly the best solution from the perspective of the
government, it was less obvious how companies should match the project
management system with their existing functional structure. What organizational structure would be most suitable for these aerospace companies?

Alternative approaches

There were two possible ways to implement the project management system:
either it would replace the existing functional structure or it would somehow
be implemented alongside that structure. Replacing the functional structure
was not seen as a good solution. Shareholders would not be keen on seeing a
firm that only consisted of projects and the functional structure delivered too
many benefits. The academic Jay Galbraith, who later theorized about the
matrix structure, suggested that in functional structures projects invariably
get delivered too late while in organizations with only a project structure new
technologies are not developed fast enough.

Thus firms found themselves moving towards a dual structure where
functions and projects lived alongside one another and individuals became
subject to two chains of command. That dual structure became known as

the matrix organization or matrix structure because individuals found themselves operating at the intersections of both structures, inside a matrix. The matrix organization has been likened to a web of relationships. Galbraith wrote:

Aerospace firms were faced with a situation where both technical performance and coordination were important. The result was the matrix design, which attempts to achieve the benefits of both forms.

Over time the company develops support mechanisms, a culture and behaviour that are appropriate for a matrix organization.

Experiments in miniature

Because it was government that forced companies' hands, the matrix structure was developed in a reactive manner. Academic Eric Trist commented: 'Project management and matrix organization have emerged as hurried improvisations rather than as thought-through transformations.' One of the first companies to experiment with a project management organization was the Martin Company in 1952–53. But the Martin Company essentially created miniature companies, each running a single project, instead of a full-blown matrix structure.

McDonnell Aircraft Company was the brainchild of Princeton and MIT trained engineer J.S. McDonnell, who had been working for a range of aircraft companies before finally being able to establish his own company. In 1952 the US Air Force had requested to deal with only one McDonnell employee, who became known as the System Program Director, in Air Force speak. Previously all functional departments had been sending their own representatives. McDonnell hired project managers as a consequence. These project managers had project engineers on their teams who served as internal 'ambassadors' to the various functional departments and to outside suppliers. As project managers grew to be more powerful, the matrix structure became the means to balance the two hierarchies. The evolution to a matrix structure then occurred spontaneously because it turned out that the hierarchies of project teams showed significant overlap with the functional hierarchies. In 1958 a general manager with a similar status to head of department was appointed to oversee the projects. By the late 1950s McDonnell had truly implemented a balanced matrix structure where neither departments nor projects dominated.

The matrix revolution

Other companies to implement a matrix structure around the same time included General Dynamics, Lockheed, and Goodyear Aircraft. At General Dynamics' astronautics division a conflict resolution mechanism was developed whereby programme directors and department managers sat down to solve issues around authority, costs, scheduling, and performance in the development of the new intercontinental Atlas missile. Lockheed moved ahead in steps. When the initial project expediter proved toothless and undermined customer relations, it introduced a project coordinator instead. Goodyear similarly went through a process of gradual systematization, first unsuccessfully trying to work with committees of functional supervisors, before settling on the matrix structure. In the 1960s the matrix structure had become the de facto standard in the aerospace industry.

The matrix structure proved to be very successful in large companies dealing with numerous complex projects because it allowed for effective communications and decisions and created projects of a workable size. The matrix has helped companies stay abreast with rapid technological changes through their functional structure yet deal effectively with customer needs through the project structure. So companies outside the aerospace industry started taking up the matrix structure as well. Sweden's Skandia, an insurance company, introduced a matrix structure in the 1970s, when it was faced with the need to diversify its range of products substantially as a consequence of changes in the social security system. Its matrix balanced regional customer-facing offices with different insurance products. Other industries where the matrix structure has made headway include consulting, IT hardware and software, healthcare, social services, and advertizing.

Another important application of the matrix structure emerged when companies started internationalizing at a more rapid pace and wanted to create more globally integrated organizations. By creating a matrix that balanced the demands of its national markets and its product divisions, companies could overcome communication and coordination problems. The so-called *transnational* model, proposed by academics Chris Bartlett and Sumantra Ghoshal and implemented by companies such as ABB, can be seen as an evolution of the traditional matrix structure, though with a heavy emphasis on the informal elements of coordination that are needed for the structure to work.

Compromise solution

Any organization that primarily runs projects, from the International Olympic Committee to a Chinese made-to-order electronic components subcontractor, will always have some sort of matrix structure in place because it must deal with multiple environmental demands simultaneously. At the same time, the matrix structure remains a compromise, because it is neither as cost efficient as a functional structure, nor as flexible as an individual project team. Being organized as a matrix means an organization incurs additional administrative costs and is somewhat limited in its flexibility.

In their 1982 book *In search of excellence*, Peters and Waterman commented that 'the formal matrix organization structure regularly degenerates into anarchy and rapidly becomes bureaucratic and non-creative.' To be fair, though, most companies have ended up avoiding the *formal* matrix: instead, they have opted for a hybrid model whereby a variety of informal and lateral mechanisms are used to 'oil the wheels' of the dual-reporting system.

Work-out groups

In the early 1980s many companies were going through a process of downsizing. Frequently, the result of business process reengineering (see pp. 35–37), was a company with significantly fewer employees, but often the same or an increasing amount of work to be done. Suddenly, employees were overwhelmed and underresourced. Worse still, while the employees could improvise and devise solutions to make their working lives easier, management had no time to authorize their suggestions.

Consequently, companies set out to find new ways of working that would help enable the employees that remained to cope with the workload, without adversely affecting the company's performance. The challenge was to be able to tap into the innovative talent of the workforce and find ways of improving organizational processes, yet do this in a way that did not tie up management for a long period of time.

One of the companies struggling with exactly this dilemma in the 1980s was General Electric, one of America's longest running and most successful corporations, and with the help of their dynamic CEO, Jack Welch, GE was looking for an elegant and innovative solution to delivering efficient organizational improvement.

Town meetings

Workout is a problem-solving process. It involves bringing together a large group of employees, from different levels of the company, who are stakeholders in a particular problem. Often the meeting will be held offsite. The group will work in small teams to develop solutions to specified issues, usually related to improving the organization's performance, with the agenda set by a member of the management team who then leaves the teams to get on with their discussions. The discussions may take several days. Facilitators may be involved at this point to help ensure maximum performance from the teams.

The next stage is that the smaller teams re-form into a large group and present their ideas to someone with decision-making authority, usually a senior manager. This meeting is often referred to as the 'town meeting' and is a critical part of the process. The senior manager is tasked with providing instant feedback in the form of three possible responses: yes, no, or I'll have to consider it more. When the manager has to consider it further he will clarify what he is looking at, and how he will arrive at a decision.

It is essential that, if workout is to be a success, the workout strategy has the full support of senior management, and that it is made clear that obstructing the process is not acceptable. There are two key strengths to workout. First, because it is both an informal organizational structure and, by definition, temporary, workout helps to generate more ideas than other organizational change initiatives. Second, because workout cuts across formal lines of authority, it generates much more commitment from all layers of the organization, compared to traditional top-down-driven change initiatives.

Let's get the workout

Accounts of the origins of the term workout are varied. What they all have in common, however, is General Electric, and the company's legendary CEO, Jack Welch. During the 1980s, Welch put his dynamic mark on GE and on corporate America. GE's businesses were overhauled. Some were cast out and hundreds of new businesses acquired. GE's workforce bore the brunt of Welch's quest for competitiveness. Nearly 200,000 GE employees left the company. Over $6 billion was saved.

Having proved that he could tear the company apart, Welch had to move onto stage two: rebuilding a company fit for the 21st century. Central to this was the concept of workout, which was launched in 1989.

Welch had turned Crotonville, GE's management development centre of 30 years, into a laboratory of process and management innovation. During 1998, Jim Baughman, head of Crotonville, reported back to Welch that, after a substantial period of staff cutbacks, employees were dissatisfied with the amount of work they were shouldering. In one conversation, one of the two reputedly said: 'Let's find a way to get work out of the system. And let's call the process "Work-Out".'

In another version the idea came to Welch as he returned by helicopter in September 1998 from an employee feedback session at Crotonville, where employees had complained about a mismatch between the espoused corporate vision and strategy, and what actually happened on the front line.

Or, alternatively, workout was the result of a chance question asked by Professor Kirby Warren of Columbia University. Warren asked Welch: 'Now that you have gotten so many people out of the organization, when are you going to get some of the work out?'

Whichever way it happened though, Welch and GE invented and pioneered the concept.

Spreading the Welch way

'Work-out helped us to create a culture where everyone began playing a part, where everyone's ideas began to count, and where leaders led rather than controlled,' wrote Welch in his book *Jack: Straight from the gut*.

It also helped many other companies. Best practice tends to get borrowed and so it was with workout. Ford was one major corporation that soon adopted the process. 'The ideas are very transferable,' said Carl Bergman, a general manager at Ford, in a 1994 article 'The Welch way', published in *Incentive* magazine. 'This isn't rocket science. It's just a simple way to solve problems, have champions of the solutions at the lower levels and make management accountable. All this drives the action.'

Also, the concept spread as executives leaving General Electric took the idea with them to their new employers. So Larry Bossidy used workout at Allied Signal, the auto parts manufacturer, where steering groups were tasked with ridding the organization of non-value-added work.

Power to the people

Workout was astonishingly successful at GE, and has been elsewhere. It helped GE begin the process of rebuilding the bonds of trust between the company employees and management. It gave employees a channel through which they could talk about what concerned them at work and then to actually change the way things were done.

People feel empowered by workout and able to voice their opinions and ideas; it is a communication tool that offers employees a dramatic opportunity to change their working lives. In *Get better or get beaten! 29 leadership secrets from GE's Jack Welch*, the author, Robert Slater, tells how, in one workout session, a secretary asked her manager why she had to stop what she was doing to empty his outbox. Instead, why not just drop the papers on her desk whenever he left the office? The manager could not think of a reason, and so changed his behaviour – easy for the boss, less work for the secretary, and it was all agreed in a cordial exchange of views.

Communities of practice

During the 1980s there was an emerging realization in the world of business that human knowledge was becoming vital to competitiveness. Financial capital had become plentiful, but *intellectual capital*, as it became known, was both scarce and valuable.

The trouble was that most companies were not actually very good at managing intellectual capital. While policies for managing the workforce had become more enlightened over the years and had sought to make the office or factory a more engaging and attractive place to be, there were few consistent attempts made to get the most out of the collective knowledge and skill base of employees. Companies lacked systems for sharing knowledge among employees, or for capturing the ideas of their experts.

Xerox, the famous inventor of copier machines, was acutely aware of this problem. Its Palo Alto Research Center had invented many of the staples of modern computing, from the mouse to the graphical user interface to the Ethernet. But it had failed to capitalize on any of them and by the mid-1980s was struggling as the sole remaining western player in a photocopier industry dominated by heavyweight Japanese competitors.

Practise it

The solution, or at least an important element of the solution, was under Xerox's nose all along. Communities of practice, as they became known, were informal groups of individuals who shared learning with one another on an informal basis around a particular area of technical expertise. Communities of practice were, in essence, the antidote to traditional structures because they operated on an informal and spontaneous basis, and they allowed knowledge to be spread among the individuals who most needed it. But they were also extremely difficult to pin down, or to manage in a structured way.

The copier repairmen

Unlike almost all the other examples in this book, communities of practice were *discovered* rather than *invented*. Indeed, one could argue that they have been around since the existence of large organizations, but it was only in the late 1980s they were formally named.

The term community of practice was coined by Jean Lave and Etienne Wenger, researchers at the Xerox-affiliated Institute for Research on Learning, in their 1991 book, *Situated learning*. While their study drew from a variety of examples including butchers' apprentices and midwives, the most vivid evidence came from Xerox itself, and more specifically from the doctoral thesis of a colleague called Julian Orr.

Orr spent a year observing the work habits of Xerox's copier technicians. He wanted to know how they learnt their trade, and how they picked up the skills of the job. While the copier technicians had a detailed manual to tell them how to repair different machines, they didn't actually use the manuals. Rather, when faced with a tricky problem, they sought out their buddies and went for a coffee. Orr discovered that across the Xerox organization there was a vast informal network of copier technicians with its own implicit hierarchy of experts, masters and apprentices. These people formed an informal community built around a specific practice area, in this case copier repairing (hence 'community of practice' though Orr did not actually use the term himself). And the group had several other important characteristics as well – it worked only on an informal basis, with its members resisting any attempts to create official task groups; and it shared knowledge through word of mouth, never through the written word.

Spreading the concept

Lave and Wenger's ideas quickly attracted interest, as companies saw the potential to nurture and develop their informal communities of practice. One such company was Chrysler, which like many other car manufacturers in the 1980s employed a linear production system, with work moving through design, engineering, procurement, and the rest of the production process in a sequential way.

The separation of functions proved costly, so in the early 1990s Chrysler changed its production process, switching to a platform-based model where all those involved in the development of a particular model would be brought together in cross-functional teams. After a while, however, there were signs that lack of communication between the platforms across functional disciplines was causing problems. To ensure knowledge was being shared among the engineers in the various platform groups, informal communities of engineers were formed, sharing best practice. The company then formalized these, creating what were termed tech clubs. Members of the tech clubs contribute to and maintain an *Engineering book of knowledge*, a database containing the knowledge accumulated by the clubs.

The combination of platforms and tech clubs allowed Chrysler to cut R&D costs and car development times by over half. And other companies had similar positive outcomes. At Hewlett-Packard, for example, a community of practice focusing on a particular piece of software standardized the software's sales and installation processes, and also created the pricing for the sales team.

By the mid-1990s several consultancies had sprung up with community of practice offerings, a sure sign that a management innovation has hit the big time. And Etienne Wenger and his colleagues published a *Harvard Business Review* article in 2000 proclaiming communities of practice as 'the next organizational frontier'.

Sense of community

Communities of practice are still very much in evidence in today's organizations. Most consultancies, for example, where there is an emphasis on intellectual capital, have put in place dozens of these communities based around key knowledge areas, and there are also virtual communities of practice that extend beyond formal organizational boundaries – such as open source software communities.

But all this attention notwithstanding, communities of practice still evade active management. The problem is they are, by definition, informal structures, so any attempts to formalize their existence, or to create incentive systems around them, is likely to end up changing their unique quality. Many companies have essentially corrupted the term community of practice, and now use it to refer to any sort of cross-cutting network structure. But for those companies still trying to create value out of communities of practice as they were originally defined, the lessons are clear: you can encourage people to create them, and you can provide resources to enable them to emerge, but you cannot actually manage them.

5

Customer and partner interfaces

What is the best way to structure relations with customers and other partners? How should activities be distributed across the value chain? The purpose of innovations in customer and partner interfaces is to create the most value in these external relationships.

 ## Introduction

This chapter examines management innovations in two related areas. First, we look at the various approaches firms have used for understanding, organizing around and serving their customers – in other words, the issues that are the primary, traditional concern of marketers and salespeople. Second, we look more broadly at the boundaries of the firm, with a view to identifying the major innovations that have led firms to either grow or shrink their boundaries, or that have led firms to develop novel ways of working with partner companies, such as alliances or consortia relationships.

There are some obvious overlaps between the management innovations discussed in this chapter and those to be found elsewhere in the book: firm boundary decisions are closely linked to strategy and also to supply chain management; recent technology-led innovations in marketing, such as customer relationship management (CRM) are intertwined with information-processing innovations such as ERP; and the section on internal structure is in many ways a reflection of the external boundary choices that are made.

Customer relationships

There are certain timeless elements to the ways in which firms relate to their customers. It seems likely that the practice of haggling over price, or the ability to assure potential customers of the quality of the product, mattered as much to ancient Greek merchants as they do to modern firms. But, of course, the approaches firms take to do such things have evolved considerably over the years – driven both by profound new insights into customer needs and behaviours, and by changes in technology. As a result, there has been enormous progress in techniques for customer management over the last century, even if those changes tend to be more incremental than radical in nature.

During the period 1880 to 1930, innovations in the management of customer relationships took place along three streams. The first was about *novel ways of gaining access to a diverse body of potential customers*. In 1886, John S. Pemberton put in place the first successful *franchising* operation in the USA, by licensing people to bottle and sell a new drink – subsequently named Coca-Cola (following an earlier attempt at franchising by the Singer Corporation). Franchising proved to be a very successful way of rapidly growing consumer businesses, and especially restaurant businesses.

A subsequent innovation in the same stream was the creation of multilevel marketing by Amway, the American Way, in 1963 – a model that incentivized independent 'associates' to distribute products to their friends and families in return for a cut of the revenues. While this approach to selling has been challenged because of its similarity to illegal 'pyramid' schemes, it has proven to be a highly effective model for certain categories of product (e.g. cosmetics) and for certain developing countries that lack a strong retail infrastructure.

Another novel way of gaining access to a diverse body of potential customers was *direct marketing*. This term was coined by marketing guru Lester Wunderman in 1961 to refer to the targeted approaches firms use to access their customers at home or through customer magazines, as opposed to traditional mass media advertizing. But the origins of direct marketing, of course, go much further back in time. Retailer Montgomery Ward launched the first mail-order catalogue in 1872, subsequently leading to the establishment of the Direct Mail Advertizing Association in 1917. Mass mailing, direct to individual homes, was the precursor to direct marketing, and led to a host of innovations that most consumers curse rather than applaud – from the coupons and vouchers that are appended to direct mail adverts through to 'no-obligation' book of the month clubs.

Divide and rule

The second stream of marketing innovations involved creative ways of dividing a body of customers into segments, so as to meet their specific needs more effectively. In the 1920s General Motors pioneered *market segmentation* by developing five distinct brands each designed to appeal to slightly different customer needs. If this seems an obvious thing to do, recall that GM's major competitor at the time was Ford, where the product range was restricted initially to the Model T – and a black Model T at that.

A related innovation was *brand management* – the idea that a single individual or team should have responsibility for how a brand is positioned and perceived in the marketplace and that internal brands are allowed to compete with one another. Brand management was introduced by Procter & Gamble in the late 1920s, and subsequently adopted by most other consumer goods firms.

Deeper dives

The third stream of marketing innovations were more technique based than management based, and concerned with *a deeper understanding of customers*. Market research is the generic name for this activity, and while there is no clear starting point for where it first emerged, a key date was the founding of A.C. Nielsen, in 1923, and the widespread application of Arthur Nielsen's powerful tools for linking sales and marketing activities to financial performance.

Progress continued to be made along all these three streams of activity through the inter-war and post-war years. But the advent of business computing in the 1970s led to dramatic changes in both the quantity of information about customers that could be held in one place, and also the way in which that information could be used. More recently, the internet has changed the type of relationship firms can have with their customers. It is now feasible to engage in an interactive relationship with them. And so database marketing from the 1980s gave way to *customer relationship management* (CRM) in the 1990s, as IT-driven ways of targeting individual customers more narrowly and more effectively. By capturing detailed information about individual customers' buying behaviour, it was possible to engage in highly tailored direct marketing campaigns, and to offer loyalty schemes or 'frequent flier' type programmes to increase the long-term value of the relationship with each customer.

Terms such as *interactive marketing*, *one-to-one marketing*, and *permission marketing* have been used to capture this important shift, though it is not yet entirely clear how the actual practices of sales and marketing are changing in response to the opportunities afforded by the internet.

Firm or flexible boundaries?

Firms have always expanded or contracted the range of activities they engage in to suit the times: there have been sole traders since the dawn of civilization, and there were prototypical diversified international firms as far back as Assyrian and Phoenician times, some 4000 years ago. So perhaps more so than any aspects of business, the innovations we observe around diversifying or focusing activities are little more than the latest cycles of change around an enduring tension between the desire for size and power, and the desire for focus and agility. But while there may not be any groundbreaking innovations of the type we have seen elsewhere, there are nonetheless seminal developments that occurred at specific times in history and led to dramatic changes across multiple industries.

It is useful to think of the scope of the firm on two dimensions – the horizontal dimension is concerned with the range and volume of products or services a firm sells, the vertical dimension is concerned with how much of the value chain of activities from raw material to final consumption the firm controls.

Take the horizontal dimension first. Many firms went through a phase around the turn of the 20th century when they sought to control their markets by merging (or at least coordinating their activities) with their competitors. In the USA such entities were called trusts, and in Japan they became known as *zaibatsu*, and became a prominent feature of the industrial landscape. But what was good for firms was not necessarily good for consumers. So in the USA and UK in particular the passing of anti-trust and anti-competition legislation saw the break-up of many of these large dominant entities – the most famous case being the splitting of Standard Oil into a series of regional oil companies. The *zaibatsu* in Japan were restructured in 1946, after the Second World War.

Faced with restrictions on their ability to grow within their industry, many firms pursued growth through diversification – by buying up businesses that had nothing to do with their core areas of capability. In the post-war years conglomerate firms such as ITT and Hanson became dominant players in the industrial system, while in Japan a structure called the *keiretsu* arose from the ashes of the *zaibatsu*.

Spin-off time

By the 1980s, however, the evidence was that most conglomerates were failures. Following a few high-profile cases of corporate 'raiders' breaking up these conglomerates for vast profits, most opted to spin off poorly fitting businesses (such as ICI's spin-off of Zeneca) or to break up entirely into three or more pieces (such as Hanson's dissolution in 1996).

Today the vast majority of firms are focused around one or a small number of related markets. The cycle of growth and diversification has come full circle.

The vertical dimension has, likewise, had its ups and downs. Firms tend to move forward (by buying up distributors) or backward (by buying up suppliers) as a means of increasing control, so the late 19th century was, not surprisingly, a period when many firms had high levels of *vertical integration*. Ford Motor Company owned its own plantations to guarantee its supply of rubber for car tyres, for example, and oil companies, then as today, controlled the entire chain of activities, from exploration through to retail.

But, just as diversification gradually fell out of favour, so did vertical integration. From the late 1970s, firms slimmed down their activities to focus on their core competences. Increasingly, they also began to engage in *outsourcing* – where a specific function or process such as IT, facilities management, or even product manufacturing, is farmed out to a specialist supplier. Some firms have become extremely lean as a result of this trend, a few even becoming virtual firms that coordinate the activities of others rather than actually making or selling anything themselves. Even Japan's *keiretsu*, and the very similar Korean *chaebol*, lack the degree of horizontal and vertical integration displayed previously.

Hybrid fashion

In addition to changes in the size and scope of the firm, a related trend that took off in the post-war years was the pursuit of 'hybrid' forms of coordination, such as alliances and joint ventures between independent firms. For example, one prominent example was the formation in 1968 of VISA, a *consortium*, a multi-firm alliance of some 10,000 banks that all agreed to coordinate their credit card issuing and billing activities. In many ways these hybrid forms fill the gaps that have been created by horizontal and vertical disintegration.

Franchising

One of the key challenges facing any growing business is how to get access to sufficient capital to move rapidly into new markets. Depending on the economic conditions at the time, borrowing money might be prohibitively expensive, and selling equity to outside investors can result in the owners losing control of their business. Expansion into new territories also raises challenges, as such tasks as finding premises, hiring staff, and sourcing suppliers all require a good understanding of local markets.

While these challenges would all be familiar to any current-day entrepreneur, they first arose in a big way during the mid-19th century in the USA, as companies began building regional and national-scale businesses. Companies as diverse as Singer Sewing Company, Coca-Cola and Ford Motor Company all faced their own versions of this problem.

Free, not easy

The solution came to be known as franchising – derived from the French word, *franche*, the feminine version of *franc*, or free. Franchising provides a mechanism for the company (the franchisor) to expand its business into unfamiliar territory by granting the local partner (the franchisee) a licence to the business concept, trademark, and other support services. The franchisee invests his or her capital in building the local franchise, and also pays a periodic fee back to the franchisor for the rights to the business concept.

There are considerable benefits for both parties. In a retail franchise, for example, the franchisee is able to start a new business more quickly than they would otherwise, with a proven business model, and expert support. The franchisor gets geographical spread, greater awareness of the brand, and a regular income stream, while retaining ownership. Plus the workforce is highly incentivized.

Sewing up the franchise

Franchising has a long and complex history. It is impossible to trace it back to one individual business. It is, however, possible to point to a number of companies that have been highly influential in its development.

Early forms of franchising have been around for a very long time. It has origins in Europe and in particular in England, in the brewery industry, for example. There tavern owners had tied agreements with brewers in return for financial assistance, and the tied public house system still exists today in the UK.

The Singer Sewing Company was instrumental in the development of the franchise movement. In 1851 Isaac Singer formed I.M. Singer and Company, to sell his recently patented sewing machine. Following patent infringement suits, Singer together with other manufacturers formed the Singer Sewing Combination, creating a patent pool in 1856, and selling licences to manufacturers for a fee of $15 per machine per year in the USA, and $5 per machine outside the USA.

In 1863 I.M. Singer became the Singer Manufacturing Company, with 22 patents and assets of $550,000. The same year the company launched its first franchise.

Another important milestone step in the development of modern franchising was the creation of the Western Automobile franchise in 1909. Franchising at this point was still little more than an agreement to supply a branded product to someone who already had sufficient industry experience to sell that product. Western Auto provided many of the other services that we associate with modern franchising, including training, merchandising, and marketing support.

It's a deal

Franchising percolated through a range of industries during the late 1800s and early 1900s. The car and soft drink industries adopted franchising fairly early on. Coca-Cola franchised its first bottling operation in 1901; Henry Ford invented the dealer franchise system to sell his Model T Ford in the early 1900s. There were 7000 dealers in the USA by 1912.

A&W Root Beer was franchised in 1924. With food added to the menu by one innovating franchisee in the 1920s, this became an early restaurant franchise. It was soon followed by Howard Dearing Johnson, a cigar salesman, who is widely credited as introducing franchising to the restaurant business in the 1930s, through the Howard Johnson's chain of restaurants in the USA. Famous franchises starting up in the 1930s and 1940s included Kentucky Fried Chicken, in 1930, and Dairy Queen, in 1940.

In the 1950s there was a franchising boom in the USA, fuelled by demand from returning servicemen, plus legislation that tightened up trademark protection. It wasn't long before franchising had taken hold in sectors as diverse as car rental and dry cleaning. McDonald's, Burger King, Holiday Inn and Budget Car Rentals were all franchising success stories of the 1950s and 1960s.

In the decade following 1961 McDonald's franchise units increased by 758 per cent. By 1975 there were some 1200 companies in the franchising industry generating over $176 billion in revenues.

Franchising the world

Franchising is not without its problems. Many retailers have struggled to retain control over quality and service in their far-flung franchise operations; and franchisees are often an additional source of resistance when a company has to make dramatic changes to its product range.

But regardless of these risks, franchising continues to grow. Today, with more people wanting to take control of their own lives, entrepreneurship on the increase across the globe, and a fresh drive for outsourcing (see pp. 136–138), franchising is bigger business than ever.

A PricewaterhouseCoopers survey for the International Franchise Association's Education Foundation, revealed that the US franchising sector generates over $1.5 trillion in economic activity, and employs 18 million people. Another survey for the same organization reported that potential franchisees can choose from over 100 lines of business. In the UK, research by NatWest Bank and the British Franchise Association revealed that the British franchising industry is worth £10.8bn, and growing twice as fast as the UK's economy.

Franchising is now a global phenomenon. As of 2005, for example, China had 2320 franchisor systems operating in the country, with a growth rate for the sector at over 10 per cent. More can be expected.

Direct marketing

Generally speaking, the more links in the value chain, the greater the cost of the finished goods or services to the consumer. So it was in post Civil War America, for example, where farmers were receiving low prices for their goods and yet paying high prices for their farming tools and equipment. Rather than sell goods via a middleman, such as the general store, or the local greengrocers, why would firms not sell directly to the market? Certainly there were enormous benefits offered by wholesalers and retailers in the scale of market they could reach, but these benefits came at a cost, and with a loss of direct information about the wants and needs of the people buying their products.

So, as consumer products companies in the late-19th century began to explore new ways of reaching the mass market, a variety of models emerged. One, as discussed already, was franchising; another was direct selling through agents or through catalogues. A third and complementary approach was the practice that came to be called direct marketing.

Live and direct

Direct marketing techniques are those that deal directly with the consumer, and focus on measurable results that can be tracked. In direct marketing, there is a call to action, that is, the consumer is required to do something – such as to call a freephone number.

Traditional direct marketing methods include telephone sales, direct mail, door-to-door sales, leafleting, cold calling, and junk email. The internet has opened up a new avenue of opportunity for direct marketers and a number of techniques, such as permission marketing.

Direct mail, also known as junk mail – solicited or unsolicited advertising sent through the mail to individuals – is one of the most popular direct marketing methods. It is used as a means of targeting potential customers by making use of mailing lists, which specify a range of criteria, including details such as age, income level, and profession. It is common, for example, in the selling of insurance, assurance, and loans to individuals. Direct mail is not, however, a particularly effective means of advertising; the response rate is generally accepted to be around 2 per cent.

Wunderman

The term direct marketing was coined by US ad man Lester Wunderman. While working at Wunderman, Ricotta & Kline, the firm he set up in New York City in 1958, Wunderman was asked to speak at the Massachusetts Institute of Technology. The event was a gathering of professors of marketing from MIT and other business schools. Before the talk Wunderman decided that he needed to find a name to describe what he did, a term that this specific audience could relate to. Until then the term direct mail was used to describe the process of pitching straight to the consumer, but Wunderman decided on a new term – direct marketing. He introduced the phrase to the group during his presentation, the press picked up on it, and, shortly after, it was entered into the congressional record when a senator of Indiana used it.

In hindsight, however, Wunderman regrets his choice of phrase. It is, he says in a video blog on his firm's website, 'not wholly accurate'. Were he to be making that speech over, he would have used 'personal advertising' instead, and not direct marketing.

It is worth mentioning that, as Wunderman pointed out, while he invented the term direct marketing, there was an industry already there waiting for a definition. The practices involved in direct marketing, such as direct mail, for example, date back well before Wunderman's involvement in the industry.

The modern concept of direct mail, for example, was conceived in part by Aaron Montgomery Ward in the USA in 1872, which produced a single sheet of paper to sell its dry-goods items direct to customers. Prior to this there are many records of mail-order catalogues or adverts dating back to the 1700s, both in Europe and the USA.

Mailing the world

In the UK direct marketing started in earnest with the mail-order catalogue of Great Universal Stores, founded in Manchester in 1900. Later in the 1950s and 1960s the Reader's Digest Company created a computerized consumer database, while Trenear-Harvey Bird & Watson became the UK's largest direct marketing agency in the 1980s.

Back in the USA, Wunderman's agency was bought by ad agency Young & Rubicam in the 1970s and, by the 1980s, had been renamed Wunderman Worldwide. Wunderman continued to be highly innovative in the direct marketing field.

One celebrated innovation of Wunderman's was the gold box response. This particular innovation was a reaction to ad agency McCann Erickson muscling in on the Columbia Record Club account that Wunderman's agency dealt with at the time. Direct marketing is about results, yet direct marketers were still struggling with ways to demonstrate both the effect that advertising in different media had, plus the relationship between their work and the consumer's response.

Wunderman came up with the idea of putting a gold box in a print ad that only made sense to consumers who had seen the TV ad. In a gold box the reader entered the number for an additional record that they got from watching the TV ad, this then gave them a free record. This allowed the agency to measure the boost the TV ad provided to the direct marketing campaign.

There is an e in mail

By 2007 Wunderman's agency was owned by global communications conglomerate WPP, and Wunderman had written his autobiography, *Being direct, making advertising pay*. In the meantime the direct marketing industry had transformed beyond recognition from the industry that Wunderman started out in back in the 1930s. To be sure, our letter boxes continue to be stuffed with direct mail advertising that rarely gets opened, but advances in customer relationship management technology have made it possible to tailor these mailshots to individual consumers. For example, Tesco has used its loyalty card data to create more than two million variations to a single direct mail campaign, through a combination of different promotion offers and lifestage-related information.

The internet, too, has created many new forms of direct marketing. Take permission marketing, a term coined by American marketing innovator Seth Godin, the former president of Yoyodyne Entertainment and ex-VP of direct marketing at Yahoo! The premise of permission marketing is that consumers will willingly give up valuable personal information and grant permission for direct marketers to send them product information so long as they are given sufficient incentive.

The internet also ushered in the era of email and its unwelcome offspring – spam. While back in the world of bricks and mortar, telesales, and junk mail are a less popular face of direct marketing.

Market segmentation

At the beginning of the 20th century Ford achieved standardization and mass production by producing as narrow a product range as possible. The Model T reigned supreme. Ford's massive Highland Park plant was opened in January 1910 and produced 15 million Model Ts between then and 1927. More than 700,000 were built in 1917 alone. It was the industrial triumph of its time.

Meanwhile General Motors was a ragbag of cars and companies, trailing desperately behind Ford's car-making colossus. This changed when Alfred P. Sloan took over GM. Sloan brought organizational nous to the company. He undertook a careful analysis of the company's products and markets, and came up with a simple but effective new organizational model. From an internal perspective the new model involved the creation of five largely autonomous divisions – this became known as the divisional structure (discussed in Chapter 4). And from the perspective of the customer, the new model allowed clear differentiation according to customer needs. This was the birth of what we now call market segmentation.

Every purse

Market segmentation involves developing a distinct set of products and services to match the needs of each customer segment. Before Sloan's arrival at GM, the various models of car had competed for the same market, but he realized that there were important benefits to be gained by differentiating GM's offerings.

Sloan's thinking was neatly encapsulated in the slogan: 'A car for every person and purpose.' This implied that GM would provide different cars for all possible price positions, ranging from the low end to the high end of the market. In essence, market segmentation involves splitting one larger hetero-geneous market, where demand preferences from different customer segments are different, into a number of smaller and relatively homogeneous markets, each of which is tackled by a separate product offering. Market segmentation helps a company close the gap between actual customer demand and its own offerings because these offerings become more precise. With market segmentation, any marketing efforts should become much more effective.

The first segments

The process of turning market segmentation from a bright idea to a management innovation began in 1920. Since GM had much catching up to do with Ford and people saw the need for these changes, 'there was little open opposition to the initial proposals for change'. GM chairman, Pierre du Pont, accepted Sloan's proposals with only minor adjustments. Two divisions, Buick and Cadillac, were performing reasonably well and had clear positions in the market. But the other three divisions, Chevrolet, Oldsmobile, and Oakland, were very much a work in progress. As Sloan reorganized these divisions, he ensured that GM as a whole would cover all price ranges and customer segments by putting restrictions on the price ranges for each of the divisions.

This was a lengthy process and it was not until 1925 that GM had positioned Cadillac as the leader among expensive cars, followed by Buick, Oldsmobile, and Oakland (now Pontiac). At the bottom end of the market it positioned Chevrolet, which was starting to attack market leader Ford. Around that time GM started referring to its segmentation system as the 'price pyramid', since it sold small numbers at high prices at the top end (Cadillac) and large numbers at the bottom end at low prices (Chevrolet). GM also began to engage in market research by developing data on the 'market and its potential in terms of population, income, past performance, business cycle, and the like'.

Juicing the orange

The segmentation approach provided a number of clear advantages. Customers could stay with GM throughout their lives, because as their income rose (or fell) they would simply move to a different segment and GM brand. GM diversified its risks since at the peaks of the economic cycle its top brands would do well, while demand for low-cost offerings would rise in recessionary times. This clearly manifested itself as the euphoria of the late 1920s turned into the Great Depression of the early 1930s. Ford meanwhile, with its exclusive focus on low prices, had started to struggle. By 1924 its profit margin per car had fallen to $2. It also suffered from the substantial second-hand market for its own Model T, which meant that fewer new cars were sold. These used cars were often actually perceived as superior, because they included add-ons like shock absorbers and gear shifts, which were increasingly becoming the standard.

After 1924 sales of the Model T continued to drop, even when Ford lowered its prices in response. In 1927 it finally decided to start working on a new model but by then the damage had been done. GM was more profitable than Ford every year between 1925 and 1986.

The car in front

Most tellingly, when Ford started to rethink its product portfolio in 1927, it also began to apply the principle of market segmentation. Neither GM nor Ford has ever doubted the effectiveness of market segmentation since. Prior to GM's introduction of market segmentation, there had long been a latent feeling in many companies and industries that different parts of the market had different demands but this had not previously been tackled so strikingly inside a single firm, although there had been all kinds of forerunners like the introduction of first, second, and third class on trains.

From the 1920s onwards most organizations started to operate some form of segmentation system. Although segmentation comes at a cost, since separate product offerings need to be developed for each segment which requires more marketers, more advertising and larger investments of all kinds of resources, many companies found that this cost was outweighed by the benefits. When firms also became better at managing multiple brands simultaneously through brand management (see pp. 128–130), this increased the effectiveness of segmentation further.

Today's segments

Academic thinking on market segmentation did not take shape until 1956, when Wendell Smith formulated the term and developed the concept. But since then market segmentation has become something of a science. Consumer-facing companies now undertake huge amounts of market research to determine which market segments they can tackle and how they should tackle them. Market segmentation is a necessary ingredient in any marketing effort. Market segments have also become ever smaller and better defined. As database techniques have been developed further, many companies are moving towards 'segments of one', using one-to-one marketing and customer relationship management techniques. Even organizations that were traditionally ignorant of their customers, like government departments and universities, have taken up segmentation. As a consumer you are willingly and unwillingly part of a market segment for each of the firms you buy from.

Brand management

In consumer marketing, brands became increasingly important in the 19th and early 20th centuries. Initially this was not a problem, as firms usually had a single brand for a single product. However, with the rise of market segmentation and merger and acquisition activity, Procter & Gamble (P&G), like other firms, found itself with multiple brands competing in a single product category. This raised the possibility that these brands could cannibalize one another, by cutting into each other's market share.

P&G created a market research department (initially called an economic research department) in 1923. The department used techniques like door-to-door research. This helped greatly in collecting and analyzing relevant data about different market segments. The need for segmentation increased further thanks to economic circumstances. The Great Depression forced P&G to think about a cheaper soap because of rapid growth in that market segment.

In the late 1920s P&G introduced a new brand of soap, Camay, next to the existing Ivory brand. Instead of substituting the old Ivory brand by Camay, received wisdom at the time, P&G decided to allow competition between the two. Unfortunately Camay's introduction proved less successful than hoped for. The fault was seen to lie with 'too much Ivory thinking', as the fear that Camay would cannibalize Ivory's market share implied Camay was not pushed as hard as it should have been. In particular, P&G blamed its advertising company for favouring Ivory over the new brand.

Ads up

The solution to this was brand management, an organizational structure in which brands are assigned to individual managers who are responsible for their performance. P&G used several sources of inspiration to build its brand management system. First, it drew from what is now referred to as functional brand management, an existing system where brand management was outsourced to outsiders like advertising agencies. This system was limited in its impact, because it did not reach into the firm's other functions. Second, the key inventor of brand management, Neil McElroy, drew on his experiences in England, where he had launched the Oxydol brand. He had observed how Unilever, P&G's main European competitor, had its brands compete with one another, albeit in a crude and ineffective manner.

McElroy, who had joined P&G as an advertising department mail clerk after graduating from Harvard Business School, managed the advertising for

Camay in the USA. Based on his experiences, McElroy developed the belief that every brand should have it own managers who could more effectively advertise and market that brand. These brand managers would be committed to the success of their individual brands, not all the different brands in a product category. A brand group could develop deep knowledge about its own product and market segment, which would be impossible for non-specialists. This way P&G could benefit from local autonomy and creativity. At the same time discipline and coordination between the different brand groups could be achieved at corporate level.

Cringe worthy

P&G started working on its brand management system in the late 1920s and formally introduced it in 1931. But McElroy faced some obstacles in the process, since as he later explained 'some of the more conservative members of the company cringed at the idea of having a punch taken at ourselves by ourselves'. P&G insiders feared the prospect of internal brand wars. McElroy first discussed his ideas with VP Ralph Rogan. Rogan was positive but suggested McElroy would need support from the very top of the firm. McElroy then took his ideas to P&G President Dupree, breaking the longstanding P&G convention that memos ought to be shorter than one page. His three-page memo convinced Dupree that it would be sensible to have specific teams in place for each individual brand.

The brand management system implied substantial changes. Brands like Ivory, Camay, Crisco, Suz, and Oxydol were the responsibility of separate groups. Each had its own funding, advertising staff and internal cohesion. Gradually, the brand management system changed the entire mindset of P&G. Because brands now ruled the day, less focus was paid to different geographical units. Brand managers became responsible not just for the marketing of their brands but also for activities like new product development and sales.

Brand management really made its name a few years later with the introduction of the washing detergent Tide. When P&G introduced Tide it rapidly overtook large and profitable existing brands. P&G pushed ahead, sticking to the philosophy that consumers should eventually determine what is best for themselves. Hence Tide completely overwhelmed its competitors in the market for washing detergents and P&G received confirmation that its brand management helped to generate well-managed, strong and lasting brands.

Boarding the brandwagon

On the back of its brand management system, P&G was able to gain a dominant position in the fast moving consumer goods industry, through the successful introduction of brands like Pampers, Ivory, and Crest.

Of course, what worked for P&G was equally applicable to other consumer goods companies, though it took competitors like Lever Brothers many years before they introduced a similar structure. Brand management became the de facto standard for how to run a consumer marketing function. This created an entirely new job title, that of brand manager, and led to the rise of marketing as a separate management area, with consumer marketing at its core. Consumer goods companies increasingly started to hire new graduates, like MBAs, to fill the position of assistant brand manager or even brand manager.

Brand power

The brand management system has been hugely successful, implemented by more or less every fast moving consumer goods company in the world as well as in other consumer-facing industries like automobiles and banks. Along the way brand management was inevitably refined. At P&G brand management produced some undesirable side-effects. Because the brands were separated and barriers placed between them, knowledge sharing between brands became very limited. Brand managers were simply not eager to share information with their major competitors. Furthermore it was not always easy for P&G to apply company-wide competences and capabilities in the various brand groups.

Other criticisms have focused on brand managers themselves. Because they are generally not very experienced, led by the numbers, and highly competitive, they can be too eager to destroy the firm's other brands. Some have gone as far as accusing them of being 'murderers of brand assets'. Smart consumer goods companies understand these limitations and have started to bring in enhancements – including employing company-wide knowledge management systems and more focus on qualitative techniques to complement the numbers. Brand management will continue to lead the way in the consumer goods industry.

Customer relationship management

The rise of market segmentation (see pp. 125–127) was a major advance in the provision of products that specific groups of customers actually wanted. Over time companies became ever more proficient in defining, measuring and servicing these segments. But, by the 1990s, it was increasingly clear that existing market segmentation approaches were falling short on two counts.

First, a segment is still a group of customers and even within that group there will be differences between individual customers. But segmentation typically aggregates the needs of individual customers, in the process making it harder for companies to service individuals.

Second, customer loyalty levels were ever decreasing. Companies were starting to realize that retaining existing customers might, in fact, be much less costly and hence more profitable than attracting new customers. So companies like Capital One, an up-and-coming credit card provider, saw an opportunity to become better at creating value for customers and generating profit for themselves.

It's all about relationships

Customer relationship management (CRM), a specific form of relationship marketing, is a way of identifying, obtaining, and retaining customers. CRM stresses maintaining and improving the relationship between the seller and the customer through the use of detailed data. Some proponents of CRM suggest it requires a strict focus on individual customers while others believe it is sufficient to define small and precise market segments and target those.

CRM relies to a substantial extent on information systems, like customer databases and internet-based applications for communication with customers. The use of information systems for automating and improving sales, marketing and customer support is often referred to as operational CRM, in contrast to analytical CRM which involves collecting data to learn from customer relations and improve business decisions. An important aspect of analytical CRM is to identify which customers are most profitable for the company and redirect efforts to relations with those customers. CRM may even lead to the termination of loss-making relations with other customers on the seller's initiative when these relations cannot be made profitable.

Other aspects of CRM include a more intimate and sustained relationship and the use of network relations, like using core existing clients to impress potential new clients. One-to-one marketing is a related term to CRM and was first introduced by former advertising executive Don Peppers and business school professor Martha Rogers. They suggested one-to-one marketing entails 'being willing and able to change your behaviour toward an individual customer based on what the customer tells you and what else you know about that customer'. Using one-to-one marketing and CRM ought to lead to improvements in both cost and sales levels because fewer customer replace-ments are needed and existing customers can be served better.

CRM's warm embrace

An early exemplar of CRM was Capital One. It was just a startup company in the early 1990s when it undertook a series of initiatives to provide a more fine-grained and tailored set of offerings to credit card customers. Capital One implemented test cell analysis, a technique whereby different direct mailings are sent out to customers in hundreds of test cells. These cells were composed based on how customers behaved and how much profit they generated for Capital One. Capital One then observed how each of the cells responded to the mailings. With that information, it developed specific offerings for the most attractive segments, and designed marketing campaigns around these offerings.

Between 1992 and 1994 credit card receivables at Capital One increased from $1.7 billion to $9 billion. Part of its CRM system was intelligent call routing, which used computers to identify which customer was making a phone call. Based on that customer's information, the grounds for the phone call would be predicted and the customer was redirected to a customer representative with specific information and recommendations for further products. This lowered the costs of communicating and increased customer satisfaction.

The direct route

Capital One was not alone. As CRM started to spread rapidly in the 1990s, others to take it up successfully included the insurance company Direct Line and the Ford Motor Company, which integrated all internal and external customer data in a single application so it could use actual customer behaviour to target its marketing. The market for software CRM solutions also grew rapidly during the 1990s. Early and important vendors included Siebel, Clarify, Oracle, and Onyx. This software initially focused primarily on automating and standardizing marketing tasks. But later it became better at more analytical tasks. In 1998 Oracle introduced what was seen as the first full CRM suite. The rise of the internet allowed for an additional communication channel with customers and CRM systems increasingly incorporate features to use the internet.

Many companies, especially those operating in business-to-consumer markets, have now implemented some element of CRM. This has raised some issues about the effectiveness of CRM. A number of reports suggest low satisfaction with CRM programmes and particularly with the software. Not unusually in the field of management innovation, implementation of CRM turns out to be harder than expected. It requires an entirely different approach to dealing with customers, based on the customer's needs, not the company's products. Information on customers is sometimes hard to acquire or bring together. And in many companies the software drove the CRM strategy rather than being part of that strategy.

Personal segments

Despite these setbacks, CRM is still actively pursued by many managers. In fact, these lessons from the past are now being used to make CRM more effective. CRM practitioners focus on four areas: salesforce automation; customer service and support; field service; and marketing automation. The ability to segment customers, as in Capital One's cell analysis, is still crucial. Another tool that has been added is customer lifetime value analysis, which helps determine the profitability of customers. Nobody doubts the key underlying ideas of CRM, that retaining existing customers is cheaper than acquiring new customers and that a marketing approach targeted to specific customers is better than a more generic approach.

Vertical integration

It was only in the 19th century that the large companies, so common in today's business world, started to emerge. Previously, many companies were crafts based, focusing on small parts of the value chain, and often highly specialized. Such businesses were very limited in their growth opportunities, because recruitment of more specialists was hard, mass production could often not be achieved, and the stages of the value chain took place in different locations. As a consequence, there was not much benefit in integrating activities.

Then came important innovations in production processes like scientific management (pp. 12–17) and the moving assembly line (pp. 17–20), in cost accounting (pp. 48–50) and professional management (pp. 75–77). These allowed for production on a much larger scale. But how could such scale advantages best be exploited? And who should be exploiting them? In pursuit of growth and profit, Andrew Carnegie of Carnegie Steel saw himself faced with this question in the late 19th century.

Up and down

Vertical integration is where a company controls multiple elements of the sourcing, production, and distribution process. This may mean controlling the entire process from raw materials extraction to distribution and sale of the final product, or just some part of it. So in theory a single company could extract or produce raw materials, refine these materials, manufacture intermediate products and finished goods, then transport these goods to wholesalers or retail outlets and through these outlets sell the goods to the consumer.

There are two types of vertical integration. *Backward vertical integration* refers to ownership and control of the inputs into the production process, like a chocolate manufacturer owning the cocoa-growing plantation. Alternatively, *forward vertical integration* involves owning and controlling the distribution and retail elements of the value chain. Vertical integration can be contrasted with horizontal integration where a firm expands at the same level of the value chain, often through mergers and acquisitions.

There are a number of explanations for vertical integration. One suggests that it is the natural model for new enterprises, and it is only as they begin to differentiate the stages of production that the value chain begins to fragment. Another suggested mechanism is that innovators find it very difficult for other companies to accept the feasibility of their innovation, so they find themselves having to take control of the value chain. The third and most prominent explanation is that vertical integration offers scale advantages and allows companies to be monopolists or pretend to be monopolists. Because they own all stages of the value chain, there is no competition until the final stage, sales to the consumer.

Tall stories

If there is any example of a company to be held up as the pioneer of vertical integration it must be one of the first and most famous examples – Andrew Carnegie's steel company Carnegie Steel. Whereas others invested in certain elements of the steel production value chain, Carnegie had a more expansive strategy.

The richest man in the world at the turn of the century – in 1901 to be precise – Carnegie accumulated his millions between the 1870s and the end of the 1800s by dominating the steel value chain, buying up a host of companies including coalmines, coke ovens, steel mills, iron ore barges, and railways. No wonder he was able to sell his steel empire to J.P. Morgan at the turn of the century for a staggering $480 million, pocketing a massive $225 million in the process. Carnegie later became a major benefactor and the namesake of such places as New York's Carnegie Hall and Carnegie Mellon University in Pittsburgh.

Crossing Ford

The vertical integration model rapidly found traction elsewhere. As the world rushed headlong into the 20th century, the car manufacturers, such as Olds and Ford, were little more than small startups. These companies were vertically integrated to the extent that they made their own tool parts, finished products and then were involved in the sales and distribution of those products. But this vertical integration was more a product of circumstance than intentional corporate strategy.

In the case of Ford, however, as the development of mass production and the assembly line got underway, it became clear that Ford required specialized tools and machinery. Naturally enough, Ford decided, given the specialist nature of the equipment, that it would be easier for the company to make the tools itself.

So, for example, initially Ford struck an agreement with the John R. Keim Mills, a producer of pressed steel, which by 1908 was supplying various parts for Ford's vehicles. Ford cooperated closely with the mill, eventually purchasing it in 1911. Then, following a strike at the Keim Mills, he removed all the machinery to Ford's Highland Park plant. Effectively, Ford vertically integrated many activities in one place, Highland Park. Ford's main competitor, General Motors, would take vertical integration even further in the period up to the Second World War.

An example of another sector that took up an extremely high level of vertical integration is the oil industry, where large vertically integrated companies like Exxon, Shell, and BP, explore and then drill for crude oil, refine that oil and then even own many of the pumps through which they retail their products. Governments also tend to be very vertically integrated.

Vertical integration remained a key strategy all the way to the 1970s, especially forward integration with companies moving into the distribution and sales of their products. Since then momentum has decisively turned against vertical integration as companies discovered the flexibility and efficiency of markets. Focus on core activities, in the 1980s, and then outsourcing, in the 1990s, replaced the belief that large scale, vertically integrated, operations are the only route to success.

Out of favour

Today the world has changed in a way that no longer favours vertical integration. In the personal computing revolution, for example, most firms that tried to control the entire value chain from component manufacturing through product design to retail, failed to capture significant market share.

Yet a few tech firms managed to bunk a trend of value chain fragmentation. Apple computers, for example, is one of a few successful tech companies designing its own products, controlling marketing, even selling through Apple stores. Samsung is another firm that is relatively vertically integrated yet highly profitable. Most other firms opted to outsource wherever possible to build flexibility and low cost into the value chain.

One strong argument for vertical integration used to be that it allowed a company to innovate more effectively. However, the tech industry has shown that it is perfectly possible to outsource innovation, whether it is to a product design company, a plasma screen manufacturer, an advertising agency or an electrical goods retailer. With no obvious benefits and several disadvantages the days of high levels of vertical integration are over, unless you have a monopoly of one segment of the value chain, such as access to raw materials or distribution to the market.

Outsourcing

For most of the 20th century, 'bigger is better' had been the guiding principle of businesses. They had diversified, sometimes into unrelated industries, in an effort to increase sales. They had vertically integrated (see pp. 133–136) many functions in the belief that increased bargaining power and more control would deliver larger profits. And they measured their strength through what they could do, not what others could do for them.

Yet by the 1970s and particularly into the 1980s this model of running a company gradually started to look outdated. Unrelated diversification proved not to be as beneficial as thought, and many conglomerates such as ITT and the Hanson Trust would be unwound. And vertically integrated companies often became highly inflexible, as IBM discovered to its cost when faced with a range of focused competitors such as Intel and Microsoft.

In the 1970s, the computer revolution had started, and this changed the way companies operated internally. Companies were now forced to set up information technology (IT) functions. But the revolution had an even bigger impact on how companies could relate to each other because IT allowed many processes to become standardized, and a range of specialist IT companies started to emerge. So when Kodak had to decide how to run its IT function in 1989, what would be the best decision?

Outsiders

Outsourcing can be defined in many ways. Some argue that outsourcing refers to any activities that are undertaken by outside suppliers. Others prefer narrower or more specific definitions, such as the purchasing of ongoing services from an outside company that a company currently provides for itself.

All these definitions imply that some outside supplier is doing work for the company. So outsourcing allows a company to tap into its supplier's production capacity, which can potentially produce lower costs, higher quality, more specific knowledge, and more innovation.

IT needs help

Like vertical integration, outsourcing has been around for as long as organizations exist. Companies have always needed to rely on the marketplace for some of their inputs. And there have always been suppliers willing to provide these inputs. Even in IT outsourcing, a much more recent phenomenon, a key provider such as EDS has been around since 1962. But in the 1980s the pace of outsourcing definitely picked up, and one outsourcing decision stood out from the pack.

Kate Hudson was the vice-president for Corporate Information Systems at Eastman Kodak when the unit was created in 1988. When Hudson looked at studies on IT at Kodak, they all screamed one clear message: 'All studies said we needed help.' Kodak had been thinking about which of its businesses were core businesses and Hudson applied a similar logic to IT.

By systematically analyzing which IT functions were core, she came to the conclusion that data centres were not core for Kodak. And it turned out that external vendors could deliver the same service at a much lower cost, because they could achieve greater economies of scale. So in 1989 an IT outsourcing deal was announced between Kodak and IBM. When IBM announced the deal, it said it was unusual. IBM would take on the work of four Kodak data centres and employ 300 Kodak employees. According to IBM Kodak's aim was to cut costs by up to 50 per cent, though eventually the number was more like 15 per cent. Kodak also outsourced other parts of its IT to Digital and Business Land.

Around the world

A deal of this magnitude, especially in terms of the numbers of people and other assets being transferred to an outside organization, had not been seen before. It had a serious impact on how companies around the world viewed

IT outsourcing. Many organizations, from BP to the US government, followed in Kodak's footsteps and decided to outsource significant parts of their IT in the early 1990s, and in some cases all of it. IT increasingly came to be seen as a commodity, rather than a mechanism for competitive advantage.

Outsourcing also spread to other business arenas. There was already significant outsourcing of manufacturing prior to the Kodak deal, but this became even more prevalent, partly fuelled by the lean manufacturing model of Toyota (see pp. 20–25) and by the way Toyota employed its suppliers. Business process outsourcing, when an entire process such as billing is undertaken by a partner company, is a more recent development, and has boasted spectacular growth in recent years. The rise of China and India as more or less unlimited reservoirs of skilled labour has helped to create a global outsourcing industry of very considerable proportions. And it has created new rising stars like Lenovo, Tata, and Wipro. By all projections outsourcing is expected to grow more over the coming years.

Transformers

Outsourcing fits current thinking on company strategy. It helps companies concentrate on their core competences and activities. When companies announce a new outsourcing deal, they almost always explain it is done to increase focus on the core business. Outsourcing also fits well with strategic alliances (see pp. 138–141, on consortia and alliances). Some outsourcing relations can be seen as strategic alliances and learning partnerships. Indeed there is much talk of moving outsourcing away from costs to strategic or transformational outsourcing.

Against this background, one would be tempted to conclude that outsourcing is always a winning strategy. That is not necessarily true. Prior to the vertical integration movement of the 20th century, outsourcing levels were much higher but then declined. Perhaps in 10 or 20 years from now companies will once again start to question the wisdom of outsourcing. Too much outsourcing, after all, is not such a great thing, as it hollows companies out and leaves them with an insufficient base to compete in the marketplace.

Consortia and alliances

In the 1970s the hierarchical divisional organization was the established standard for most companies. But some cracks were starting to appear in this model. On the one hand, hierarchy reduced a firm's flexibility in handling the multiple and competing needs of its customers; and, on the other hand, some projects were so large that even one company could not handle them alone. This was particularly a concern in cases where a technological or administrative standard had to be set on an industry-wide basis. Going it alone in such cases was often not the right solution as other companies might not be willing to take on the proposed standard.

The advent of the computer also began to create a change of mindset. Early work was taking place on computer networks, and scenario planning envisaged a more networked world in the future, where organizations would be cooperating more, even when they competed in other respects. How then could managers of banks, for example, who needed to set up coordinated payment systems, find ways to combine concepts such as decentralization and cooperation?

Extra medium

One solution was a radical rethinking of the concept of the corporation and its boundaries. Consortia and alliances are means for firms to work together to achieve some joint goal. They can be defined as a partnership of two or more organizations that organize or acquire control of a separate organization. Consortia and alliances depart from the principles of the hierarchical organization in important ways. They acknowledge that not all knowledge and resources reside in one company. They create some sort of new medium to facilitate the cooperation between partners. And this new medium draws on the knowledge and resources of the partners.

Dee Hock, founder and CEO of VISA, came up with a more specific term – *chaordic alliances*. The word 'chaord' is derived from the first syllables of the words 'chaos' and 'order'. Hock uses the term to describe any system of organization that exhibits characteristics of both chaos and order, dominated by neither. In his book *Birth of the chaordic age,* Dee defines chaordic:

1. The behaviour of any self-governing organism, organization, or system that harmoniously blends characteristics of order and chaos. 2. Patterned in a way dominated by neither chaos nor order. 3. Characteristic of the fundamental organizing principles of evolution and nature.

VISA waver

In 1968, Dee Hock secured his place in the history of the financial services industry when he created a new global system for the electronic exchange of value, which would become VISA. To facilitate this innovation in the world of finance he also created a highly innovative new organizational form, the consortium: a profit-making, decentralized, membership organization owned by financial institutions across the globe.

Hock described the formation of this radical new enterprise in a 1998 speech, that encapsulated the essence of his innovation:

In the beginning, no one thought such an organization could be brought into being. But, in June, 1970, we proved ourselves wrong and the VISA Chaord came into being: a non-stock, for profit, organization with ownership in the form of irrevocable, non-transferable, rights of participation. It transcends language, currency, politics, economics and culture to successfully connect a bewildering variety of more than 20,000 financial institutions, 20 million merchants and a billion people in 220 countries and territories. Annual volume approaches $1.8 trillion, continuing to grow in excess of twenty-percent compounded annually with no end in sight.

As the organization skyrocketed past $100 billion of volume, it was coordinated by less than 500 people, none were recruited from business schools, none could own shares or acquire wealth for their services. Yet those people, without consultants, selected the VISA name and completed the largest trademark conversion in commercial history in a third of the time anticipated. They created the prototype of the present communications systems in ninety days for less than $30,000. Those systems now clear more electronic transactions in a week than the entire US Federal Reserve System does in a year.

I tell you these few things to make a single point that we have somehow lost sight of in our present organizations: The truth is, that given the right chaordic organizations, from no more than dreams, determination and the liberty to try, quite ordinary people consistently do extraordinary things.

Chaords everywhere

Consortia and alliances started to spread in a wide range of industries, first slowly but from the 1980s in an increasing pace. They suited the mood of the times. Consortia and alliances were a way to exploit the core competences of various partners, as each partner can bring its own specialized ability to the table. As companies increasingly focused their activities around their core competences, consortia and alliances were an ideal vehicle for sourcing others' competences. And they also facilitated the creation of industry-wide technology standards.

Consortia and alliances were also particularly appropriate in an era of fast-changing industry dynamics. For a large company, alliances with small firms (rather than acquisitions) can help to preserve the entrepreneurial spirit of the smaller partners. And as industry boundaries blur, companies start to compete and cooperate with other companies outside their own industry. In such cases alliances are a vastly superior solution to mergers and acquisitions. Finally, alliances have proven to be very useful when entering new countries like China. Working with a local partner, many western companies have more effectively negotiated the local environment.

As far as Hock is concerned, in 1984 he left VISA to pursue his interests in both the evolution of organizations and the development of new management practices. As well as VISA's becoming a business, simultaneously, Hock's vision has become a lifetime's passion. One of his accomplishments after leaving the company was the creation of the Chaordic Alliance, a global institution linking people and organizations in order to develop, disseminate and implement new, more effective and equitable concepts of commercial, political and social organization. The Chaordic Alliance has since morphed into the Chaordic Commons, a global network of individuals and organizations, carrying on Hock's original vision: pioneering new ways to organize.

Order and chaords

In a world where innovation is a primary competitive driver, organizations are forced to look outside themselves for sources and triggers of innovation. In an increasingly networked world, organizational forms disperse and become more fragmented, organizational boundaries are blurred, and strategic alliances arise along the lines that Hock originally envisaged. Procter & Gamble's connect and develop initiative (see pp. 154–157) is a good example of this.

Another example is Pfizer, which has engaged in a number of collaborations with other pharmaceutical companies to produce leading products such as Lipitor, a cholesterol reducing drug, which it co-marketed with the Warner Lambert group, and a blood clot busting drug with Eisai, a Japanese pharmaceutical company, to name a few. In fact, Pfizer has its own group set up to focus solely on managing the company's strategic alliances.

And as strategic alliances have become common competitive currency, so has VISA, Hock's original creation, continued to prosper. Today Hock's original chaordic organization has over 20,000 member financial institutions, with 1.55 billion VISA cards in circulation, contributing to $4.6 trillion (US) in global sales.

6

Innovation and strategy

How do companies become more innovative? What is the best way to create superior long-term strategies? The purpose of innovations around innovation and strategy is to improve the ability of the company to be successful in an evolving market.

 ## Introduction

How does a firm chart its long-term direction? And what does it have to do to remain relevant and successful as its markets evolve? These are big questions that have always preoccupied business leaders.

Today we typically make a clear distinction between *strategy,* which refers to the choices firms make about where and how they play in the marketplace, and *innovation,* which refers to the implementation of new products, services, businesses and working practices. But they are two tightly interlinked concepts, because both are concerned with how the firm adapts to its changing business environment. So in this chapter, we consider them together.

As with other aspects of business, it is a fruitless exercise to try to identify the first firm that had an explicit strategy, or the first to take innovation seriously. The concept of strategy dates back at least to the Ancient Greek military, and firms have been innovators for as long as they have existed. It is nonetheless possible to chart the emergence of specific management innovations that either formalized the implicit activities of strategy and innovation, or which helped push these processes in new directions.

Innovation management

Consider first how firms develop new products. The late 19th century saw some significant changes in government policy towards business innovation. The most important was the formalization of intellectual property rights, especially patenting, which provided real incentives for firms to invest in new technologies. In addition, antitrust legislation in the USA led to the break-up of industry-wide cartels, and heightened the importance of innovation as a competitive weapon. Partly as a result of these changes, the first years of the 20th century saw GE, DuPont, Bayer and a number of other large companies investing in *industrial research labs*.

Thomas Edison, the Wizard of Menlo Park, was one of the key figures. Rather than being the lone genius of popular myth, Edison was actually a highly capable manager of others, and his systematic approach to innovation yielded a stream of new products for his parent company, GE. By the 1920s all major firms in such fields as electricity, chemicals, automobiles and telephony had their own research labs. These labs increasingly spanned the entire spectrum of activities from basic research through to product development.

During the first half of the 20th century firms became increasingly accomplished at managing what became known as the 'research and development' (R&D) process, and the additional pressures for rapid technological innovation during wartime further drove their efforts. But just as with any other process, the R&D process started to become bureaucratic and slow.

This problem came to a head in 1943 in the USA, when aircraft manufacturer Lockheed committed to developing a jet engine within 180 days – a far faster time than its internal processes would normally have allowed. Lockheed responded to this challenge with a focused team of engineers who disregarded the formal process – with great success. Known in Lockheed as the *skunk works*, this form of ad hoc research and development group subsequently became commonplace in large firms. Tracy Kidder colourfully described a similar ad hoc group in his award-winning book, *The soul of a new machine*, and both IBM and Apple made use of skunk works teams in the early 1980s in the development of their personal computers.

These two different approaches to innovation – one relying on formal process, the other relying on small focused teams – have continued to coexist over the last 60 years, and both have been gradually improved over the years. On the formal process side, the stagegate model was introduced in the late 1980s as a way of sharpening the decision making around large R&D investments. By dividing the work into a series of 'stages', and by formalizing the criteria at each 'gate', the intention was to better prioritize funding and also more effectively to kill off projects that were not going to make it.

On the informal side, *corporate venturing* took off in the late 1960s as a way of bringing venture capital-style thinking into large companies. Corporate venture units were similar to skunk works in many ways, but they typically also included some outside funding and/or decision making from venture capitalists. Early pioneers here were DuPont and Exxon, and, more recently, such companies as Shell, Unilever, and Intel have also created their own unique models of corporate venturing. Another variant on the informal model is pharmaceutical firm GSK's experimentation with research centres of excellence which are autonomous drug discovery operations that are managed as if they were small biotechnology companies (with incentives to match) while still being part of the large GSK organization.

What are the next trends in innovation? The biggest current transformation underway is towards what is increasingly called *open innovation*. This is the idea that firms can no longer afford to do everything themselves, and that networks of linked firms and individuals can often outperform the formally controlled hierarchy of an IBM or a Siemens. Procter & Gamble is perhaps the best known pioneer here with its '*connect and develop*' model of innovation in which relationships have been built with tens of thousands of scientists around the world; other similar initiatives include Sun's Java Development Community, and Lego's attempts at building its next-generation products by collaborating with its customers. It is not yet clear what this new model will look like, but the success of open source software collaborations such as Linux suggests that firms will end up operating a hybrid that draws from both its traditional models as well as from open source models.

And there is further speculation, at the time of writing, that Google is charting new territory with its own highly innovative approach to management and organization. It is too soon to judge these efforts, and Google will surely have its own problems sooner or later, but the systematization of the management innovation process is an important challenge facing companies today.

Strategic management

The other stream of management innovations concerned with shaping the firm's long-term direction is in the area of strategic management. Some of the relevant innovations here are concerned with dividing the firm up into a series of *strategic business units* each facing its own distinct target market, and choices firms make about diversifying or refocusing their portfolios of businesses through outsourcing or vertical integration. Such innovations are examined elsewhere, when we discuss firm boundaries. The focus here, instead, is on those innovations that changed the ways individual businesses analyzed, conceptualized, and implemented their own strategies.

The foundation here was *management by objectives* (MBO): a system for translating high-level business goals into individual objectives. Developed in the early 1900s, and popularized by Peter Drucker in the 1950s, MBO helped to create alignment between all the different activities of the firm.

But the biggest single innovation in strategy was probably *strategic planning*, a sophisticated process for gathering and analyzing data about a business' competitive situation, and formulating an appropriate set of choices to respond to that situation. Strategic planning emerged in the post-war years, thanks in part to the techniques developed during the war, and it became the dominant way of working in large firms through the 1960s and 1970s. As in many other areas, GE is credited as one of the original pioneers of strategic planning. And it was helped by the introduction of a range of new analytical techniques, such as the BCG 'growth share' matrix, which identified businesses as cash cows, dogs, question marks, or stars.

A complementary innovation that also emerged in the late 1960s was *scenario planning*, which had its origins in the work of Hermann Khan and his colleagues at the RAND institute before being formally implemented by Shell Oil in the lead up to the oil crisis of 1973. Scenario planning was essentially a way of thinking through the implications of hypothetical future events and how the firm would react to them, rather than simply looking at the future as a linear extrapolation of the past. Shell's superior level of preparedness for a tenfold increase in oil prices led many other firms to adopt their own version of scenario planning.

By the early 1980s formal strategic planning was falling out of favour – perhaps because it was seen as being too distant from the markets it was serving, perhaps because it was overly bureaucratic. Throughout the 1980s, and again beginning with GE, firms gradually moved away from the rhetoric of strategic planning and adopted more decentralized and less formal models for analyzing and responding to market trends. The analytical techniques developed in this era – most notably the concepts of industry analysis and competitive advantage developed by Michael Porter – offered greater precision for those involved in strategic thinking, but they were not dramatically different to what had gone before.

What have the innovations in strategy been in the last 20 years? There has been considerable innovation in the nature of strategic *thinking*, with such concepts as industry analysis, core competence, and strategic innovation all having enormous influence, but there have been few, if any, dramatic innovations in the *practice* of strategy – in the actual activities and efforts put in by people responsible for strategy. Strategy workshops have become a popular technique used by firms for taking a group of senior managers offsite to work through their strategic issues, but to some degree this practice has always been in existence. *Benchmarking* arose as a key way of tracking the activities and performance of other companies in the late 1980s, but again its origins go way back. More recently such companies as EDS and Nokia have experimented with democratizing the strategy process by getting up to 500 people in the firm involved in analyzing and evaluating the trends and challenges facing the firm. Perhaps strategy is completing its own full circle by returning to the intuitive roots from which it started but this time using the intuitions of everybody, not just the chosen few.

 # Industrial research labs

In the 1880s and 1890s large companies on both sides of the Atlantic started to emerge in such industries as chemicals, cars, and electrical products. By investing ahead of demand in such areas as manufacturing and distribution, many of these companies went on to achieve unprecedented economies of scale. And, by pursuing mergers and cartel-like relationships, these major companies, such as Standard Oil in the USA and IG Farben in Germany, often came to dominate and control their industries.

But two important areas of legislation changed the rules of competition for these large companies. First, regulatory advances in the field of property rights, beginning with the German Patent Act in 1876, gave inventors of new technologies an exclusive period in which they could profit from their inventions. Second, governments started imposing restrictions on market dominance, and antitrust laws such as the 1890 Sherman Act forced companies to rethink their policies of market control.

These changes led major companies to start taking innovation seriously – as a way of sustaining their positions in their existing markets. Before this, innovation had been driven by lone geniuses, such as Alfred Nobel or Werner von Siemens, rather than by any sort of organized activity. For example, AT&T, one of the most celebrated technological innovators of the 20th century, had a policy of not doing original research until 1907. The challenge, therefore, was to design a vehicle that could help establish a pipeline of new products.

Into the lab

The solution – as developed independently by Bayer, General Electric, and AT&T – was the creation of industrial research laboratories, housing a large number of trained scientists and engineers and separated from production and other departments. Together these people worked towards the creation of new science and technologies that could be applied inside the business. Thomas Edison thought of the laboratory as a variant of the machine shop, where independent entrepreneurs and mechanics also shared ideas. While the scientists were under some pressure to come up with something useful, they were not expected to sell their inventions directly into the marketplace. Their objective was to contribute to the long-term development of the company, especially its ability to innovate.

Research labs started to produce innovations in a quantity not seen previously. The lab at GE, for instance, came up with electric lighting advances like the development of ductile tungsten that allowed GE to become leader in that industry. Other innovations included laser light and x-ray tubes. The labs helped companies attract the best scientific talent. They also changed the way in which invention and innovation took place because the scientists were protected from direct commercial intervention. And because smaller firms did not have the resources in place to operate labs, the labs also enlarged the difference between the haves and have-nots.

The job of research

In 1876, faced with a crisis in its core dye stuff trade business as well as the new German patent laws, Bayer decided to start employing more scientists in its plants to develop new products. One of the Bayer directors, Carl Rumpff, hired three recently graduated chemical doctors and sent them to different universities where they were supposed to work as postdoctoral researchers on projects for Bayer. This did not quite pan out as hoped, and the three returned to Bayer in 1884. There, one of them, Carl Duisberg, discovered new dyes that were deemed to be 'of the utmost commercial importance'. As a reward for his discoveries, Duisberg was allowed to become a full-time researcher, detached from operational issues. He was also provided with research assistants. By 1888 Duisberg was a board member and, in effect, a separate research division had emerged, its mission being to invent new colours. The job of researcher had been established in the process.

But in spite of these successes, research was still physically located in whatever room happened to be available. In 1889 Bayer decided to formalize its commitment to industrial research by building a laboratory to house researchers. Duisberg helped design this building, which cost 1.5 million German Marks. In 1891 the building was completed. After 15 years of gradual growth the industrial research lab was born at Bayer.

Lab land

Other large European companies also introduced research labs in the late 19th century. In the United States, various companies went through a similar process some years after Bayer. GE's Charles Steinmetz had taken his education in Germany and Switzerland and was therefore familiar with what companies had done there. In July 1897 Steinmetz proposed that GE should build an electrochemical laboratory, because there seemed to be opportunities and he himself was interested in arc lighting. By September 1897 he had encountered resistance from GE President Coffin and the board of directors, who did not see an immediate business benefit in spending money on a lab. In 1898 he tried again, pointing to the threat of new competitors, but failed once more. In response Steinmetz enlisted support from others in 1899, notably the head patent attorney Albert David and vice-president Edwin Rice. But it was not until September 1900, when GE became really concerned about competitors' research activities, that Steinmetz managed to get his detailed proposal accepted, first by Elihu Thompson, who had founded GE, and then finally by the board. Some board members still did not believe the initiative was going to succeed and agreed only because they foresaw a swift collapse.

Research labs were also introduced around that time at DuPont and AT&T. DuPont directly followed the lead of the German chemicals producers, most prominently Bayer. It also believed it could benefit by attracting leading scientists in the USA who would want to do non-academic work. Although the decision at DuPont did not attract the same opposition as at GE, DuPont had to adjust to managing scientists. AT&T, a Bell subsidiary, built its lab in 1911 in part because existing patents had started to run out.

Industrial research labs produced most of the key product innovations in the 20th century across many areas like electronics, chemicals, defence, pharmaceuticals, and computers. They managed to combine specialist knowledge and expertise with the ability to post, exploit, and enforce patents inside commercial firms. Labs have also had an effect on manufacturing processes and methods.

Working their labs

Today, all large manufacturing companies continue to employ large numbers of scientists who help them create new products. Industrial labs have become so taken for granted that it is very hard to imagine these firms being successful without a lab. Labs have also significantly increased the entry barriers into industries, making it very hard for new entrants and small entrepreneurial firms to compete with large incumbents even when these entrepreneurial firms had brilliant ideas.

Recently, though, the tide has started to turn. Some of the most well-regarded labs in the world, including AT&T's Bell Labs (now part of Alcatel-Lucent) and Philips' research labs, shifted their focus during the 1980s and 1990s away from basic research and towards much more applied product development. In the drug industry, small biotech startups began to challenge the established pharmaceutical firms with much leaner and more focused research operations. And many software firms have also been successful on a smaller scale.

These changes have led many large firms to rethink their innovation strategy. Today the buzzword is open innovation (pp. 154–157) – the idea that even large firms need to become better at tapping into the technologies and ideas outside their boundaries, rather than attempt to do everything in-house. This strategy is unlikely to entirely supersede the industrial research lab approach, but it makes clear that there are limitations to trying to do everything oneself.

Skunk works

As the Second World War went on, participating countries increasingly tried to use advanced technology to outdo opponents. This had also been the case in previous wars, especially the First World War, but the pace of technological innovation had accelerated. In 1943 reports emerged that Germany had introduced a jet fighter in its attempts to gain control over European skies. This German speed advantage severely threatened Allied use of fighters and bombers, which were needed to support any land-based offensive.

The Allies had their own jet engine in place, constructed by Britain's DeHavilland, but the United States had no plane in which the engine could be fitted. To make matters worse, time was clearly not on the side of the Americans. The US Army Air Corps commissioned Lockheed to come up with a solution. Lockheed's top engineer Clarence L. 'Kelly' Johnson promised to deliver a prototype within 180 days. But Lockheed and other aircraft producers did not have structures or processes in place to design new planes in such a short period of time.

Shielding the skunk

The solution, which later became known as a skunk works, lay in getting the maximum creativity out of a small group of creative people in the minimum amount of time, by separating them from the rest of the organization. Unlike the industrial research lab, a skunk works focuses on a very specific problem with the intent to come up with a commercial solution. And skunk works are shielded from the rest of the organization even more than industrial research labs, although they may draw from company resources. Skunk works typically also have a different culture from the rest of the company, which gets formed during a project. In some cases they even work without the commitment or knowledge of top management.

Brewing up

At Lockheed, Johnson went to the company president, Robert E. Gross, and managed to 'steal' 23 engineers and 103 shop mechanics from other projects. Johnson was given free rein on aircraft design and methods. Separated from the rest of the company, the team set up in a small assembly shed in Lockheed's Burbank, California, plant, and set to work intensively. After 143 days the XP-80 prototype jet was born. It became the first US jet fighter and was capable of exceeding 500 mph. The overall development cost was $9 million, which was very low given that some 9000 related aircraft were eventually produced.

There are two versions of how the name skunk works came about. Some have said that there was a strange smell around the shed where the XP-80 was developed. But Kelly Johnson himself later said that outsiders who asked about what went on in the shed were told some brew was being stirred up. This brought up a parallel with a factory from Al Capp's 'Li'l Abner' comic strip where Hillbilly characters chopped up skunks to brew strange potions. Seven success factors were later identified that make skunk works successful:

- clear focus on the mission
- extensive up-front planning efforts
- critical analysis of customer needs
- leveraging of project overlaps
- early involvement of suppliers

▨ team empowerment

▨ breaking the rules.

Planet skunk

The skunk works' next project, the Saturn, was not as successful but because of low development costs this was not much of a problem. Lockheed retained its skunk works unit, and Johnson remained its head until 1975. More recently the company has developed the F-117A Stealth Fighter.

Other companies also took up the skunk works concept. DuPont successfully used the concept in 1987 on a development project that was intended to replace rubber in disposable nappies with Lycra Spandex, as did Steve Jobs in the development of the Apple Mac, and IBM in the development of its personal computer. Many technology-based companies that needed to develop radically new solutions within a limited period of time turned to skunk works. A key advantage is that the invention and commercialization phases can become almost indistinguishable.

The modern skunk

Ben Rich, who took over from Johnson at Lockheed, comments:

Skunk works should be part of a large organization, as we are at Lockheed. In today's business climate, I do not think a skunk works would be feasible if it could not rely on the resources of a larger entity. It needs a pool of facilities, tools and human beings who can be drawn upon for a particular project and returned to the parent firm when the task is done.

There are other limitations associated with the skunk works model, because it can create a divide between the haves and have-nots, and it can lead the firm to avoid investing in a truly innovative organizational climate. Eventually skunk works can undermine the effectiveness of the overall organization. And they can be hard to manage, vulnerable, and fragile.

Yet skunk works remain the best solution available for certain types of innovation. When a radically different solution is needed, especially if there is time pressure, skunk works are likely to produce the best outcomes. Top executives now realize this and have become more involved in the setting up and resourcing of skunk works units, although they still acknowledge that these units must remain independent and shielded from the corporate bureaucracy.

Corporate venturing

How can large companies encourage entrepreneurial behaviour among their employees and still retain them under the corporate umbrella? And how can they create new businesses at the same time as running their established businesses?

These issues have been the subject of perennial attention and semantic invention. The term corporate venturing first entered the business vernacular in the mid-1960s, and dozens of large companies on both sides of the Atlantic created 'venture units' or 'new venture divisions' to incubate their promising new business ideas. Since then, interest in corporate venturing has waxed and waned with the business cycle, and new terms have been invented along the way. For example, Gifford and Elizabeth Pinchot heralded the arrival of the 'intra-corporate entrepreneur' in 1978, and Gifford Pinchot is credited with coining the term 'intrapreneur'. Said Pinchot: 'Alert leaders recognize that to compete in today's dynamic marketplace they must release the intrapreneurial spirit of their employees. The only question is how.' His book, *Intrapreneuring: Why you don't have to leave the corporation to become an entrepreneur*, came out in 1985; and the American Heritage Dictionary added the term 'intrapreneur' in 1992. Intrapreneuring has grown up and become subsumed within the broader realm of corporate venturing.

The venturing concept

Corporate venturing is an approach to new business development used by many large firms, in which they establish a separate organizational unit (a corporate venture unit) that invests in and nurtures startup business ventures. The UK's Centre for Business Incubation defines corporate venturing as 'a formal, direct relationship, usually between a larger and an independent smaller company, in which both contribute financial, management or technical resources, sharing risks and rewards equally for mutual growth'. These relationships may take the form of intrapreneurial ventures, as when large companies spin-off new businesses and/or technologies. However, they may also involve the provision of equity and/or non-equity investment to small, independent ventures.

Chemical giant DuPont was one of the first companies to create a formal corporate venture unit. As described by Russell Peterson in a 1967 *Harvard Business Review* article, the company decided to 'place new ventures in a separate development-oriented organization possessing the climate that fosters change and encourages positive bold thinking'. Other early experiments with this approach were tried at 3M Corporation and Exxon.

The downside of adventure

But as DuPont discovered, corporate venturing was no panacea for the problems of bureaucracy and short-term thinking, and this experiment was halted in the early 1970s.

Researchers identified many problems with this first wave of corporate venture units. These included: not giving the venture unit enough independence in choosing which ventures to invest in and sell; not providing sufficiently clear objectives; and not giving the venture unit enough time or money to deliver on its objectives.

But this was not the end of the story. Corporate venturing took off again in the mid-1980s, before being halted by the 1987 stock market crash, and then again in the bull market of the 1990s before once again grinding to a halt when the dotcom bubble exploded. But rather than learning from earlier mistakes, the companies throwing money at corporate venturing during these eras made the same errors as before.

But there was one difference in the most recent corporate venturing wave, namely the increasing use of tricks from the venture capital industry, including careful staging of seed money, and equity-based reward structures for venture managers.

'While they may do well to mimic certain VC practices, corporate venture structures ultimately will only work if they can deliver strategic benefits to their sponsoring companies,' asserts innovation guru, Henry Chesbrough. 'They must leverage the potential advantages of corporate ventures.' Those advantages include corporations' much longer lifespan, he says, which in turn enables them to support longer range ventures. Major corporations may also have the ability to finance larger scale projects that would be beyond the capacity of independent venture funds.

Adventures now

Venture units today are typically more focused, more selective, and more streamlined than they were in the late 1990s. And their executives have enough self-assurance to know when to resist the inevitable meddling of parent company executives. Of course, this increased maturity does not guarantee survival, but it certainly helps. After all, many venture units just need time: time to figure out what they are really doing and where their priorities lie; and time to grow their ventures through their most fragile years and into viable businesses.

Open innovation

Innovation is a critical organizational competence. 'Today the only way to have an advantage is through innovation,' observed Harvard Business School guru Michael Porter. 'Top quality, reasonable price and good service merely get you into the game; they're not enough to allow you to win. Innovate or die,' says Tom Peters with characteristic bluntness.

While companies used to be able to draw a direct link between their investment in R&D on the input side and the flow of new products on the output side, the link became more tenuous during the 1990s. Take the pharmaceuticals industry, for example: through the 1990s the pharma giants spent more every year on drug development, but they did not see a return on that investment: in fact between 2002 and 2004 drug approvals by the FDA in the USA fell by 47 per cent. The drug pipeline had begun to dry up.

Similar problems were being encountered in other industries. Through the 1980s and early 1990s, telecoms giants such as BT in the UK, Ericsson in Sweden and Lucent in the USA continued, as they always had, to build their own proprietary technologies with their own in-house teams of software engineers. But they discovered that the groundbreaking innovations in their industry were often coming from small startup companies in entirely unexpected places.

Faced with a proliferation of new technologies, new competitors, and new centres of expertise around the world, large companies began to face up to an uncomfortable question: was the traditional in-house approach to R&D, which had served them well for over a century, valid any longer?

Open logic

The alternative to a proprietary and secrecy-based model of innovation was, of course, open innovation – the idea that individual firms can harness insights and ideas from multiple sources. To some extent, open innovation has always been part of the technology landscape, but it became a major force during the 1990s. One driver was the open source software movement, which turned the notion of intellectual property on its head by publishing its computer source code on the internet for anyone to see. It even allowed programmers to take the code and modify it thus contributing to the final product. The result was, in many people's eyes, not least the consumers, a better product. The Linux operating system, the Firefox web browser, the Thunderbird email client, these are all extremely functional open source software products.

As Henry Chesbrough at the Haas School of Business, University of California, Berkeley, and a leading authority on open innovation, says:

We have moved from closed innovation to a new logic of innovation: open innovation. *This new logic builds upon the recognition that useful knowledge is widely distributed across society, in organizations of all sizes and purposes, including nonprofits, universities, and government entities. Rather than reinvent the wheel, the new logic employs the wheel to move forward faster.*

It is a case, as Chesbrough points out, of companies realizing, 'not all the smart people work for us.' As he notes: 'Their realization is that, in a world of abundant knowledge, hoarding technology is a self-limiting strategy. No organization, even the largest, can afford any longer to ignore the tremendous external pools of knowledge that exist.'

Connecting and developing

With the rise of open source software, as well as the emergence of small biotechnology players in the pharmaceuticals industry, large companies began to rethink their approach to innovation. Some of the earliest converts were in the telecommunications industry. For example, Lucent created two corporate venture units in the 1990s to bring open innovation thinking to the famous Bell Labs – one unit made seed investments in hot new startups, the other created spin-off companies using non-core technologies, and both were highly successful. In Europe, BT, Siemens, Nokia and Ericsson all adopted their own versions of these models as they sought to keep up with the changing rules of the innovation game.

But perhaps the most comprehensive change in innovation strategy to be adopted by an established company is by Procter & Gamble. Under the stewardship of CEO A.G. Lafley, in 2000 P&G announced its 'connect and develop' strategy. This represented a wholesale realignment of the people working in its labs: where previously they had been responsible for doing research and developing products from that research, the new model was to tap into new ideas wherever they existed, and to use those ideas to drive product development. The target was to bring in half of P&G's innovation from sources outside the organization.

To get to its ambitious target the idea was to leverage different innovation networks. The company uses InnoCentive, for example, an online network of over 75,000 scientists founded by pharma giant Eli Lilly. It has also helped pioneer networks such as YourEncore, a network of retirees from over 150 companies.

P&G's new strategy is paying dividends. Over 50 per cent of the organization's innovations now originate outside the organization compared to under 15 per cent when Lafley first announced his target in 2000. 'Connect and develop' has helped propel more than 250 products into the marketplace, generating billions of sales.

The pharma companies are also inching their way towards alternative innovation models. Whether it is through licensing, alliances, or joint venturing the pharmaceutical companies are unlocking the doors of their research labs. In 2002 the top 20 pharma companies derived 17.5 per cent of their total brand-named prescription (ethical) sales from licensed products. That figure was up to 19.5 per cent by 2004. It is expected to grow to 26 per cent by 2010. If the pharmaceutical companies can manage to add value through new innovation models, so too can most other industries.

Market forces

Now commercial corporations in all sectors are being urged to embrace the collaborative principles of open innovation. In an article in *Harvard Business Review*, 'Open-market innovation', Darrell Rigby and Chris Zook identify several benefits associated with open innovation: more ideas are generated and a broader base of expertise accessed leading to improvements in the 'cost, quality and speed' of innovation; licensing new innovations to third parties may provide a needed stimulus within the organization to make more use of internally generated ideas; exported ideas may receive more intense scrutiny and so a more rigorous test of the economic viability of the idea.

Open innovation has spread beyond the open source movement, into many different sectors. In the electronic consumer goods market, for example, many of the leading players realize that it is not possible to keep pace with the consumer's insatiable appetite for new products without adopting a more open innovation model.

The net gainers are companies like Quanta Computer in Taiwan and Wipro in India. Companies like these are known as original-design manufacturers (ODMs). They design and assemble electronic equipment for the major brand names like Dell and Sony. And, where once they might have built to design specs supplied by the client, increasingly they are driving the design innovation themselves.

Such outsourcing of R&D is not without risk. Motorola used ODM BenQ Corporation in Taiwan to design and build mobile phones. BenQ subsequently moved into the China mobile phone market selling its own branded products, though this strategy proved to be less than successful. There is also investor sentiment. When a company has outsourced just about everything including the innovation, what is left of proprietary value other than the brand?

The upside

Most companies, no matter how progressive, may take some time to adopt a completely open approach to innovation. Indeed, they may never do this. Ensuring a fair exchange of value between innovation partners is still a challenge. There are real risks involved in open innovation, alliances, joint ventures and partnering arrangements that simply do not exist in licensing and in-house R&D. Not least the risks of unwanted technology transfer and spillover, or lengthy, costly, legal disputes. Until firms find ways of managing these and other risks, new innovation models may remain just a great idea rather than a business reality.

While there is some risk, however, there is also a huge upside in terms of competitive advantage through innovation. Many commentators and industry practitioners were convinced that innovation was one thing that couldn't be outsourced. Various arguments were put forward, from the need to stay close to the customer, to the risk of giving away intellectual property. The innovation outsourcing revolution currently underway suggests the doubters were wrong.

 # Management by objectives

The rapid growth in companies that occurred during the first half of the 20th century created inevitable problems in control and coordination. The CEO of a 100-person company knows everyone personally, and can coordinate and monitor performance informally. But the CEO of a 1000+ person company has to build formal structures and policies to be confident that everyone is aligned to the broader objectives of the company. What sort of approaches did companies adopt to achieve such alignment? One approach was to break the company up into divisions and business units with clear and discrete goals. Another, as we discuss in Chapter 7, was to use information systems to standardize activities.

But perhaps the most important, though most easily overlooked, mechanism for achieving alignment of effort was simply through good, old-fashioned, management. The key task of the manager, it can be argued, is to make clear what the objectives of each subordinate are supposed to be, and to monitor and evaluate the subordinate's output against those objectives. This basic concept came to be known as management by objectives, or MBO for short.

Management by definition

Stephen Carroll and Henry Tosi define MBO in their book *Management by objectives: Applications and research* published in 1973. 'Management by objectives is a process in which members of complex organizations, working in conjunction with one another, identify common goals and coordinate their efforts towards achieving them. Emphasis is on the future and change, since an objective or goal ... is a state or a condition to be achieved at some future time,' say the authors.

With MBO, the assumption is that $a + b = c$; that there is a goal that is attainable, and that it can be reached via objectives **a** and **b**. By setting clear objectives it becomes easier for the individual to deliver, even though the journey may be difficult.

The original Drucker

While the underlying idea that a company should achieve alignment by setting specific objectives for its people is as old as the hills, the origins of the term 'management by objectives' are very well defined.

In 1937, after working as a journalist in London, Peter Drucker, who would become the world's leading management guru, moved to America and wrote *The concept of the corporation* in 1946. This groundbreaking work paved the way for Drucker's later work and involved an examination of the intricate internal working of General Motors that revealed the auto giant to be a labyrinthine social system rather than an economical machine.

In 1954 Drucker published *The practice of management*, one of the seminal books in management. The book contained a number of important concepts. And of the many ideas contained in the book, the one that was greedily seized on by business was management by objectives. 'A manager's job should be based on a task to be performed in order to attain the company's objectives ... the manager should be directed and controlled by the objectives of performance rather than by his boss,' wrote Drucker.

Lacking the populist trend for snappy abbreviation, Drucker always referred to 'management by objectives and self-control'. His inspiration for the idea of MBO was Harold Smiddy of General Electric whom Drucker knew well. He also acknowledged Alfred Sloan, Pierre du Pont amd Donaldson Brown of DuPont as practitioners of MBO.

Managing by simplicity

As MBO became popularized, interpretations became narrower than that proposed by Drucker:

The performance that is expected of the manager must be derived from the performance goal of the business, his results must be measured by the contribution they make to the success of the enterprise. The manager must know and understand what the business goals demand of him in terms of performance and his superior must know what contribution to demand and expect of him – and must judge him accordingly.'

In practice, however, the personal element in Drucker's interpretation of MBO was subsumed by the broader corporate agenda. Instead of being a pervasive means of understanding, motivation and satisfaction, MBO became viewed by many as a simplistic means of setting a corporate goal and heading towards it.

The concept was disseminated through the business world by the work of a number of people including US academic George Odiorne, and, in the UK, consultant John Humble. Hewlett-Packard was one company where MBO made a big impact. 'No operating policy has contributed more to Hewlett-Packard's success than the policy of management by objective,' noted HP founder David Packard.

Back to MBO

MBO was one of the big ideas of the late 1950s and 1960s. Today, while it still has its supporters, it has been criticized from a number of corners.

In practice, MBO demanded too many data. It became overly complex and also relied too heavily on the past to predict the future. The entire system was ineffective at handling, encouraging, or adapting to change. MBO simplified management to developing the managerial equivalent of highways, in order to reach objectives quickly with the minimum hindrance from outside forces.

Companies soon found, however, that not only was the road far from straight, but that the route was often changed mid-journey. 'The confusion of means and ends characterizes our age,' Henry Mintzberg, management guru and strategy expert, observes. Today, the highways are liable to be gridlocked, and managers left to negotiate minor country roads to reach their objectives. And then comes the final confusion: the destination is likely to have changed during the journey. Strategy does not stop and start, it is a continuous process of redefinition and implementation.

Equally, while MBO sought to narrow objectives and ignore all other forces, success (the objective) is now less easy to identify. Today's measurements of success can include everything from environmental performance to meeting equal opportunities targets. Success has expanded beyond the bottom line.

Strategic planning

Until the Second World War, business strategies had typically been devised based on intuition and prior experience. But as circumstances changed, strategies were adapted accordingly. Companies had planned and formalized some of their activities but these were primarily internally oriented activities like operations. In the decades following the war, companies increasingly started to recognize the limitations of their intuitive approach to strategy, such as a lack of foresight into what might happen and the use of outdated information and resources.

In 1945, when Henry Ford II became its president, Ford Motor Company was losing $10 million every month, because its financial systems, plants, and products were outdated and its engineering staff was too small as a consequence of the poor management of his grandfather, Henry Ford, in his later years. Henry Ford II felt the company needed to remake and modernize itself.

It was then that Ford started to implement a system of strategic planning. Strategic planning involves the creation of plans for how a company can best utilize the opportunities that exist in its environment and overcome sudden environmental changes. Strategic planning is a systematic approach for a company to define its vision of the future and objectives and to translate these objectives into specific actions and allocations of resources like money, managerial talent and production facilities. This planning process takes into account both customer needs and competitor positions. Because strategic planning is a top-down process, it also has the potential to change power structures in a company through reallocation of resources.

Whiz kids

In 1946 Ford struck on a group of 10 young men, who were offering their services to businesses. These men were led by Colonel Charles 'Tex' Thornton and became known as the 'Whiz Kids'. The Whiz Kids, including Robert McNamara, later Secretary of Defence under John F. Kennedy, had all worked in the US Army Air Force where they had learned statistical and formal techniques in the war. In the military these techniques were, for instance, used to predict the development of weapons systems and enemy moves. Because of their successes at the Office for Statistical Control, Thornton had suggested applying similar methods in business. The group were very young, mostly still in their 20s, but had levels of confidence and experience that matched people 20 years their senior. At Ford, the Whiz Kids had a broad remit to look at capital spending, organizational charts, the creation of profit centres and product divisions (see Chapter 4), product plans and job descriptions.

When the Whiz Kids went to work they tried to piece together all the information they could possibly find inside Ford. They believed planning could replace the guesswork and intuition that characterized Ford at the time. This method proved as successful at Ford as it had been in the military. By introducing planning, they managed to modernize Ford's organization greatly.

It took Ford some time to develop its approach to planning. By 1956 it had embraced a broader type of strategic planning and Ernest Breech, its chairman, commented: 'The development of product planning procedures – like organizational planning – depends much upon individual personalities and the type of products to be designed. Our own procedures have come about through a gradual evolution. Maybe I should call it trial and error.' Breech summarized Ford's planning approach:

In our business, long-range facilities planning, to put it simply, means analyzing the market for our products over a certain period of years, determining what percentage of the market we think we can get, determining the type of products that will be characteristic of those years, and translating those findings into plant requirements. In other words, we ask what facilities we will need to produce standard volume.

Ford became much more analytically focused.

Electric strategy

Another firm that is strongly associated with strategic planning is General Electric. GE had grown rapidly during the 1940s. CEO Charles Wilson asked his successor-to-be, Ralph Cordiner, to propose some changes. Cordiner realized that more planning would have to be at the heart of these changes. During Cordiner's years at the top, from 1950 to 1963, GE developed its own strategic planning approach. It evolved around identifying customer needs in specific product markets, a focus which would eventually result in the development of the strategic business unit (see Chapter 4). These customer needs and market opportunities were then translated into strategic and operational objectives and resources were distributed accordingly.

Post-1945, and especially into the 1970s, companies found themselves faced with ever increasing levels of environmental turbulence. And as the complexity of decisions, as well as the amount of information available to take them, increased strategic planning, along with scenario planning (see pp. 162–165) proved to be an interesting solution for large numbers of companies. And there was evidence that strategic planning seemed to work. Igor Ansoff, who was the first guru to write and speak about strategic planning extensively, showed that firms using planning obtained a superior and more predictable performance than the non-planners. McKinsey consultant and future IBM CEO Louis Gerstner wrote about ways to make strategic planning more effective in 1972. Strategic planning became very popular in large companies through the 1970s and 1980s.

What could be?

Over the last 20 years though, strategic planning has fallen into disrepute for a variety of reasons. Strategic plans were often not translated into decisions and actions. This is often called 'paralysis by analysis'. At lower levels in the organization there was often resistance to the introduction of strategic planning. Other objections levied against planning included its inability to deal with rapid and unexpected change and too much focus on the existing business. Gary Hamel and C.K. Prahalad argued: 'In our experience, strategic planning typically fails to provoke deeper debates about who we are as a company or who we want to be in ten years' time. Strategic planning almost always starts with "what is". It seldom starts with "what could be".'

Companies still need to engage in strategy making. But from the rise and fall of strategic planning we have learned that a strict focus on making plans can actually undermine the creativity that is needed to set successful strategies. At the same time, strategic planning has been useful in moving the basis for strategy making from mere intuition towards analysis based on facts and figures. Smart strategists today realize that such analysis is a good starting point, but it is not a panacea for success.

 # Scenario planning

Taking decisions when the future is well known is easy. Unfortunately, the future is almost always uncertain. This uncertainty became an increasing problem after the Second World War and resulted in the creation of strategic planning. Strategic planning allowed companies to think about the future and plan ahead. Yet strategic planning avoided answering the question: *What if there are multiple possible futures?*

This was a problem that oil company Shell faced in the late 1960s. The oil industry was dominated by the Seven Sisters, of which Shell was seen as the ugly sister as it neither had large reserves nor an exclusive relationship with one of the Arab nations where oil drilling took place. Much of its performance came from smart trading. Although Shell was a stable company, and oil prices had been equally stable in recent years, the Arab nations were becoming increasingly vocal about getting more money and influence out of the oil business. And in 1975 the Teheran agreement, which specified terms between oil companies and the oil-producing OPEC countries, was going to expire. How could Shell possibly set a strategy in the face of this type of uncertainty?

What if …?

The solution lay in scenario planning – a process that helped companies explore and anticipate alternative futures. If external, or even internal, conditions change, scenario planning helps to predict what effect various strategies will have on a company's performance. Unlike the predictions or forecasts that are essential to strategic planning, scenario planning helps to create an approach to managing risk. Scenario planning may, for instance, involve the comparison of a scenario that extends the past into the future through extrapolation with a scenario where the future is radically different from the past. A key advantage is that this allows for more open-minded thinking about the future, often in the form of brainstorming sessions, because the company does not commit itself to any of the proposed futures. And as the world changes, the company will have thought through a wider range of options and will be better positioned to respond.

Pushing the envelope

The importance of thinking through different possible future scenarios came, as so often, from the military world. In the immediate aftermath of the Second World War, Herman Kahn led the development of scenarios for military strategy at the Rand Corporation, and he subsequently started applying his methods to the broader changes in the wider political and social world.

In the late 1960s Shell started working on its version of scenario planning. In 1965 Shell had introduced unified planning machinery, its version of strategic planning that looked six years ahead. Ted Newland, a former Royal

Air Force pilot working at the planning department, was asked in 1967 to develop a view of Shell's operations. Newland was impressed by the work of Kahn, and convinced his boss Jimmy Davidson that it held much in store for Shell. In late 1969 Davidson convinced the board of managing directors that Shell should start adopting scenario methods.

In 1971 Newland was joined in London by Pierre Wack, a former magazine publisher and graduate of the prestigious École des Sciences Politiques. Wack had done some work with Kahn's methods to assess the French market. Wack and Newland developed four explanatory scenarios in 1971, using Kahn's methods. These scenarios did not produce a clear course of action but did allow for certain futures to be deemed impossible. Yet Frank McFadzean, a former head of planning, said that he 'could have done as well on the back of an envelope'. In 1972 the scenario team, now consisting of 20 members, composed six scenarios, focusing on the oil price and taking into account the behaviours of oil producers, consumers, and companies. They also found out that 'soft' data would need to be included.

In September 1972 two families of scenarios were presented. As Wack later recalled:

We quantified both the A- and B-family scenarios in terms of volume, price, impact on individual oil producer and consumers, and interfuel competition. Our presentation gained the attention of top management principally because the B-family of scenarios destroyed the ground many of them had chosen to stand on. Management then made two decisions: to use scenario planning in the central office and the larger operating companies and to informally advise governments of the major oil-consuming countries about what we saw coming.

Wack turned out to be the sort of 'intellectual maverick' needed to make local Shell managers understand the need for scenario planning. Meanwhile, Davidson created the atmosphere and facilitated the background conditions required for Newland and Wack to do well.

Then the first oil crisis came in 1973, on the back of ever increasing demand and pressure by the oil-producing OPEC countries to increase their ownership in production facilities. Prices shot up, just as some of Shell's scenarios had envisaged. None of Shell's competitors was prepared for such a situation. This initial price shock would be followed by many years of unstable oil prices and volumes, continuing to this day. And partly on the back of the insights it gained from scenario planning, Shell developed strongly, becoming Exxon's largest competitor by the 1980s. Arie de Geus, who would later become Shell's leading scenario planner, gave the following example: 'The price of oil was still $27 in early January 1986. But on February 1 it was $17 and in April it was $10. The fact that Shell had already visited the world of $15 oil helped a great deal in that panicky spring of 1986.'

Following the future

Of course, Shell's successes with scenario planning attracted many followers. In the 1970s many firms took on scenario planning to better predict the future, especially in the oil industry but also in other industries where leadtimes are long, assets specific and uncertainties abundant. But because the scenarios were often quite simplistic and the economic recession led to layoffs, many firms also rapidly abandoned scenario planning. It proved hard to surprise managers through the contents of a scenario.

Over time, lessons have been learned that make scenario planning once again an interesting methodology. Companies have learned that the preparation of good and insightful scenarios is of crucial importance for their effectiveness. And scenarios should lead to more than just discussion. To achieve real action on the basis of scenarios, companies need to build flexibility into their strategy implementation function. These days, specialist consultants often work with their clients to create tailor-made scenarios and use their own scenario planning methodologies. Since uncertainty continues to haunt business decisions, scenario planning remains well suited as a process supporting strategic decision making.

Benchmarking

Business is competitive. Companies vie to produce the best products and services at the most competitive prices. But how does an organization know that it is using the best practices, operating the most efficient processes, and employing the most cost-effective means of producing its goods and services? These are key questions even when a company is doing well. They are even more important when a company's competitors are doing better.

In the 1970s the Japanese car manufacturers, notably Toyota and Honda, outperformed US automakers, triggering the decline of the US car industry. At the same time Japanese manufacturing firms in other industries from consumer electronics to motorbikes began to outperform their US counterparts. Naturally, US corporations began to wonder how the Japanese companies managed to steal a march on them.

What was needed was a structured means of gathering and analyzing information that explained where a company could make improvements to its business.

Bench presses

One of the key solutions that emerged was benchmarking – the comparison of one company's performance against that of another company, or against an industry average. It involves the detailed study of productivity, quality, and value in different departments and activities in relation to performance elsewhere.

The principle behind benchmarking (or best-practice benchmarking as it is sometimes known) is very simple. If you want to improve a particular aspect of your organization or the service it provides, find someone else who is good at the activity you want to improve, and use them as a benchmark to raise your own standards. In effect, it's a way of pulling up performance by the bootstraps.

Typically, a database of relevant performance measures is drawn up from looking at similar activities in other parts of the firm and in other firms. This information is then used to compare the performance of the unit being reviewed with the range of experience elsewhere. So, for example, a manufacturing company might benchmark its transport and delivery performance against other business units it owns and against a transportation specialist such as one of the courier companies.

Copycats

As with many other management innovations, benchmarking existed as an informal activity for many years before it was actually named. The first mentions of benchmarking in the management literature came in the early 1980s when the concept was associated with Xerox. An article in the *Training and Development Journal* in 1984, written by two employees at Xerox, describes how 'for the past two years the Xerox Corporation has focused its attention on two targets: employee involvement and competitive benchmarking.'

According to Xerox, benchmarking 'means analyzing what the company does against what its strongest competitors do, to learn the most important lessons each competitor can teach'.

Then, in a 1987 *Harvard Business Review* article 'Ideas for action: How to measure yourself against the best', the authors described how Xerox started using benchmarking in 1979 in order to analyze unit production costs in manufacturing. The idea was to determine whether the Japanese plain paper copier competitors had relative costs as low as their relative prices.

The people at Xerox compared operating capabilities and features and stripped the machines to check out the components. The result of the comparison showed production costs in the USA were much higher. Xerox adopted the costs of its Japanese competitors as targets. Senior management decided that all business units and cost centres in Xerox should use benchmarking.

Cataloguing benchmarks

As Xerox discovered, it is not easy for a company to compare itself to its competitors. However, it is still a worthwhile exercise to make comparisons with non-competitors. An early example of this was the company's work with the sports goods retailer, L.L. Bean. In 1980 and early 1981 Xerox conducted a benchmarking exercise with L.L. Bean. While the results of the benchmarking were beneficial for Xerox, there was also a positive outcome for L.L. Bean. The company was so impressed with the success of Xerox it decided to use benchmarking as part of its planning process.

Once benchmarking was widely reported in the management literature, such as the *Harvard Business Review*, other companies began to incorporate benchmarking into their organizations.

The concept also evolved within Xerox, as it was used at different locations around the world. For example, although benchmarking was usually applied to costs, in late 1993 managers at Rank Xerox's headquarters in Marlow, England, decided to apply it to the revenue side of the equation.

The project, led by 'Team C', which comprised people from across the company's operating divisions in Europe, the Middle East and Africa, was highly successful. For example, by copying France's best practice in selling colour copiers, Switzerland increased sales by 328 per cent, Holland by 300 per cent, and Norway by 152 per cent.

Benchmarking goes global

Benchmarking is a global practice today, adopted by many organizations, across a wide range of functions. The Global Benchmarking Network, for example, founded in 1994, is an alliance of 23 benchmarking centres in 22 countries, representing over 25,000 businesses and government agencies.

Today there are three main techniques used in benchmarking. Best demonstrated practice (BDP), a technique used successfully for the last 15 years, is the comparison of performance by units within one firm. For example, the sales per square foot of a retail outlet in one location can be compared with the same statistic for a store in another location, within the same chain.

Relative cost position analysis looks at each element of the cost structure (e.g. manufacturing labour) per dollar of sales in firm X compared to the same thing in competitor Y. Finally, best related practice is similar to BDP, but takes the comparisons into related (usually not competing) firms, where direct comparisons can often be made by cooperation between firms to collect and compare data.

7

Information efficiency

How can companies obtain the right information needed to take decisions? What are the best decisions, given the available information? The purpose of innovations in information efficiency is to improve the availability and use of information throughout the company, using formal tools and mechanisms.

 ## Introduction

One of the core tasks of management is information processing. Effective managers are good at picking up information from disparate sources, making sense of that information, and acting on its insights. And while certain types of information can only be gained through face-to-face meetings, there is still enormous value for firms in creating systems that codify and analyze information on the manager's behalf.

This chapter focuses on management innovations that enable the efficient and effective processing of information, and particularly information that is quantitative in nature. Some of the innovations use statistical or mathematical techniques, and most of them benefit from the ever increasing power of computers. They deal, in effect, with the science, rather than the art, of managerial decision making (although some might say you can not start making scientifically based decisions unless you master the art).

The dramatic increases in information processing power that have occurred over the last 50 years make this section of the book rather more easy to write than most. So, for example, innovations in people management are always – to some degree – reinventions of earlier ideas because the basic nature of the employee has not changed that much. But innovations in information management, contrariwise, are often radical improvements over what came before because of the possibilities opened up by technological change.

The story of information-based innovations begins with Frederick Taylor's scientific management, which is dealt with in detail in Chapter 1 (pp. 12–17). By measuring work processes and collecting detailed information about the nature of the employee's work, Taylor the engineer was able to produce dramatic productivity improvements.

Armed with a stopwatch, Taylor examined in intimate detail exactly what happened at work and how long it took. For example, he calculated that a theoretical pig iron handler called Schmidt could load 47 tons a day rather than the more usual 12½ tons. This information meant workers would know exactly what was expected of them, and managers would know exactly how much should be produced. It also meant that more accurate piecework rates could be set with more reliable bonuses and penalties. The introduction of Taylor's ideas at the Watertown Arsenal reduced the labour cost of making certain moulds for the pommel of a packsaddle from $1.17 to 54 cents. Schmidt increased production by 400 per cent while receiving 60 per cent more pay. The power of information could not have been more powerfully made.

The next key development in the application of quantitative techniques to the world of business occurred in the 1930s with the rise of *operations research*, also known subsequently as management science. Operations research, which emerged from the innovative analytical techniques developed by Britain's Royal Air Force, allowed analysts to develop mathematically optimal solutions to complex and ambiguous problems – such as those found in the world of management. Operations research made it possible to turn management (or at least one aspect of management) into a domain of applied mathematics.

In the 1950s and 1960s operations research spawned a range of related techniques, such as simulation. By simulating and modelling production flows, or other management problems, managers could understand how an intervention would change an entire system. Another innovation of the 1960s was *yield management*, also know as revenue management, which attempted to identify the best possible price for goods. For example, American Airlines was the first airline to introduce yield management in flight bookings, aimed at 'selling the right seats, at the right prices, to the right customers'.

But the potential of operations research for the field of management could only be realized when businesses were able to afford their own computers. So in parallel with the rollout of mainframe computers across the population of large firms in the late 1960s and 1970s, materials requirement planning (*MRP I*) and then manufacturing resources planning (*MRP II*) took hold. These systems were designed to control and manage the flow of materials and other resources, particularly in manufacturing environments.

The introduction of the personal computer (PC) in the late 1970s spawned the next wave of management innovations in information processing. End-user computing involved transferring the ability to use computers from the corporate centre to the actual users: it is why millions of office workers around the world find themselves sitting behind a screen every day. End-user computing had enormous implications for the *management* of companies. Observers speculated that end-user computing would eliminate the need for 'middle managers' who had previously been the primary information conduit between frontline employees and senior managers, and while this did not happen, the increased access to information across the firm nonetheless led to dramatic changes in the relationships between employees and managers.

In the 1980s a plethora of management information systems were developed, of which expert systems became the best known. Expert systems involved the use of computers to address complex problems by programming a set of decision-making rules that simulated the knowledge of experts. While such systems never proved to be quite as effective as their proponents had hoped, they became extremely useful for certain well-defined applications.

In the mid to late 1980s the cutting-edge in information systems innovation shifted to interorganizational systems. Early examples of these included American Airlines' Sabre and American Hospital Supply's ASAP system. These interorganizational systems allowed for effective communication between organizations, and often the transfer of sales data.

In the early 1990s *enterprise resource planning* (ERP) was introduced. ERP was a system for processing and managing transactions. It facilitated integrated and real-time planning, production, and response to customer demands. ERP also increasingly became an interorganizational system. A related development, that drew to a large degree on the methods and concepts of ERP, was customer relationship management (CRM), which we discussed in Chapter 5 (pp. 130–133).

On the surface, it would seem that the management of information has become more fundamental to the job of management. There are certainly many more ways available today for gathering and managing information than there were even 20 years ago. But, as always, the challenge is as timeless as its achievement is elusive: to gather information efficiently in terms of cost and time and to translate information into improved performance.

Operations research

The first half of the 20th century was not only a period of prolific technological innovation, but also one of substantial military conflict. In 1934, the British Royal Air Force (RAF) realized that Germany was building up its military power, which might eventually lead to a conflict with Britain and perhaps even an airborne German invasion of the island itself. To prevent that invasion it would be helpful to have an early warning system in place. In December 1934 the RAF set up a Scientific Survey of Air Defence to 'consider how far recent advances in technological knowledge can be used to strengthen the present methods of defence against hostile aircraft'.

Any army is faced with the problem of how to mobilize and deploy its forces in the most efficient manner possible. In the case of Britain in the build-up to the Second World War, though, that problem was much more pronounced than normal. After its experiences in the previous war, Britain had established a professional army. It also had more advanced technological equipment than before, including aircraft, tanks, support equipment, submarines, and other vessels. This raised the question how best to allocate these scarce resources. What was the most efficient planning scheme?

Optimal solutions

The answer would prove to lie in the use of operational research (OR), later renamed operations research in the United States. OR used scientific analysis to study complex problems, which are normally systems involving multiple components. This leads to decisions that are substantially better than the subjective decisions that result from letting an individual decide solely based on that person's intuition and experience. In fact, OR analysis aims to produce what is known as the optimal solution, the best possible outcome given the information available and the decision parameters that are imposed. It draws on a variety of mathematical and statistical (probabilistic) techniques including simulation and linear programming.

Following its survey the RAF started experimenting with integrating radar into an early warning system at Biggin Hill (1936) and Bawdsey (1937). To do this effectively, OR analysis of the control room and communication system turned out to be indispensable. In 1938 Albert Rowe, who headed the radar development organization, first started using the term operational research. There had been some previous use of scientific techniques in the military, including Thomas Edison's use of statistics for the evasion and destruction of submarines, but the problems now faced required a new approach. The academic mathematician Patrick Blackett, who later became Lord Blackett and a Nobel Prize winner, had been a member of the investigating committee in 1934. In 1940 Blackett was charged with setting up the Antiaircraft Command Research Group, the RAF's first OR group. It would come to be called 'Blackett's Circus'. Large numbers of scientists were called upon to help in solving OR problems.

OR employees would attend staff meetings at operational headquarters to understand normal decision-making methods and conditions and then turned these into OR problems that they solved. The radar system turned out to be an important reason why Britain succeeded in repelling the German Luftwaffe during the so-called Battle of Britain in late 1940. As a consequence Blackett managed to push the use of OR techniques throughout the RAF and the coastal commands. From 1942 Blackett became Director of Naval Operational Research and also applied OR to naval problems especially in the U-boat war, including setting the best size for convoys, the most effective setting for depth charges against submarines and the efficient servicing of long-range aircraft. OR came up with counterintuitive solutions, for instance showing that large convoys worked better than small ones because convoy escorts would be more effective.

Winning the war

When the USA got drawn into the war as well, it immediately took up OR techniques, on an even larger scale than the UK. OR was used in four areas: the investigation of the effectiveness of weaponry; the analysis of operations that had taken place; the prediction of future operations; and the analysis of organizational techniques. At the end of 1942 OR had become a key part of the operations of the US Navy and the US Army, helping the Allies to win the war eventually.

After the war there was initially not very much business interest in OR. But in the academic world the journal *Operational Research Quarterly* first appeared in 1950. In it, Blackett argued that OR would be most effective if researchers would work at 'executive levels as observers and potential critics'. Blackett believed that his wartime experiences could simply be replicated in business and other civil applications. But in civil society, decision making turned out to be substantially less centralized and much harder to control than in the military so Blackett's vision of OR as the key decision-making mechanism never came true. Nonetheless OR spread to all kinds of sectors, like transportation, where it is used in scheduling, and manufacturing, where it is, for instance, used in determining optimal inventory levels. OR showed its value in a wide range of settings. Before 1960 most key OR techniques had been established in at least a basic form. In the 1960s and 1970s many businesses set up separate OR groups. Yet when the economy went into recession in the 1970s and 1980s, these groups were abolished just as quickly.

And/OR

OR has survived to this day in the worlds of business, the military and academia because there remains a range of problems for which it is best suited. These are problems where information can be quantified and decision parameters are well defined. Recent examples include how British Airways used OR techniques for lowering engineering inventory, saving £21 million in the process, and the use of OR in optimizing the operations of call centres. And there are specialized software suppliers and consultants who deliver OR solutions to clients. However, the idea that OR could one day guide the overall strategy of a company has long been abandoned.

Yield management

As industries developed, companies producing perishable goods encountered special challenges. Faced with an inventory of perishable goods, the firm selling the goods had to optimize returns on the sale of those goods, before the goods perished. To do this it needed to match supply and demand in the most efficient way, by understanding consumer behaviour, and by predicting and reacting to consumer demand.

Thus airlines in the 1970s, for example, were faced with the challenge of optimizing their return from airline ticket sales, or managing revenue from inventory. Flight tickets were perishable, of course, as once the flight departed they had no value. Here there was a difficult problem matching supply and demand, which differential real-time pricing might help solve.

Customers might have expected unsold seats to be sold at a cheaper price closer to the flight takeoff time. However, if there was sufficient demand for a few seats, this might not have been the case. Equally, airlines might have expected to charge a premium for guaranteeing a seat, however, as supply might have outstripped demand early on, a cheaper price might be more appropriate. What is clear is that there is a highly complex set of calculations and decisions that needed to be made.

Yields of gold

This is the challenge that yield management, also known as revenue management and real-time pricing, was developed to deal with in the 1970s. In essence, yield management is a technique for determining the optimal pricing policy for a product or service. It uses real-time computer modelling and forecasting of behaviour to predict the demand for a product or service in a particular micro-segment.

Yield management is not just used for individual products and services, it may be used across a group of goods, an individual market or an entire operation. Forecasting methods for yield management systems will factor in a wide range of information, including details about weather patterns, historical demand pattern, and competitive information such as pricing.

Luck yields dividends

Innovation is often the product of happenstance and chance connections. So it was with yield management. American Airlines, through American Airlines Decision Technologies, began its research into the subject in the early 1960s.

Its interest in yield management was, in many ways, the result of a chance conversation between C.R. Smith, president of American Airlines and R. Blair Smith, a senior sales representative for IBM.

In 1953 Smith and Smith met on an American Airlines flight from Los Angeles to New York, and the talk turned to the travel industry. Wouldn't it, the two agreed, be much simpler for all concerned, both passengers and airlines, if it were possible to create a data-processing system that provided a comprehensive airline seat reservation solution, and that any travel agent could access electronically at any time from anywhere.

It wasn't until six years later, though, that the fanciful idea became a reality. In 1960 the then computer giant IBM, and one of America's leading airlines, American Airlines, announced that they were, together, intending to develop the electronic passenger reservation system that Smith and Blair had envisaged – the semi-automatic business research environment, for simplicity's sake, Sabre.

The advent of Sabre paved the way for the development of an automated yield management, DINAMO – dynamic inventory allocation and maintenance optimizer – in 1988. The aim was, as American Airline's 1987 annual report described it: 'selling the right seats, at the right prices, to the right customers,' – and at the right time. The introduction of DINAMO was estimated to have led to $1.4 billion extra revenues in the three years between 1989 and 1991.

The first cut

The Sabre network got underway in 1960 when the first Sabre reservations system was installed in Briarcliff Manor, NY. Over the next four years the network was slowly extended across the USA, from east to west coast and from Canada to Mexico. At the time of its completion in 1964, it was the largest real-time data-processing system outside the government's own SAGE system.

In 1976 Sabre was installed in a travel agency for the first time. With a travel booking system that extended across the country, linking up the various travel agents, the company was able to use the system to gather real-time information about bookings.

The automated yield system DINAMO was a direct result of both the rollout of Sabre, plus the deregulation of the airline industry in 1979, which led to the bigger airlines introducing differential pricing of seats, such as American Airline's ultimate supersavers, to compete with the cheap fares of low cost carriers.

Before long it became clear that airlines would struggle to survive without yield management systems. Carriers slow to adopt the system, like People Express, went out of business.

Donald Burr, the CEO of People Express, remarked:

We were a vibrant, profitable company from 1981 to 1985, and then we tipped right over into losing $50 millions a month. ... What changed was American's ability to do widespread yield management in every one of our markets. We had been profitable from the day we started until American came at us with Ultimate Super Savers. That was the end of our run because they were able to underprice us at will and surreptitiously.

By the early to mid-1990s yield management had spread throughout the global airline industry, and then began to be adopted in other sectors, both in the USA and Europe.

Today's yield

Today, yield management is used across a range of industries and has become an indispensable competitive tool, particularly for pricing perishable inventory. Lines of business where yield management plays an essential role include the sale of hotel rooms, airline seats, and car rentals.

More recently, ethical concerns have been raised about the use of yield management. For example, one issue relating to yield management, which has caused unease in recent years, is price discrimination. By factoring in personal information into the yield management pricing process, it may be possible to use the information about an individual to predict that they would be willing to pay a price above the market price, and then use variable pricing to charge them more than another person buying a similar product at the same time.

MRP I and MRP II

Dramatic improvements in the efficiency of manufacturing processes had taken place in the first half of the 20th century. As we described in Chapter 1, innovations in mass production and lean manufacturing had allowed manufacturers in many industries to prosper. But the methods used to manage the flow of goods and information within the company, and between companies, remained underdeveloped in the 1960s. Companies such as J.I. Case and IBM were used to working with what was called production inventory control, but that method was largely intuition driven and required much manual processing. How could these companies become more efficient in processing flows of information and goods?

Round the loops

The solution came to be known as material requirements planning (MRP I) – a logically related set of procedures, decision rules, and records, which were translated into a master production schedule. This schedule was then used to produce specific requirements for any given time period and a plan for obtaining the necessary component inventory items. Enabled by the introduction of first-generation computers into large companies, MRP I emerged as a substantially improved way of managing materials and production, leading to lower inventory costs, higher reliability, better order tracking, and more efficient production.

Manufacturing resource planning (MRP II) was a further improvement on MRP I. It was a closed-loop system focusing on the management of all resources of manufacturing companies, including materials and shopfloor control, requirements planning, finance, marketing, engineering, and even personnel decisions like staffing and payrolls. MRP II made it possible to simulate the impact of various possible decisions and thus helped to support effective decision making. And because of its zero inventory goal, MRP II could be aligned with just-in-time systems (see Chapter 1). MRP II also extended MRP I in other ways – by including control and feedback loops, and by offering a much broader functionality.

Copernican theory

Of course, concerns about inventories and production planning did not start in the 1960s. For example, in the 1940s control departments in the airframe industry used techniques similar to MRP I. But with the advent of business computing and the establishment of the American Production Inventory and Control Society (APICS) in 1956, the ground was prepared for a step change. IBM consultants Joseph 'Joe' Orlicky and Oliver Wight were involved in the gradual development of computer systems around the Bill of Materials, which Orlicky implemented in 1961 at J.I. Case Company's Racine, Wisconsin, tractor plant. Using an IBM 305 RAMAC with a 15 million character disk file capacity and a specifically written software program, the system produced an inventory record (either automatically or on demand) and a weekly overview. At an APICS conference in 1966, Orlicky first met Wight and George Plossl, another consultant, to find out they had essentially been working on the same things. They teamed up and 'MRP I' was born. Orlicky himself likened it to a 'Copernican revolution' – an entirely new way of managing the flow of materials in a business setting.

But the limitations of MRP I gradually surfaced, and MRP II was developed in its place. Because computer-based systems tend to develop gradually, it is hard to point to a single moment in time when MRP I evolved into MRP II, but in 1978 Oliver Wight, who had now established his own consultancy firm, is said to first have used the term MRP II in a meeting in his living room. MRP II really took off in the early 1980s, with US manufacturing firms facing a lot of competitive pressures from Japanese and other overseas competitors.

Tools and technology

APICS, with its network of members, proved to be a fertile breeding ground for the spread of MRP I throughout the USA and abroad in the late 1960s and early 1970s. But MRP I proved significantly less precise and successful than hoped for. It required significant computing power by the standards of the time and was often run only once or twice a month. As circumstances changed regularly, because of breakdowns or unexpected shortages, the production schedule would rapidly become obsolete. One estimate in 1972 suggested MRP I was only successful at 2 per cent of the companies in which it had been implemented.

MRP II proved to be a much greater success, as it was more accessible for medium sized and large companies. Tim Vlach, the manufacturing manager of Megatest Corporation, California, said that 'inventory reductions alone freed up $7 million for more productive investment, while labour-related efficiencies yielded another $1.5 million', a lot for a company with $40 million sales. Managers at Toyota also embraced MRP II, because they found that MRP II could support their just-in-time function when ordering from suppliers. So MRP II started to show its potential for improving the entire supply chain, not just for the flow of goods within a single company.

But MRP II also had its own limitations, and these started to emerge in the 1980s. The biggest single problem was the lack of interconnectivity between systems, so that the MRP II system in a manufacturing plant often could not connect with the systems in other plants, let alone the logistics or billing systems run by different departments. And during this period computer processing power took off exponentially, so the MRP I- and MRP II-based systems rapidly became outdated. The scene was set for another innovation: the emergence of enterprise resource planning (ERP) systems.

MRP now

The management of inventories and manufacturing has become considerably more precise and less problematic these days, partly thanks to the dramatic increases in computer processing power over the last two decades. Moreover, many supply chains are global in nature, and many traditional manufacturing companies are now focusing increasingly on services. For these reasons, MRP I and MRP II are now primarily historical lessons in how to deal with operational problems. Companies still face the problems that MRP I and MRP II tackled, but today the solutions to these problems are so standardized that there are few managerial challenges left in this area. The focus has shifted to higher order questions such as how to get more innovation out of the company's supply chain.

 # Enterprise resource planning

After the implementation of MRP I in the 1970s and of MRP II in the early 1980s, companies had computer systems in place to manage their flow of resources like inventories and information. But these systems were far from perfect. MRP systems were usually standalone legacy systems, developed in one part of one company. This created compatibility problems with outside suppliers, and it led to enormous internal problems during mergers or reorganizations because, even within the same company, subsidiaries would have wildly different systems in place. The interconnectivity of these systems, while existing in theory, was actually very limited in practice. Moreover, the user friendliness of MRP systems was limited, as was the amount of information they produced that could actually feed into managerial decision making. What could be done to overcome these limitations of MRP systems?

ERP means integration

The solution came to be known as an enterprise resource planning (ERP) system. As the name suggested, ERP systems were designed to embrace the entire enterprise: they used computers to process and manage transactions and facilitate integrated and real-time planning, production, and response to customer demands. ERP systems also produced all the accounting information needed to fulfil customer orders and to invoice them.

The greatest strength of ERP systems was their ability to integrate flows of information. They operated through a series of specialized modules, which allowed for 'end-to-end' connectivity and information sharing between functions and organizational units. It was also possible to integrate information flows across companies, by linking a supplier company's ERP system to a customer's system. And because ERP systems were standardized applications, problems with incompatibility were greatly diminished.

The birth of ERP

Gartner Group had been analyzing the market for MRP II solutions on behalf of its manufacturing end users. In the late 1980s these users became increasingly frustrated with the limitations of existing solutions. In its search for new technologies and new providers, Gartner started describing the new systems as ERP systems, integrated manufacturing suites. From here on, the term became commonly used, even though the systems on offer were nowhere near the ideal Gartner described. Various companies then started marketing their systems as ERP, the most prominent of which were SAP, Baan, Oracle, J.D. Edwards, and Peoplesoft. By the early 1990s Germany's SAP had emerged as the market leader in ERP systems. SAP's success was in part a reflection of the technical quality of its software, but it also stemmed from the ability of the company to work with both hardware manufacturers *and* with consultants (who were required to install and customize SAP's software).

New releases

In 1992, SAP brought out the R3 ('Release 3') version of its product, and during the mid-1990s came to dominate the ERP market, at least among large companies. But it quickly became apparent that implementing SAP R3, or the offerings of competitors, was far from straightforward. Many large companies took up to three years to implement their ERP systems, and spent a small fortune on consultants to customize the software to their particular needs. However, the potential improvements from using ERP were also enormous, both in terms of direct savings and because ERP systems forced the different functions, divisions and businesses inside large companies to start operating in a more integrated manner. In the mid-1990s few large companies had the courage not to implement an ERP system, and SAP was usually the safe choice.

ERP today

There have been several attempts to rename ERP systems into something more contemporary yet but to date none has stuck. Almost all large companies operate some form of ERP system today. Of course, more functionality has been added over the past 10 to 15 years, such as internet compatibility and more advanced information for decision making, but, in essence, the underlying system still performs the same tasks that SAP's R3 first introduced. Implementation costs have come down, as even the interfaces between organizations have become more standardized and companies have learned from their costly implementation projects in the past. SAP and its competitors have started catering to the market of small and medium sized companies much more. And ERP is no longer as hyped up as it was in the mid-1990s. Yet it is still a central part of how companies manage their entire flow of information.

Conclusion:
The management
innovation agenda

 ## Introduction

What are the common elements that crop up time and time again across the 50 case histories in this book? This question is a form of Rorschach test, in that the reader is likely to pull out those themes that fit his or her existing belief system. A psychologist would probably point to the personalities and backgrounds of the key individuals in each case; an institutionally minded historian would likely focus on the social or political environment at the time that allowed the innovation to take hold. Our bias is essentially practical: we prefer to focus on the tangible steps taken by the individuals in each case, the ways they came up with their new ideas, and the approaches they used to build support within their organization.

We started this book by promising to deliver the answers to two questions practitioners have asked us. First, what are key management innovations that have been produced over the past 150 years? We have detailed 50 innovations across various areas. In the process we have given insights into how they affect today's practice and how they can be used to discover the problems tomorrow's management innovations will deal with. Second, how does management innovation happen? In this conclusion, we describe the management innovation process to answer this second question. Specifically, we see management innovation as occurring in five steps:

- explicit dissatisfaction with the status quo
- inspiration from the outside
- a conceptual breakthrough
- internal selling and validation
- external selling and validation.

Explicit dissatisfaction with the status quo

Management innovation always seems to start with a problem or challenge that everyone can relate to. Alfred Sloan was seeking to pull together five disparate organizations in the mid-1920s, and everyone could see that this was a complex challenge. Or, for a more recent example, in 2003 UBS Wealth Management, the private banking arm of the Swiss giant, was looking to grow after several years of painful cost cutting. The executives started looking into the blockers – the things that were standing in the way of the growth agenda – and they realized that the budgeting process was a key problem area. CFO Toni Stadelmann noted at the time: 'Budgeting is highly defensive – it is cumbersome, and it is fundamentally *against* growth. It is about negotiating down the targets that are proposed by the centre. And it causes people to talk about numbers not about clients and market opportunities.' This realization led to a complete rethinking of how individual client advisors worked and the elimination of the traditional budgeting process. Wealth management has been growing rapidly ever since.

Inspiration from the outside

Management innovators need inspiration – examples of what has worked in other settings, analogies from different social systems or unproven but alluring new ideas. For example, Dee Hock founded VISA with a unique cooperative organizational model that drew more from the principles of Jeffersonian democracy than from traditional hierarchical thinking. And Lars Kolind, creator of Danish hearing-aid company Oticon's 'spaghetti organization', built on his experiences as a scout leader to create a mission-driven, collaborative model of working.

A conceptual breakthrough

It is customary to assume that every innovation has a 'eureka' moment – when the inventor makes the key conceptual breakthrough or proposal that everything else follows from. 3M's Art Fry famously came up with the Post-it® Note concept at his local church as he sought to keep track of multiple pages in his book of hymns. However, the evidence suggests that such eureka moments are rare. Invention is a process in which the innovator brings together the various elements of a problem (dissatisfaction with the status quo) with the various elements of a solution (which involves some inspiration from outside plus a clear understanding of the internal situation and context), but the manner in which these elements are brought together is typically iterative and gradual.

Take the case of 'Connect and develop', Procter & Gamble's radical approach to building an external network of scientists around the world as a means of 'turbocharging' its internal R&D. This major organizational innovation took the best part of 10 years to put together. Larry Huston, the key architect of the model explained:

Back in the mid-1990s I was interested in how to develop a new organization form where people would be fluid and could swarm to the good projects, yet protect the base business. We spent time actually thinking through the detailed, entire organization design and I actually made a concept video. Then in 2000 my boss said we want you to create the new business model of innovation. Building on my earlier work I started to create the conceptual positioning for connect and develop. A lot of it starts with experiments; making concepts and storyboards and films, just like you would do if you're making a product. People just think this stuff falls to the ground, they don't realize that these big management systems are constructed. It takes a lot of skill to do that.

Internal selling and validation

In one important respect, management innovation is just like every other form of innovation: it involves change and uncertainty, and as a result it encounters resistance from people who don't understand or don't value the proposed innovation. And it is impossible to predict accurately whether any innovation's benefits will exceed its costs. A critical element, then, is for the management innovators to generate validation for their new idea among their internal constituencies. Consider Oticon's development of its radical 'spaghetti organization' with no formal hierarchical reporting relationships, a resource allocation system built around self-organized project teams and an entirely open-plan physical layout. In the early 1990s, this new model helped Oticon to achieve dramatic increases in profitability over the rest of the decade. CEO Lars Kolind's first step in putting this new organization in place was to persuade the owners of the company that a radical change was necessary to confront the challenge posed by giant competitors like Siemens and Philips. Once that had been achieved, he embarked on a massive internal selling programme to explain the nature of his proposed changes to the employees. He used radical slogans such as 'think the unthinkable' and visual symbols, such as a large transparent chute in the middle of the building.

External selling and validation

Finally, management innovation benefits enormously from a stamp of approval from an independent observer, such as an academic, a consultancy, or a media organization. This external 'validation' is important because of the uncertain and ambiguous nature of most management innovations. The lack of hard data to prove that a particular innovation is working means that companies frequently seek external validation as a means of increasing the level of internal acceptance. This process of validation also typically increases the visibility of the innovation to competitors or companies in other industries, which tends to reinforce the innovation further.

Management innovation as a conscious activity?

These themes suggest an important final point: If we can identify the conditions that have allowed management innovations to transpire serendipitously, is it possible for companies to recreate those conditions and accelerate their own process for management innovation? Do we have to leave this all to chance, or can we create some sort of hothouse where by tending the soil, fixing the light, and setting the humidity these innovations will sprout up more quickly and more vigorously?

We believe the hothouse model has real merit, and at the time of writing we are in the process of putting it into practice – our very own management innovation, if you will. Called the Management Innovation Lab (MLab), this venture is a collaborative research endeavour in which forward-thinking companies and distinguished scholars work together with the goal of inventing the management processes and practices that will define competitive success in the 21st century. MLab's mission is to accelerate the evolution of the practice and the theory of management. Giant steps in management: past, present, and future.

Resources

Scientific management

Stewart, T.A., Taylor, A., Petre, P. and Schlender, B. (1999) The businessman of the century. *Fortune*, 22 November.

Taylor, F.W. (1903) *Shop management.* Harper & Row, New York.

Taylor, F.W. (1911) *The principles of scientific management.* Harper & Row, New York.

Moving assembly line

Hounshell, D.A. (1984) *From the American system to mass production, 1800–1932: The development of manufacturing technology in the United States.* The Johns Hopkins University Press, Baltimore, MD.

Lacey, R. (1986) *Ford: The men and the machine.* Heinemann, London.

Williams, K., Haslam, C. and Williams, J. (1993) The myth of the line: Ford's production of the Model T at Highland Park, 1909–16. *Business History*, 35(3), 66–87.

Lean manufacturing

Ohno, T. (1988) *Toyota production system.* Productivity Press, University Park, IL.

Udagawa, M. (1995) The development of production management at the Toyota Motor Corporation. *Business History*, 37(2), 107–119.

Womack, J. and Jones, D.T. (1996) *Lean thinking.* Simon & Schuster, New York.

Total quality management

Deming, W.E. (1982) *Out of the crisis.* MIT Center for Advanced Engineering Study, Cambridge, MA.

Feigenbaum, A.V. (1983) *Total quality control.* McGraw-Hill, New York.

Juran, J.M. (ed.) (1995) *A history of managing for quality: The evolution, trends, and future directions of managing for quality.* ASQC Quality Press, Milwaukee, WI.

Cellular manufacturing

Berggren, C. (1994) NUMMI vs. Uddevalla. *Sloan Management Review,* 35(2), 37–49.

Miyake, D.I. (2006) *The shift from belt conveyor line to work-cell based assembly systems to cope with increasing demand variation and fluctuation in the Japanese electro.* CIRJE F-Series CIRJE-F-397, CIRJE, Faculty of Economics, University of Tokyo.

Mass customization

Da Silveira, G., Borenstein, D. and Fogliatto, F.S. (2001) Mass customization: Literature review and research directions. *International Journal of Production Economics,* 72(1), 1–13.

Pine, B.J. (1993) *Mass customization: The new frontier in business competition.* Harvard Business School Press, Boston, MA.

Business process re-engineering

Hammer, M. (1990) Reengineering work: Don't automate, obliterate. *Harvard Business Review,* 68(4), 104–112.

Hammer, M. and Champy, J. (1993) *Reengineering the corporation: A manifesto for business revolution.* Nicholas Brealey Publishing, London.

Hammer, M. and Stanton, S. (1999) How process enterprises really work. *Harvard Business Review,* 77(6), 108–118.

Supply chain management

Christopher, M. (1992) *Logistics and supply chain management.* Financial Times/Pitman, London.

Macbeth, D.K. and Ferguson, N. (1994) *Partnership sourcing: An integrated supply chain approach.* Financial Times/Pitman, London.

Schonberger, R.J. (1990) *Building a chain of customers.* The Free Press, New York.

Six sigma

Harry, M. and Schroeder, R. (2000) *Six sigma: The breakthrough management strategy revolutionizing the world's top corporations.* Doubleday, New York.

Kumar, S. and Gupta, Y.P. (1993) Statistical process control at Motorola's Austin assembly plant. *Interfaces,* 23(2), 84–92.

Linderman, K., Schroeder, R.G., Zaheer, S. and Choo, A.S (2003) Six sigma: A goal-theoretic perspective. *Journal of Operations Management,* 21, 193–203.

www.mikeljharry.com/story.php?cid=4

Cost accounting

Cooper, R. and Kaplan, R.S. (1998) *Cost & effect: Using integrated cost systems to drive profitability and performance.* Harvard Business School Press, Boston, MA.

Kranowski, N. (1977) The historical development of standard costing systems until 1920. *Journal of Accountancy,* 144(6), 66–73.

Return on investment

Fiedlob, G.T. and Plewa, F. J. (1996) *Understanding return on investment.* John Wiley, New York.

Henrici, S.B. (1968) Eyeing the ROI: A fresh look at what qualitative techniques, backed by judgement, can do. *Harvard Business Review,* 46(3), 88–97.

Johnson, H.T. and Kaplan, R.S. (1987) *Relevance lost: The rise and fall of management accounting.* Harvard Business School Press, Boston, MA.

Discounted cash flow

Dulman, S.P. (1989) The development of discounted cash flow techniques in US industry. *Business History Review*, 63(3), 555–587.

Pezet, A. (1997) The development of discounted cash flow and profitability of investment in France in the 1960s. *Accounting, Business and Financial History*, 7, 367–380.

Wright, M.G. (1990) *Using discounted cash flow in investment appraisal*. McGraw-Hill, New York.

Beyond budgeting

Hope, J. and Fraser, R. (2003) *Beyond budgeting: How managers can break free from the annual performance trap*. Harvard Business School Press, Boston, MA.

Hope. J. and Fraser, R. (2003) Who needs budgets? *Harvard Business Review*, 81(2), 108–115.

Lindsay, R.M. and Libby, R. (2003) Svenska Handelsbanken: Accomplishing radical decentralization through 'beyond budgeting'. Case study available at www.ssrn.com/abstract=9214784.

Activity-based costing

Anderson, S.W. and Young, S.M. (2001) *Implementing management innovations: Lessons learned from activity based costing in the US automobile industry*. Kluwer Academic Publishers, Dordrecht.

Cooper, R. and Kaplan, R.S. (1988) Measure costs right: Make the right decisions. *Harvard Business Review*, 66(5), 96–103.

Cooper, R. and Kaplan, R.S. (1998) *Cost & effect: Using integrated cost systems to drive profitability and performance*. Harvard Business School Press, Boston, MA.

Balanced scorecard

Kaplan, R.S. and Cooper, R. (1998) *Cost & effect: Using integrated cost systems to drive profitability and performance*. Harvard Business School Press, Boston, MA.

Kaplan, R.S. and Norton, D.P. (1996) *The balanced scorecard: Translating strategy into action*. Harvard Business School Press, Boston, MA.

Stata, R. (1989) Organizational learning – the key to management innovation. *Sloan Management Review*, 30(3), 63–74.

www.schneiderman.com

Economic value added

Black, A., Wright, P., Bachman, J.E., Davies, J., Maskall, M. and Wright, P. (1998) *In search of shareholder value: Managing the drivers of performance*. Financial Times Management, London.

Knight, J.A. (1997) *Value-based management: Developing a systematic approach to creating shareholder value*. McGraw-Hill, New York.

Stewart, G.B. (1991) *The quest for value: The EVA management guide*. Harper Business, New York.

www.sternstewart.com

Corporate welfarism

McCreary, E.C. (1968) Social welfare and business: The Krupp welfare program, 1860–1914. *Business History Review*, 42(1), 24–49.

Nelson, D. and Campbell, S. (1972) Taylorism versus welfare work in American industry: H. L. Gantt and the Bancrofts. *Business History Review*, 46(1), 1–16.

Zahavi, G. (1988) *Workers, managers, and welfare capitalism: The shoeworkers and tanners of Endicott Johnson, 1890–1950*. University of Illinois Press, Chicago.

Professional managers

Gourvish, T.R. (1970) Captain Mark Huish: A pioneer in the development of railway management. *Business History*, 12(1), 46–58.

Micklethwait, J. and Wooldridge, A. (2003) *The company: A short history of a revolutionary idea*. Modern Library, New York.

Mintzberg, H. (1971) Managerial work: Analysis from observation. *Management Science*, 18 (2), 97–110.

Business education

Copeland, M.T. (1958) *And mark an era: The story of the Harvard Business School*. Little, Brown & Company, Boston, MA.

Crainer, S. and Dearlove, D. (1999) *Gravy training: Inside the business of business schools*. Jossey-Bass, San Francisco, CA.

Micklethwait, J. and Wooldridge, A. (2003) *The company: A short history of a revolutionary idea*. Modern Library, New York.

www.aacsb.edu/ The Association to Advance Collegiate Schools of Business.

Performance-related pay

Brown, M., Heywood, J.S. and Sharpe, M.E. (eds) (2002) *Paying for performance: An international comparison*. M.E. Sharpe, New York.

Lesieur, F. (1958) *The Scanlon Plan: A frontier in labour–management cooperation*. MIT Press, Cambridge, MA.

McGregor, D. (1961) *The human side of enterprise*. McGraw-Hill, New York.

Meyer, H.H. (1975) The pay-for-performance dilemma. *Organizational Dynamics*, 3(3), 39–50.

Assessment centres

Keil, E. C. (1981) *Assessment centers: A guide for human resource management*. Addison-Wesley Longman, Reading, MA.

Riggio, R.E. and Mayes, B.T. (1997) Assessment centers: Research and applications. *Journal of Social Behavior and Personality*, Special Issue 12(5), 85–108.

www.assessmentcenters.org/ International Congress on Assessment Centre Methods

T-groups

Argyris, C. (1964) T-groups for organizational effectiveness. *Harvard Business Review*, 42(2), 60–74.

Bennis, W. (1993) *An invented life*. Addison-Wesley, Wokingham.

Kleiner, A. (1996) *The age of heretics.* Nicholas Brealey, London.

Lundberg, C.C. and Bowen, D.D. (1993) Iphigenia, or on the fate of T-groups. *Journal of Organizational Change Management,* 6(5), 7–14.

Quality of work life

Kleiner, A. (1996) *The age of heretics.* Nicholas Brealey, London.

Trist, E. and Murray, H. (1993) *The social engagement of social science: Volume II.* University of Pennsylvania Press, Philadelphia, PA.

www.moderntimesworkplace.com/archives/archives.html

Mentoring and executive coaching

Collins, E. G. and Scott, P. (1978) Everyone who makes it has a mentor. *Harvard Business Review,* 56(4), 89–101.

Douglas, C. A. (1997) *Formal mentoring programs in organizations: An annotated bibliography.* CCL Press, Greensboro, NC.

Zey, M. (1991) *The mentor connection: Strategic alliances in corporate life.* Transaction Publishers, New Brunswick, NJ.

360-degree feedback

Edwards, M. and Ewen, A.J. (1996) *360-degree feedback.* AMACOM, New York.

Handy, L., Devine, M. and Heath, L. (1996) *360-degree feedback: Unguided missile or powerful weapon?* Ashridge Management Research Group, London.

Lepsinger, R. and Lucia, A.D. (1997) *The art and science of 360-degree feedback.* Jossey-Bass, San Francisco, CA.

The divisional structure

Chandler, Jr. A.D. (1962) *Strategy and structure: Chapters in the history of the industrial enterprise.* MIT Press, Cambridge, MA.

Fligstein, N. (1985) The spread of the multidivisional form among large firms, 1919–1979. *American Sociological Review,* 50, 377–391.

Sloan, A.P. (1963) *My years with General Motors.* Doubleday, New York.

Strategic business units

Hall, W.K. (1978) SBUs: Hot new topic in the management of diversification. *Business*, 21(1), 17–25.

Mintzberg, H. (1994) *The rise and fall of strategic planning* (2nd edn). Prentice Hall, Hemel Hempstead.

Matrix organization

Barham, K. and Heimer, C. (1998) *ABB: The dancing giant.* Financial Times/Pitman, London.

Campbell, A., Goold, M. and Alexander, M. (1994) *Corporate-level strategy.* John Wiley, New York.

Davis, S. and Lawrence, P. (1977) *Matrix.* Addison-Wesley, Reading, MA.

Galbraith, J. (1977) *Organization design.* Addison-Wesley, Reading, MA.

Sy, T. and D'Annunzio, L.S. (2005) Challenges and strategies of matrix organizations: Top-level and mid-level managers' perspectives. *Human Resource Planning*, 28(1), 39–48.

Workout groups

Byrne, J. (1998) How Jack Welch runs GE. *Business Week,* 8 June.

Lowe, J. (1998) *Jack Welch speaks.* John Wiley, New York.

Vicere, A. and Fulmer, R. (1998) *Leadership by design.* Harvard Business School Press, Boston, MA.

Communities of practice

Brown, J. Seely, and Duguid, P. (1991) Organizational learning and communities-of-practice: Toward a unified view of working, learning, and innovating. *Organization Science*, 2(1), 40–57.

Lave, J. and Wenger, E. (1991) *Situated learning: Legitimate peripheral participation.* Cambridge University Press, Cambridge.

Wenger, E., McDermott, R. and Snyder, W. (2002) *Cultivating communities of practice.* Harvard Business School Press, Boston, MA.

Wenger, E.C. and Snyder, W.M. (2000) Communities of practice: The organizational frontier. *Harvard Business Review,* 78(1), 139–145.

Franchising

Dicke, T.S. (1992) *Franchising in America – The development of a business method 1840–1980.* University of North Carolina Press, Chapel Hill, NC.

Hall, W.P. (1964) Franchising – New scope for an old technique. *Harvard Business Review,* 42(1), 60–72.

Spinelli, J.R., Rosenberg, R., Birley, S. and Spinelli, S. (2003) *Franchising: Pathway to wealth creation.* Financial Times/Prentice Hall, London.

Direct marketing

McCorkell, G. (1997) *Direct and database marketing.* Kogan Page, London.

Nash, E.L. (2000) *Direct marketing: Strategy, planning, execution* (4th edn). McGraw-Hill, New York.

Market segmentation

Chandler, Jr. A.D. (1962) *Strategy and structure: Chapters in the history of the industrial enterprise.* MIT Press, Cambridge, MA.

Smith, W.R. (1956) Product differentiation and market segmentation as alternative marketing strategies. *Journal of Marketing,* 21(1), 3–8.

Tedlow, R.S. (1990) *New and improved: The story of mass marketing in America.* Basic Books, New York.

Brand management

Dyer, D., Dalzell, F. and Olegario, R. (2004) *Rising tide: Lessons from 165 years of brand building at Procter & Gamble.* Harvard Business School Press, Boston, MA.

Low, G.S. and Fullerton, R.A. (1994) Brands, brand management, and the brand manager system: A critical-historical evaluation. *Journal of Marketing Research,* 31(2), 173–190.

Schisgall, O. (1981) *Eyes on tomorrow: The evolution of Procter & Gamble.* Doubleday, New York.

Customer relationship management

Agarwal, A., Harding, D. and Schumacher, J. (2004) Organizing for CRM. *McKinsey Quarterly,* 3, 80–91.

Peppers, D. and Rogers, M. (1993) *The one-to-one future.* Currency Doubleday, New York.

Peppers, D., Rogers, M. and Dorf, B. (1999) Is your company ready for one-to-one marketing? *Harvard Business Review,* 77(1), 151–160.

Vertical integration

Livesay, H.C. and Porter, P.G. (1969) Vertical integration in American manufacturing, 1899–1948. *Journal of Economic History,* 29(3), 494–500.

Ruhnke, H.O. (1984) Vertical integration: Trend for the future? *SAM Advanced Management Journal,* 31(1), 69–73.

Outsourcing

Harvard Business School Publishing (1991) *Eastman Kodak Co.: Managing information systems through strategic alliances.* Harvard Business School Press, Boston, MA.

Loh, L. and Venkatraman, N. (1992) Diffusion of information technology outsourcing: Influence sources and the Kodak effect. *Information Systems Research,* 3(4), 334–358.

Mol, M.J. (2007) *Outsourcing: Design, process, and performance.* Cambridge University Press, Cambridge.

Venkatesan, R. (1992) Strategic sourcing: To make or not to make. *Harvard Business Review,* 70(6), 98–107.

Consortia and alliances

Doz, Y.L. and Hamel, G. (1998) *Alliance advantage: The art of creating value through partnering.* Harvard Business School Press, Boston, MA.

Hock, D.W. (1998) An epidemic of institutional failure. Keynote address, Organisation Development Network Annual Conference, New Orleans, LA, 16 November. Available at www.hackvan.com/pub/stig/etext/deehock—epidemic-of-institutional-failure.html

Hock, D.W. (1999) *Birth of the chaordic age*. Berrett-Koehler Publishers, San Francisco, CA.

von Clemm, M. (1971) The rise of consortium banking. *Harvard Business Review*, 49(3), 125–141.

www.chaordic.org

Industrial research labs

Hargadon, A. (2003) *How breakthroughs happen: The surprising truth about how companies innovate*. Harvard Business School Press, Boston, MA.

Meyer-Thurow, G. (1982) The industrialization of invention: A case study from the German chemical industry. *Isis*, 73(3), 363–381.

Reich, L. S. (1985) *The making of American industrial research: Science and business at GE and Bell, 1876–1926*. Cambridge University Press, Cambridge.

Skunk works

Gwynne, P. (1997) Skunk works, 1990's style. *Research Technology Management*, 40(4), 18–23.

Rich, B. (1995) *Biographical memoirs, Clarence Leonard (Kelly) Johnson, Volume 67*. www.nap.edu/readingroom/books/biomems/cjohnson.html.

Single, A. W. and Spurgeon, W. M. (1996) Creating and commercializing innovation inside a skunk works. *Research Technology Management*, 39(1), 38–41.

Corporate venturing

Block, Z. and MacMillan, I. (1993) *Corporate venturing*. Harvard Business School Press, Boston, MA.

Buckland, W., Hatcher, A. and Birkinshaw, J.M. (2003) *Inventuring*. McGraw-Hill, New York.

Pinchot, G. (1985) *Intrapreneuring: Why you don't have to leave the corporation to become an entrepreneur.* Harper & Row, New York.

Pinchot, G. and Pellman, R. (1999) *Intrapreneuring in action: A handbook for business innovation.* Berrett-Koehler Publishers, San Francisco, CA.

Open innovation

Chesbrough, H. (2003) *Open innovation: The new imperative for creating and profiting from technology.* Harvard Business School Press, Boston, MA.

Huston, L. and Sakkab, N. (2006) Connect and develop. *Harvard Business Review*, 84(3), 58–66.

Rigby, D. and Zook, C. (2002) Open-market innovation. *Harvard Business Review*, 80(10), 80–89.

Management by objectives

Carroll, S. and Tosi, H. (1973) *Management by objectives: Applications and research.* MacMillan, New York.

Drucker, P.F. (1946) *The concept of the corporation.* John Day, New York.

Drucker, P.F. (1954) *The practice of management.* Harper Collins, New York.

Greenwood, R.C. (1981) Management by objectives: As developed by Peter Drucker, assisted by Harold Smiddy. *Academy of Management Review,* 6(2), 225–230.

Strategic planning

Bracker, J. (1980) The historical development of the strategic management concept. *Academy of Management Review*, 5(2), 219–224.

Gerstner, L.V. (1972) Can strategic planning pay off? *Business Horizons,* 15(6), 5–16.

Linstone, H.A. (2002) Corporate planning, forecasting, and the long wave. *Futures*, 34(3), 317–336.

Mintzberg, H. (1993). *The rise and fall of strategic planning.* Prentice Hall, London.

Scenario planning

De Geus, A. (1997) *The living company*. Harvard Business School Press, Boston, MA.

Schwartz, P. (1991) *The art of the long view*. Doubleday, New York.

Van der Heijden, K. (1996) *Scenarios: The art of strategic conversations*. Wiley, Chichester.

Wack, P. (1985) Scenarios: Uncharted waters ahead. *Harvard Business Review*, 63(5), 73–89.

Benchmarking

Bendell, T., Boulter, L. and Goodstadt, P. (1997) *Benchmarking for competitive advantage*. Pitman, London.

Boxwell, R.J. (1994) *Benchmarking for competitive advantage*. McGraw-Hill, New York.

Camp, R.C. (1989) *Benchmarking: The search for industry best practices that lead to superior performance*. ASQC Quality Press, New York.

Operations research

Kirby, M. W. (2003) *Operational research in war and peace: The British experience from the 1930s to 1970*. Imperial College Press, London.

Slack, N., Lewis, M. and Bates, H. (2004) The two worlds of operations management research and practice: Can they meet, should they meet? *International Journal of Operations & Production Management*, 24(3/4), 372–387.

www.theorsociety.com

Yield management

Ingold, A., Yeoman, I. and McMahon, U. (2000) *Yield management: Strategies for the service industries* (2nd edn). Cassell, London.

McGill, J.I. and Van Ryzin, G. J. (1999) Revenue management: Research overview and prospects. *Transportation Science*, 33(2), 233–256.

Smith, B.C., Leimkuhler, J.F. and Darrow, R.M. (1992) Yield management at American Airlines. *Interfaces,* 22(1), 8–31.

MRP I and MRP II

Karmarkar, U. (1989) Getting control of just-in-time. *Harvard Business Review*, 89(5), 122–130.

McKay, K. N. (2003) Historical survey of manufacturing control practices from a production research perspective. *International Journal of Production Research*, 41(3), 411–426.

Plossl, G. (1994) *Orlicky's material requirements planning* (2nd edn). McGraw-Hill, New York.

Wight, O. W. (1983) *The executive's guide to successful MRP II.* John Wiley, New York.

Enterprise resource planning

Davenport, T. H. (1998) Putting the enterprise into the enterprise system. *Harvard Business Review,* 76(4), 121–131.

O'Leary, D. E. (2000) *Enterprise resource planning systems: Systems, life cycle, electronic commerce, and risk.* Cambridge University Press, Cambridge.

Ptak, C. A. and Schragenheim, E. (2000) *ERP: Tools, techniques, and applications for integrating the supply chain.* St. Lucie Press/APICS, New York.

And finally

The MLab
www.managementinnovationlab.com

Julian Birkinshaw, Co-founder and Research Director
M +44 (0)7966 908 718
jbirkinshaw@london.edu

Gary Hamel, Co-founder and Managing Director
T +1 650 851 2095
ghamel@woodsideinstitute.com

Alan Matcham, Executive Director
T +44 (0)20 7000 8755
M +44 (0)7966 908755
amatcham@london.edu

Michael J. Mol, Visiting Researcher
mmol@london.edu

Fran Husson, Operations Manager
T +44 (0)20 7000 8818
fhusson@london.edu

Index